# A man walks into a barn

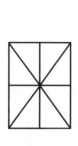

# A man walks into a barn

*Navigating Fatherhood in the Flawed*
*and Fascinating World of Horses*

## CHAD OLDFATHER

TRAFALGAR SQUARE
North Pomfret, Vermont

First published in 2021 by
Trafalgar Square Books
North Pomfret, Vermont 05053

Parts of this book have been previously published in some form by *The Chronicle of the Horse* (www.chronofhorse.com).

**Disclaimer of Liability**
The author and publisher shall have neither liability nor responsibility to any person or entity with respect to any loss or damage caused or alleged to be caused directly or indirectly by the information contained in this book. While the book is as accurate as the author can make it, there may be errors, omissions, and inaccuracies.

Thank you to Elizabeth Penta, Emcee Artist Management, and The Wood Brothers for permission to reprint select lyrics from the song "Luckiest Man."

**Library of Congress Cataloging-in-Publication Data**
Names: Oldfather, Chad, author.
Title: A man walks into a barn : navigating fatherhood in the flawed and
   fascinating world of horses / Chad Oldfather.
Description: North Pomfret, Vermont : Trafalgar Square Books, 2021. |
   Summary: "A smart, funny memoir exploring the evolution of a man and his
   relationship with his daughters as they grow up in the grips of the
   equestrian life. Nineteen years ago, Chad Oldfather found himself the
   father of a two-year-old girl who, out of nowhere, became obsessed with
   horses. Plenty of dads just "write the checks" and steer well clear of
   the barn; Oldfather instead embraced his daughter's interest, spending
   hours sitting ringside and many more in the car, commuting to lessons
   and competitions. Soon enmeshed in the sport with his younger daughters
   similarly afflicted with cases of "horse-crazy," Oldfather found himself
   learning not just about the animals that so inexplicably drew them, but
   also about people and parenting, and to his surprise, how to better do
   his job as a law-school professor. As he shared experiences with
   individuals from all walks of life, from custodians to billionaires, and
   befriended those just learning to ride as well as Olympic medalists,
   Oldfather discovered many things about the horse world that he
   loved...and many that he hated. Filled with the joys, heartbreaks, and
   life lessons that come from training, competition, and time in the
   company of horses, this is mostly a book about family, and the strong
   bonds that can form when parent and child join hands and pursue a
   passion together"-- Provided by publisher.
Identifiers: LCCN 2021012097 (print) | LCCN 2021012098 (ebook) | ISBN
   9781646010554 (paperback) | ISBN 9781646010561 (epub)
Subjects: LCSH: Horse sports--United States--Biography. | Hosemen and
   horsewomen--United States. | Fatherhood--United States. | Fathers and
   daughters. | Law schools--Faculty--United States.
Classification: LCC SF294.25 .O43 2021  (print) | LCC SF294.25  (ebook) |
   DDC 798.092 [B]--dc23
LC record available at https://lccn.loc.gov/2021012097
LC ebook record available at https://lccn.loc.gov/2021012098

Book design by *Katarzyna Misiukanis–Celińska (https://misiukanis-artstudio.com)*
Cover design by *RM Didier*
Typefaces: *Adobe Text Pro* and *Metropolis*

Printed in the United States of America

10 9 8 7 6 5 4 3 2 1

TO ADA, AUDREY, LAURA, AND LEA

*You're up against*
*Too many horses*
*And mysterious forces*
*What you don't know is*
*You are the luckiest man*

—— THE WOOD BROTHERS ——
**"Luckiest Man"**

# INTRODUCTION

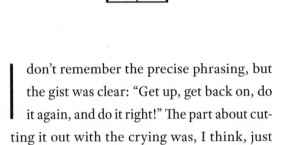

don't remember the precise phrasing, but the gist was clear: "Get up, get back on, do it again, and do it right!" The part about cutting it out with the crying was, I think, just implied. Strongly.

Those were the words by which my daughter Ada and I received our welcome into the world of equestrian sport.

Ada was five. Already her fascination with horses had consumed over half her life. For at least a year she'd pleaded with us to sign her up for riding lessons. This moment was the near-culmination of her campaign.

It was 2006, and still the early days of the internet, so simply locating a lesson barn took some effort. Neither my wife Lea nor I were horse people, and we had only recently moved to Milwaukee, Wisconsin. The phone book (remember those? ) was only minimally helpful. A combination of Google searches and word of mouth netted me a handful of leads, most of which didn't pan out. One barn no longer existed. The others wouldn't take a student who was only five-and-a-half years old. "We find that they just aren't able to pay attention," one instructor said to me.

Only Bernadette Ruckdashel, owner of Appy Orse Acres in Fredonia, Wisconsin, seemed totally unfazed by my request. She invited us to come out to watch a lesson. Then, if we were still interested, we could get Ada on the schedule. I was confident that it was not a matter of "if," but I imagined there must be kids out there who turn out to like the idea of riding lessons more than the reality. And this was all new to me. If watching a lesson was what you did before taking a lesson, then that was what we would do.

Appy Orse was about a thirty-minute drive from our house. We had driven by the farm a few days earlier when we were in the area, our entire family of five—Lea, me, Ada, and her three-year-old twin sisters Audrey and Laura—piled in our minivan, trying to imagine what this next step would hold. It was, I later realized, kind of like visiting a college as a prospective student. You're looking at an unfamiliar set of buildings in an unfamiliar place and trying to imagine what it's like to be a part of the community that fills those buildings. You might become part of that community, or you might not. Will this be a place where my life will be transformed? Or will it be a place I never visit again? How do I know which one it should be?

I don't know what everybody else was thinking as we drove back and forth along Willow Road that day. I was so focused on trying to stay between the ditches while following the directions that Bernadette had given me that there wasn't much room for me to let my brain stretch into the future, let alone gauge the family mood. But the excitement was palpable. It seems strange to say it now, given how quickly the years have flown by, but at the time this moment seemed to have been a long time coming. Finally, at long last, it would happen. Horses. Ridden. By Ada. A step into a great, exciting unknown.

We could hardly wait.

When the big day came Ada and I drove to Appy Orse. Our instructions were to go into the barn and ask for Bernadette. Over the coming months and years we would come to know the people of Appy Orse—the boarders and lessoners and their parents, grandparents, and friends—as a second family. And so it's a little puzzling to me that I don't know who it was who greeted us when we first walked into the barn, and I'm not sure that we ever saw her again. But she was clearly no stranger to the place. Bernadette was in the indoor ring, the woman told us, teaching one of the two consecutive hour-long group lessons on tap for that morning. She would take us there.

We followed her up a slight hill across the yard to a green-and-white corrugated-steel building perhaps seventy-five yards from the barn. The building's door featured a sign asking entrants to sound their voice before entering, which was not something I'd seen before. "Door!" the woman called out. A beat or two later we got, "Okay!" in response. We stepped in, closed the door behind us, and got the signal from someone who was unmistakably Bernadette (because, as I had already sensed from our brief phone call, Bernadette was unmistakable) to "wait right there."

We were just inside the door, in one of the corners of an indoor riding ring, our eyes adjusting to the lower light as we tried to get our bearings. Bernadette stood close to three horse-and-rider pairs stationed near the opposite corner. A rider on a white horse went behind them toward the far end of the ring, then turned to come back our way.

If I watched it now, I could provide a fuller description. *Was the turn balanced? Did she find a good distance to the first jump? Get the right number of strides in between them?* I could answer those questions and more. But my thoughts then were less complex, more like, "That's interesting—they're gonna jump some jumps," and then, "I hope she doesn't run into the wall."

Horses turn out to be pretty good at not running into walls. They'll usually make a sharp turn or a hard stop, both of which can be a problem for a rider who hasn't planned for them. This rider had made no such plans. The horse stopped, and inertia took over. The rider fell.

It happened right in front of us, and it wasn't gentle. When the rider hit the ground, her body was a lot closer to horizontal than to vertical. As a newcomer, unaccustomed to how these scenes play out, it registered mostly as a blur. Now, with the benefit of experience, I can confidently guess that it was the sort of fall where a little bit of the riding surface, known as "footing," ends up in the rider's mouth and a lot of it ends up in her waistband, with bruising likely to follow.

Experience also tells me that she didn't *actually* get right back up and get right back on, even though that is how it registered at the time. Falls would turn out to be a very common part of riding, and at Appy Orse, in particular, the rule is to stay on the ground as long as necessary to confirm that there are no serious injuries. But in the moment Bernadette's reaction seemed instantaneous, and not what I would have expected: The rider would not be taking a break, or pausing to collect her thoughts, or walking off the minor wounds to her body and pride. She would get back on the horse, and she would do the line of jumps again. This time, if things went according to plan, she would do it right.

I said nothing to Ada or the woman who'd led us into the building and remained standing with us, but what I thought remains one of the more vivid parts of the memory. It began with "Holy" and ended with a series of exclamation points.

The lesson continued with no sense that what had occurred was anything other than business as usual. Bernadette eventually directed us to take a seat in some chairs in a corner of the ring. There were blankets folded nearby if we got chilled—it was early February and well below freezing, and the ring was not heated. Horses cantered past just a few feet in front of us, stirring up cold air and sometimes showering us with footing as they made the turn. Other riders made mistakes, then—like the faller—repeated whatever it was they had been trying to do until they got it right. Bernadette did not soft-pedal her critiques. I spend my days as a law-school professor, so I'm familiar with teaching methods that aren't exactly soft. But this was truly "old school."

I wasn't sure how Ada would react. I suddenly appreciated the reluctance of the other trainers I had called, and the wisdom of Bernadette's inviting us to watch a lesson before signing up our daughter. The *idea* of taking lessons might have been one thing and the reality—with its falls and mistakes and critiques—something entirely different.

But Ada was transfixed. "I want to stay," she told me as the first lesson wrapped up. I promised her we would stay as long as there was something to watch.

We sat through the next lesson, which featured no dramatic falls but otherwise more of the same. After an hour or so it ended, and I broke the news to Ada that it would soon be time for us to leave. But then something unexpected happened. Bernadette asked the youngest rider in the lesson to dismount. Then she invited Ada over to where she stood.

Often, in a situation like this, a child will look to a parent for reassurance that it's okay. But that's a gamble, because what if the reassurance doesn't come? Ada took no chances. It wasn't clear what was about to happen, but there was a horse involved, and she didn't cast a single glance my way as she got out of her seat.

I watched as Bernadette asked the young rider who had gotten off the horse for her helmet, which Bernadette then put on Ada's head. An adjustment or two later, Ada climbed a mounting block, and a moment after that she sat on the horse, for the first time in her life riding one that wasn't being led or attached to a motorized walker.

I'm at least sometimes a person whose face conveys messages that don't correspond with what's going on in my mind. I was surprised, certainly, because this hadn't been part of the plan. But I was likewise thrilled because I knew how exciting this was for Ada. My expression, though, must have read as nervous. The woman who'd acted as our guide offered reassurance.

"This horse is barely awake," she told me. "She'll be fine."

I wasn't worried, and Ada was more than fine. She rode around the ring proud as could be.

She delivered her verdict the moment the car door closed for the trip home: "I want to ride here."

And so it began.

This is a book with several topics. One of them is parenthood, and its challenges, and how it involves a constant journey into the unknown, with each decision about what to do next made under conditions of considerable uncertainty. That's true in general. And the questions take on a sharper form when passion, talent, and drive make an appearance. *What's the goal? Is it the right goal? Is this the right path to reaching it? Should I push? Should I hold back? Just how committed to this dream*

*are we going to be? What shape should the dream take? When will we know that we've achieved it?*

"Success" can be measured in many ways. Familiar benchmarks focus on winning—ribbons, trophies, and other awards. But that sort of success can be a moving target. The satisfaction of succeeding at one level turns into a desire to do it again at the next level. Even the thrill of standing atop the Olympic podium no doubt wears off at some point, and then the gold medalist starts to seek ways to add to her legacy. Only one person can be the "greatest of all time," so anyone who measures success solely by awards and recognition is likely to come up short. Other measures focus more on intrinsic rewards. It's satisfying to do something for its own sake. This book could end up being read by hardly anyone and I'll still have enjoyed the process of writing it. If that was all I were after, though, these words would appear only in my diary. The fact is that I *want* people to read it, and that I sometimes allow myself to think unrealistic thoughts about just how many people might *want* to read it and what they might think when they do.

My motivations, like anyone's, are mixed. I write because I enjoy doing it *and* because I enjoy the recognition that follows from having done it. I write because there'll come a time when I'm not around, and I'd like to leave a little something for people to remember me by. I write for reasons I don't fully understand. Can I know, as I write this, what it will take for me to know whether this book is a success? Not entirely.

It's a struggle that each of us faces in our own lives, whether our goals relate to being successful in a career or in a hobby, or more fundamentally, to having a happy and fulfilling life. As I reflect on my own path it's clear I could easily have made worse life choices than I have. (And one way I keep myself feeling young is to remind myself there's still time to make bad choices.) It's also clear I could have made choices that were better in terms of professional achievement and wealth, though they would have come at the cost of being able to be an involved and present parent. Did I make the right call? I think so. The process of navigating our own lives is not easy, but at least the consequences of the decisions we make about our own paths fall mostly on us.

It's different as a parent. The consequences of the decisions I make in that capacity fall primarily on my kids. That raises the stakes. If I make a life choice that ends up with me living under a bridge? I'll figure out how to deal with it. If it ends up with my kids living under a bridge? Whole different story.

I often recall a comment on a social media post from a then moderately famous musician who'd just had a daughter: "Congratulations. It is the solemn duty of all parents to f*** up their children as little as possible. Give it your all!" In spirit, at least, that gets it exactly right. But how do you do it? How do you f*** up your children as little as possible? If you find yourself the parent of a child with a passion, and with dreams that grow out of that passion, where do you take it? Should you resist, knowing that, most likely, those dreams won't lead to Olympic glory, or should you provide your support? What's the right amount of support, and what becomes overbearing?

You won't find answers to these parenting questions in these pages, at least not in any pat form. But maybe you will learn from my own struggle with them.

This is also, of course, a book about horses, and the people who like horses. That may seem like a subject with only niche appeal. But there are all sorts of ways in which the subculture I write about here parallels lots of other subcultures in our society. The world is filled with little communities that mostly escape our notice, each with its own vocabularies, complexities, and controversies. They are all different, yet they are all the same. The questions Lea and I faced as horse parents are not so different than those faced by hockey or theater or orchestra parents.

It's not just parenting. One of the striking and truly unexpected benefits of my three daughters' activities—which would eventually include figure skating in addition to equestrian sports—was the extent to which what I learned from their experiences shaped my own professional life. As a law school professor, I've come to understand the activity we might call "doing law" is something that at a fundamental level is like riding. True mastery of either requires a nuanced understanding, a feel, that can be developed only through repetition over time. It's a simple-enough-sounding insight, but one that's often overlooked in a world that tends to value only that which can be measured. And it's an insight that has influenced my teaching. You might not think that what works in the riding ring would also work in the law school classroom, but some of it does. You might not imagine that long days at horse shows would influence how a legal scholar thinks about judging in the legal system, but they have.

The lessons run in both directions. Many of the things we think about in law could be put to work in the horse world. Some of that has to do with how we teach. Some of it has to do with how judges judge and what sorts of processes and systems could help them judge better. I work on those problems a lot in my day job, and I've been asked to speak about that work to audiences of state and federal judges across the country. There are important ways in which the jobs of judges at a horse show parallel the jobs of judges in law. So I will talk about that in this book as well.

And then there are the people. It's easy for many of us to spend our days around people who are fundamentally like us—similar incomes, similar habits, similar world views. A passion for horses cuts across those lines. No doubt the equestrian world has its lines of division and exclusion, by wealth and otherwise. Its diversity is, at best, incomplete.

These issues deserve, and are starting to receive, attention. Even so, my daughters' participation in the sport helped take me out of one bubble I might otherwise have remained in. It led me to routinely cross paths with people whose lives and perspectives were different from my own. There's value in that. Those people and those interactions have enriched my life in ways large and small. I can't say I'm a fan of every person I've met in the horse world, but I'm a fan of most of them. They have made all the lessons I've learned—and thus this book—possible. ⑨

1

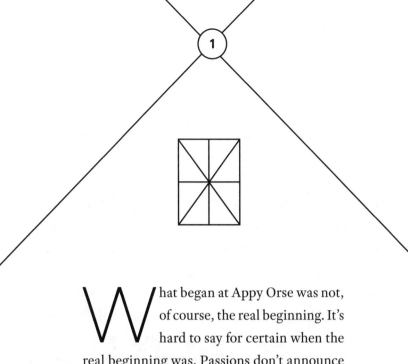

What began at Appy Orse was not, of course, the real beginning. It's hard to say for certain when the real beginning was. Passions don't announce their arrival. Even a passion that first manifests itself at a very young age—two years old, in Ada's case—is at least partly the product of forces that have accumulated over time.

Some of those forces came through from my own childhood. I was, at least for a while, a farm kid. I grew up in and around the unfortunately named Kiester, Minnesota. It's a tiny farming town in the south-central part of the state, with a population that never hit four figures and now sits somewhere in the four hundreds. The town is bordered on all sides by fields, close only to the Iowa border and other towns of roughly the same size. When I was growing up in the late seventies and early eighties, the nearest traffic light was a thirty-minute drive away.

Like many dots on the Midwestern portions of the United States map, Kiester exists because early railroads needed places to stop every so often. It enjoyed its heyday during the era of family farming, the brief moment in history that came just after technology made the horse obsolete and before things progressed to the point where comparatively little human labor is needed either. I arrived just as that era was coming to a close and my life's trajectory was affected by all of the larger forces at play. I spent roughly the first half of my childhood as a farm kid while my dad tried to make a go of it on eighty acres, just as Secretary of Agriculture Earl Butz urged farmers to "get big or get out." "Getting big" was not an option, so my dad got out. We moved into town when I was about ten.

Main Street was still a busy place then. An incomplete list of businesses located in a two-block stretch included two grocery stores, two hardware stores, two cafes, a drug store, a clothing store, a movie theater, a barbershop, a furniture store, a bar, a gas station, a farm-implement dealer, a bank, a doctor's office, and a dentist's office. (I did not make the connection until later, but the dentist's nephew was Robert Pirsig, the author of the book *Zen and the Art of Motorcycle Maintenance*.) A bakery, an appliance and TV store, and a third cafe had closed recently enough that I remembered them. Just off Main Street there was another bar and a bowling alley with its own restaurant. The town's car dealerships had been closed for what registered to my young mind as "a long time," but you could still buy a snowmobile. There were also several businesses related to farmers, as well as three more gas stations, along the southern and eastern edges of town. The rule was, "If you couldn't get it in town, you didn't need it."

The social and economic changes that had impeded my dad's ability to make a go at farming were at work more generally. Equipment became larger and more powerful, allowing—and in a sense compelling—farming to take place on a larger scale. Over time that meant fewer farms, which meant fewer farm families, which in turn meant fewer customers for the businesses in town and fewer kids in the school. The census numbers tell one part of the story. Kiester was founded in 1900 and hit its peak around 1960, when the census counted 741 residents in town itself and another 1,344 on the farms in the surrounding thirty-six square miles of township. By 1990 the town had shrunk to 606, but the real losses were on the farms in the township, the population of which was down to 317. The school population tells another part of the story: I graduated from high school in a class of fifteen, with ten of us having made the entire journey from kindergarten together. Classes a couple decades earlier had approached three times that size.

The consolidation of rural school districts had been underway for a decade or so by then, and the year after my graduation, the school combined its sports programs with Bricelyn, five miles to the west and our long-time rival. The year after that the two school systems consolidated completely, and they've since joined a couple other towns.

Though the decline of Kiester and towns like it was well underway by the time I came along, enough from the glory days remained that I had a thoroughly rural childhood. I still had family members who lived on farms, and most of my summer jobs were farm-related. I'd help bale hay, which involved standing on a moving flatbed wagon, grabbing and stacking the bales as they came out of the baler, or stacking them in what was usually a hot and dusty barn. You learned after the first time that it was best to wear long pants and long sleeves no matter how hot it was. If you didn't you ended up sporting a dense web of scratches.

"Walking beans" was another task that paid. It entailed walking up and down the rows of a soybean field, pulling weeds. You wanted gloves for this job, not so much to prevent blisters as to avoid the unremovable stink of buttonweed on your hands.

Both jobs tended to start early, before the day got too hot. The usual arrangement, for those not old enough to drive themselves out to the farm, was to meet the farmer in front of the school at what always seemed an impossibly early time. Often there would be a group of us kids, and we'd pile into the open bed of a pickup truck for the ride to where we'd be working. Safety wasn't always first. And if you were lucky, you might get paid minimum wage for your trouble.

None of this gave me much exposure to horses. That's a mildly astonishing fact given that fifty years before I was born there were horses everywhere in Minnesota. An aunt doing genealogical research went through the archives of the local newspaper and sent me portions of several issues from 1913 and 1914. Even though it wasn't her focus, the extracts included a surprising number of stories concerning locals injured in horse-related accidents. From those issues I learned that a farmer named William Nehring got knocked down when his team ran away on him, and that in late August 1913, a motorcycle ran into a team of horses just west of town. This happened because "the motorcycle was running at a fast clip and without lights." The paper bemoaned the way things had somehow become: "Not so long ago an automobile driver was arrested and charged for a lesser offense than driving without lights." My favorite story from the bunch, as much because of the way it's written as because of the content, appeared in the February 27, 1913, issue of the *Kiester Courier*:

> *As a general rule mules don't run away very often, but Will Ozmun*
> *has a team that does. As he started west from the livery barn*

*Wednesday morning with wagon and hay racks the donks took a notion to warm up a bit and started. Will pulled so hard that one line broke, the rack tipped and he was forced to jump to the hard ground, with the result that both his ankles were severely wrenched and he has been more or less done up since. The mules came out of the fracas with a few scars and the wagon was somewhat demoralized. Will will be able to work again, sometime.*

Sometimes I wonder how it all turned out for Will.

Those horse and "donk" days were long gone by the time I arrived. I can tell you a story about nearly every non-residential building in Kiester, but I have no idea which one was the livery stable or if the building is even still there. While it's of course true that the ubiquitousness of horses was not just a rural thing—cities had just as recently been filled with them, too—their near-complete absence on the farms of my youth somehow seems, in retrospect, to have been a minor crime against the species, a failure to express appropriate gratitude for horses' role in a centuries-long partnership. None of that occurred to me at the time. I was vaguely aware that one of my grandfathers had farmed with horses, but it was, as I saw the world then, something that happened in the "olden days," and thus might as well have happened a million years ago. Traces of that world remained—old tack, coated in dust, sitting in the corner of a barn or shed, usually next to some impossibly old tractor or car that had also been abandoned, all part of an inaccessible past. Grandpa still had some model horses on his shelf, outfitted with custom tack made by one of my uncles. And pretty much any time a horse appeared while he was watching TV (or so it seemed to me) he'd remark on how nice-looking it was. If there were other family members around, he'd get a chorus of laconic agreement. I tended not to weigh in. My brain could identify "horse," and it had room as well for differences in color and size. But nice-looking versus not-nice-looking? I had to take their word for it.

There were actually, of course, a few horses around had I wanted to go to the trouble of finding them. The parents of a girl who was in my class for most of elementary school had several, though I never knew exactly what they did with them. There were two or three girls a few years older who rode, and at least one a few years younger. There were horses in parades and at the county fair, and the nearby town of Bricelyn had a horse show as part of its annual Fourth of July celebration. I never went. (The host of the show, Dr. Jack Peterson, recently died at age eighty-six, having practiced veterinary medicine in Bricelyn for over fifty-eight years.)

It's not that I was a stranger to animals. I climbed on the backs of some of the cows we had during the years on the farm, and I'm nearly certain I tried to ride some of our sheep. But horses were, at best, on the periphery. I focused on more mainstream pursuits—playing sports like baseball and football, finding someone who would buy us beer, and driving to a nearby town to make sure there was nothing much happening there, either. (Unless you grew up in a very small town it's hard to appreciate just how big a deal it was if a carload of kids from a different town showed up. It was cause for excitement and tension. There could easily be a fight, because that's of course the natural, rational reaction to an encounter with people from as far as ten or maybe fifteen miles away. It was a world in which—and I swear to you this is true—we could recognize people's cars from several blocks away, at night, based on the configuration of the headlights. Anything new was notable.)

I also rode a horse—twice that I can remember. But I don't have interesting stories. Or at least what I've got are the sort of stories that are interesting only to me. Charles Zwicky, who was my daughters' second trainer, says that he often tells people he meets at parties that he's an insurance salesman. He's found that if he tells others what he actually does for a living, they feel compelled to tell him the story of the one time they rode as a kid. And the story they tell is always the same: They got on the horse, they were nervous, the horse spooked, they fell. Sometimes there's a low-hanging tree branch involved, and sometimes there isn't.

My two stories are both, more or less, that story—and I'm of course going to tell them to you anyway.

The first one is short. One of my uncles had a horse and a pony, and there came a day when somebody thought it would be a good idea to put me and a couple of my cousins on the pony—at the same time. The pony did not think it was a good idea, and we all ended up on the ground. I'm pleased to report that I didn't cry.

The second story came a few years later. I was at a different cousin's house for a birthday party or some other sort of gathering. He had a horse, and somebody decided the kids should take turns riding the horse around the fenced-in yard. When my turn came, things went pretty well—for about five or six steps. That's when I must have inadvertently asked for the trot.

No doubt you've had unexpected things happen to you, and so you know how it goes. Your field of vision shrinks to whatever specific thing you happen to be looking at. Your brain is overwhelmed by what seems to be a million unfamiliar inputs—and by the fact that it doesn't have a plan for dealing with any of them. It attempts to pick between fight or flight, but neither one seems workable when you're on top of what seems to be a "runaway horse." Did I whimper? Did I scream? I'm not sure. But I can still see us headed straight for the fence that enclosed their yard.

I didn't die that day, obviously. We didn't jump the fence. And the story ends in such an anticlimactic way that I can no longer remember just how the tale of the boy and the runaway horse came to its conclusion.

The point is simply this: As a kid I could find my way around a farm. I wasn't inherently afraid of large animals. But I certainly was not a horse person.

That I was comfortable on farms also did not mean I embraced the life-style. Sometimes genes take a while to manifest themselves. Sometimes they skip a generation entirely. I was the sort of kid for whom the farm, and the rural life, held no intrinsic appeal. I was drawn to the city. Once or twice a year I'd find myself on a school bus headed to the Twin Cities for a school field trip or the annual Little League end-of-season Twins game. We'd travel north on Interstate 35, the landscape gradually changing from rural to suburban, the two-hour drive seeming to take an eternity.

There's a short stretch, along the southern boundary of Minneapolis, where the interstate joins with State Highway 62, turning from its general northerly course to run east for a mile or so before peeling off to resume its route toward downtown. Shortly after that the road reaches a crest and the Minneapolis skyline snaps into full view. I loved that moment as a kid. I couldn't imagine what happened in those buildings, but I wanted to find out. The moment catches me still when I drive that road as an adult, except that now I see not possibility but a part of my past. I spent several years working in one of those buildings, most of it in an office that looked out over the city toward that very stretch of road.

This matters to the story, too. Not because it has anything to do with horses, but because being drawn to the city stands among the many ways in which I differed from my dad. One summer, shortly after Lea and I had moved to Minneapolis, my parents were in town to help us move from a downtown apartment to one on the edge of downtown. As we drove a load down Franklin Avenue my dad, unprompted, said, "I don't know why anyone would want to live here." The city was not for him.

On the whole, my dad and I had just the right combination of deep similarities and stark differences, lined up in just the right way, to make for what was not a good relationship. I'm sure I was not an easy child to raise, being introverted and inclined toward the intellectual in a way that, because I had no idea how to go about it, often ended up badly misdirected. I have a few memories of a "time before," of sorts, in which I happily rode with him in his pickup truck, eating peanuts he bought for me at one of the local gas stations and marveling at sunsets that, to my young eye, looked as if someone had spilled orange soda ("pop," as we call it in Minnesota) in the sky. But mostly I remember "after"—a vast expanse including most of my youth when we really didn't speak unless I was in trouble for something, in which case it was only one of us speaking. I have no memory of what caused the transition from one time period to the other. It might just have been something we settled into, with my sensing—rightly or wrongly—that I somehow wasn't and didn't know how to be the kid that he wanted, and that the best course was simply to keep my distance. But these things are always a two-way street, and I've often remarked as an adult that I'm glad I didn't have to raise myself.

Whatever the reason, the experience was regrettable. At the time, it was just how things were. We reached a rough detente in my adult years but never had the sort of relationship that many of my friends have had with their dads. "The child is the father of the man," I recall one of my college professors saying. No doubt my childhood shaped me in all sorts of ways— some good, some bad, some I'll never admit to anyone but myself, and some completely invisible to me. (My mom, I should emphasize—and understand that what I'm about to say is no exaggeration—is one of the most patient, selfless, and generally admirable human beings ever to walk the planet. If we were all like her the world would be an infinitely better place. I owe her everything, and I fall short of her example every single day.)

I was hardly alone in feeling mildly disaffected. The homecoming king and queen perhaps excluded, most everyone's adolescence includes spells of feeling like a misfit. I certainly wasn't the only kid I knew who was looking forward to leaving Kiester and seeing the larger world. I had plenty of conversations with friends about it. We weren't entirely sure what was out there, but we wanted to find out. What we didn't talk about, or at least not completely, was what we hoped to leave behind. Nobody talked about their relationships with their parents, maybe because none of us yet had the perspective to understand that things could be any way other than how they were. That sort of realization takes time. (During my senior year in college my life intersected with that of a then-second-year law student named Barack Obama. One night I found myself in a long conversation with him, and our talk turned to our life stories. It's hard for me to believe it now, but I distinctly remember describing my upbringing as "pretty normal," which it certainly wasn't if measured by the standards of the Harvard crowd we were part of then.)

The gist of all this? You would not have met the teenaged or twenty-something version of me and predicted I would someday be a horse parent. You would have been justified in predicting that I would not even be a dedicated parent, much less a good one. I certainly entertained my own doubts, and, at first, brought a real hesitancy to the task.

Friends started having kids before we did. At first it was friends who lived in other cities, and visits to them became like trips to a foreign land. A weekend of carousing in Madison, Wisconsin, differed from similar weekends in the past in that the friend I stayed with had a young son. The boy was still in that stage where age gets measured in months—old enough to walk and say a few words, but still as much baby as child. We had our moments of fun, he and I, as he showed me some of his toys. But then I got to leave.

A year or so later Lea and I traveled to Milwaukee to visit her parents, and while there spent an afternoon with a friend of hers who had recently had a baby. On past visits we would have met at a restaurant or bar. This time we met at her house, and we didn't leave. Her husband was at work and she could go nowhere without the baby. I came away from the day with one great realization, a revelation only in the mind of a twenty-something who hadn't before given it much thought: Parental responsibility was constant. This wasn't like getting a pet, which could be left on its own. Every moment had to be accounted for. Parenthood was nothing to take lightly.

Another year or so down the line I got invited to breakfast with two friends. They were a couple years older than me and together formed the up-and-coming core of our practice group at the law firm where we all worked. I assumed our meeting had some work-related purpose. Instead, one of them broke the news that he was soon to become a father. We offered congratulations, but also some thinly masked condolences. After all, his life was about to be over.

He was the canary in the coal mine. More and more of our friends had children. There was a learning curve associated with this. And as much as I hate to feed gender stereotypes, it was primarily a male phenomenon. My still-childless friends and I came to understand that it wasn't enough to arrive home and report simply that another set of friends were expecting. It was apparently important also to learn—and remember—the due date. Then, once the child was born, the announcement, "They had their baby," would be received with questions. It turns out that "human" is not the right answer to "what is it?" I was supposed to know its gender and name. Some basic statistics, too.

None of this came naturally.

I was in no hurry to join the crowd. But the momentum gathered, and eventually it became our turn. We shopped for cribs and car seats and all the various other accoutrements of parenthood. We took classes and did all the things you're expected to do when you're expecting, and probably a few more. By this point I had a pretty good handle on what was in store, and my reluctance, or my fear, or whatever it was, remained. After we toured neighborhood daycare centers, I favored the one that was open the longest each day.

What I've just told you is all true, but like a lot of truths, it's incomplete. And like a lot of people, I'm a bundle of contradictions. When the day of Ada's birth came, I excitedly bought copies of as many newspapers as I could find to save as mementos. I brought a portable CD player to the hospital so I could ensure that the first music our daughter heard would be of my choosing. (True to form for a young lawyer, the choice was deeply pretentious.)

I know that the script calls for me to say that all my apprehension fell away at the moment of birth, and that it was love at first sight. And while that's probably right, I can't say it went down the way I expected. For me, anyway, the real bond started to form once we got to know each other a little bit, once I knew how she liked to be held and she knew that I liked to hold her. Still, I remember the delivery room, and I remember the moment she entered the world. I remember the following day, and a session that the hospital held for all that day's parents and newborns. And I remember uncertainty, and a certain amount of fear that I would screw this up. (One of my most vivid memories is of sweating profusely as family members looked on while Ada cried at the top of her lungs as I struggled to strap her into her car seat for the drive home from the hospital.)

Probably all parents imagine they're going to shape their kids to a greater extent than reality tends to allow. Probably all parents, whether consciously or not, tend to make a list of what they regard as their own shortcomings and do their best to raise children who don't share them.

Probably all likewise try to build on what they regard as their strengths. And, of course, they look back to their own childhood, to the things their parents did and the things their parents didn't do, and try to adjust accordingly. We might have big dreams but the core goal is basic: F*** them up as little as possible.

I suppose I can't speak for anyone else, but for me the uncertainty and the fear of screwing up have never gone away. Parenthood is a kind of performance, and like most performances, it takes three forms. There's the parent you plan to be, the parent you actually are, and the parent you wish you had been. There may be people for whom it all goes how they thought it would, and there may be people who depart this world certain that, even if they had a chance to do it all again, they wouldn't change a thing about how they parented. If it happens, I'm willing to bet the children rarely agree. It's definitely not true for me. Whatever plan I brought with me got ripped up a long time ago, and I've done many things I'd do differently if I had a do-over. I look back on my worst moments as a parent and hope they're not the ones my daughters remember.

The uncertainty rarely appears in as stark a form as it did while I fumbled around trying to buckle newborn Ada into her car seat, but it's always there. So many segments of the journey are new ones, even for second and third children, and so many of the paths that present themselves lead to uncertain destinations. Is this next step the right one? How will we know? Good choices can produce bad results, and vice versa. And, of course, it's not just about selecting paths, but also how you approach them. Sometimes guidance is good. Other times the best approach is to back off. It's a complicated process of trying to read both the world and the kid. Perfection is unattainable. Life happens whether you're ready for it or not.

Ada was born in Minneapolis, but we moved to Oklahoma City when she was nearly two so that I could begin a career as a law school professor. Her twin sisters Audrey and Laura arrived not long after, and I often describe the change in terms of a hockey analogy: Lea and I went from being on the power play to being shorthanded. It was a busy time.

So, it's no surprise that we can't pin down the precise moment when Fate put us on the path to the barn. Was it the time, when we still lived in the Twin Cities, that we'd gone to the Wisconsin State Fair and walked through the horse barn? We paused to look in a few of the stalls, me lifting Ada high enough for her to see, getting her close but remaining mindful of the signs asking us not to touch the horses. Something about that moment led me, for the first time in my life, to pause to appreciate the majesty of these animals, and even to remark on it to Lea. I'm not generally one to get mystical, but it was a remarkable coincidence...if that's what it was.

Was Ada's infatuation something that just gradually developed? We'd consistently worked our way through animal-themed picture books, sure. But we had also gone through a phase where she was fascinated by airplanes, and on a trip to Washington, DC, I made a special journey to the National Air and Space Museum to take advantage of an especially good selection of children's books. In the Twin Cities she had been briefly intrigued by birds, and then by our neighbor's dog Schmidty, whose name—minus the "m"—she endearingly enjoyed saying out loud, over and over. Each interest seemed to arrive by chance, burn brightly for a time, then fade away as something else came to replace it. The first few days she showed a special interest in horses, we imagined, were just the start of another phase.

My first distinct memory is of a moment probably a couple weeks into the not-just-a-phase. I was on the floor in what we called "the playroom," building a barn-like structure out of Legos. It was a variation on getting the cart before the horse, because we had nothing to put in the barn. Breyer horses hadn't yet become ubiquitous, so a trip to Target to find appropriately sized toy horses turned up nothing. But, we figured, we lived in Oklahoma City. There had to be a place.

And that was how our entire family ended up in Stockyards City, historically (no surprise) the location of stockyards and a packing house, and now home to a variety of restaurants and businesses including a couple of saddle shops. Surely, we thought, they would have what we were looking for. It was a cold winter day with a brisk Oklahoma wind, and we parked the minivan across from what our study of the yellow pages suggested was the most promising option. Two memories remain for me. The first is of just how strong that wind was, and how unpleasantly cold it was crossing that street with a daughter in each arm. The second is of opening the door to that store and immediately understanding that we were out of our element. There were rows and rows of saddles and walls covered with bridles. Rack after rack held brightly colored Western apparel. None of it was anything we knew anything about.

Some people are comfortable in unfamiliar environments. Lea and I are not those kind of people. We tentatively made our way into the store, apparently throwing off enough "we don't belong here" vibes that nobody ever asked us if we needed help. Probably they figured we were just looking to get out of the wind. We eventually found the inevitable selection of Breyer model horses. It was nowhere near as large as many we'd eventually encounter over the years, but we left with a couple of the smaller Stablemates models. They were almost the perfect size for the Lego barn. They were also, we quickly learned, too fragile for a two-year-old. The floors of our house were soon littered with two- and three-legged plastic animals.

The years that followed involved variations on the theme of haphaz-ardly attempting to find ways to spend time around and learn more about horses. It wasn't long after the Stockyards City trip that Ada and I set out to get her first book exclusively about horses. Even by then we had started to grasp the magnitude of what we were dealing with, and the trip brought a sense of excitement. It was winter, with the sky already dark in the early evening. Ada noticed the moon, and then noticed it again after we had made a couple turns. "The moon is following us, Daddy," she reported from her car seat as we drove along the Northwest Expressway. She kept track of it during the rest of our trip, and we paused to admire it when we got out of the car. The book we got, called simply *Horses,* by Laura Driscoll, became required reading, often multiple times per day. Eventually we had turned its pages so many times that it fell apart and we had to replace it. Countless other horse books followed, many of which Ada would recite from memory.

Family outings often bore some relationship to horses. We became members and frequent visitors to the outstanding National Cowboy & Western Heritage Museum. (I don't know if you can still buy the *All About Cowboys* videos in the gift shop there, but if you can, I'm pretty sure you can thank me for putting that idea in the suggestion box.) We made multiple trips to Garth Brooks's hometown of Yukon, Oklahoma, to visit the Express Clydesdales, a less famous but equally impressive counterpart to the Budweiser Clydesdales. A mounted police officer com-ing down the street in front of our house was a drop-everything event. Ending up in the Bricktown entertainment district meant, at the very least, keeping an eye out for horse-drawn carriages, and on a lucky day, getting to pet a horse. We discovered that Oklahoma City bills itself as the "Horse Show Capital of the World" and made our way to the state fairgrounds, where our whole family wandered into the coliseum, unsure of where to sit and not knowing that pretty much anywhere would have been fine. It was the national show for some breed or other, and we'd shown up for something called "halter classes." That was interesting...for a little while. But everyone in our family wondered when they'd actually start riding the horses. We left without ever finding out.

One day there were pony rides at a festival in the park a block away from our house. I couldn't tell you what the festival was for or what else was there. But I'll never forget that the pony rides were only a dollar and that hardly any kids, other than my daughter, seemed to want one. We quickly burned through the five dollars I had in my pocket and walked home to get more. For the most part Ada was the only customer, and she kept the ponies moving. She rode them all enough times to develop a clear ranking of her favorites. We stayed to watch them load up and go home. That was a good day.

We talked about it for weeks.

And then there were the rodeos. I'll start with a short digression. My first rodeo—in the literal sense—had come a few years before. One of Lea's sisters lives in McKinney, Texas, north of Dallas, and once while we were in town we made a trip to the Fort Worth Stockyards. At the time, none of us yet had kids. There, among other things, we got tickets to a rodeo. We meant it as a bit of a lark, a chance to do a thing we'd do only "that once." I took advantage of the opportunity to have my first Frito pie. Lea discovered very quickly that something in the arena was a major allergy trigger—something that would matter as our journey unfolds. And we all witnessed the kids' event, which involved some version of all the present and willing youngsters chasing an unimpressed sheep around the ring. The chaos of dozens of running and screaming kids didn't sit well with one of the bulls standing in a chute nearby. That would have been fine if the gate to the chute had been fully secured.

But it wasn't, and suddenly there was a rodeo bull in the ring with dozens of children. You don't often see a crowd's mood change from entertained to terrorized in an instant. This one did.

The announcer urged calm. We newcomers began to speculate about the possibility that somebody might have to shoot the bull right in front of everyone. But then the bullfighters (otherwise known as rodeo clowns) did their thing, the danger passed, and nobody got hurt. The entire episode probably lasted less than two minutes, even though it seemed longer. You could tell which of the little cowboys and cowgirls were not at their first rodeo by the way some of them climbed the fence alongside the ring—same as bull riders do, once they've been thrown off a bull.

I was no connoisseur of rodeos, but I knew the only thing I needed to know for our purposes: *Rodeos have horses.* A colleague suggested the Lazy E Arena in Guthrie, Oklahoma, and soon enough we were near-regulars. At the time we didn't appreciate that we were seeing competition at its highest level, though the contrast later became apparent when we attended a local rodeo after moving to Wisconsin. What mattered was that there were horses. Some were untamed and bucking. Some were trained to do specific things and to do them well. Some were the trusty companions ridden by the pickup men (whose job was to get cowboys out of the way of a bucking bull or horse after a ride had ended) or maybe the announcer. Nearly always I was alone with Ada—just the two of us. Laura and Audrey were still too young for such adventures, and Lea's allergies proved strong enough that the one trip she took to the Lazy E could be only a short one. Ada and I would arrive early and stay until the end. Ada remained focused the whole time, asking questions, soaking up as much as she could, and angling for a trip to the gift shop on our way out the door.

Our bedtime routine involved reading a book or two, then turning out the light and talking about the horses we had read about, the horses we had seen, the horses we would see, the horses Ada would one day ride and own. I made up horse-themed lyrics to familiar songs. "I've Been Working at the Rodeo" (in place of "railroad") was a particular favorite.

My early anxieties about parenthood receded. Neither the inclination nor the aptitude comes naturally to everyone, as a look around the world quickly reveals. But it wasn't the burden I had feared. It's a strange thing because as my daughters have now reached adulthood I've found myself mostly back where I started: Kids in small doses are fine, but I'm certainly not going out of my way to spend time around them. And so I can't tell you why I found joy and satisfaction and an infinitely deep well of love in having kids of my own, any more than I can tell you why I really like the taste of chocolate and caramel together. Some things, so far as we can tell, *just are.* That bond, from the beginning, took its own form for each of my daughters: Ada liked to be talked to at bedtime, Laura preferred to be held for a while as I walked around the room, and Audrey liked to have a conversation even before she was able to use words, often bolting up from what had seemed to be the early stages of sleep to share something that seemed important but that was in a verbal code known only to her.

There's a special sort of magic when everything is still to come. A new town, a new job, or even just a new project brings back the thrill of the new notebooks on the first day of school. The pages contain no words; there's nothing but endless possibility. Parenthood means getting to experience that on the grandest scale. There's an entire life ahead. Everything is new and much of it is fascinating. *Anything could happen.* That sensation alone is thrilling. And, in my case, it was coupled from nearly the beginning with a child's interest, the intensity of which was something I had never experienced for myself. Lea and I didn't know everything about what the future would hold, but we knew it would include horses. ✺

2

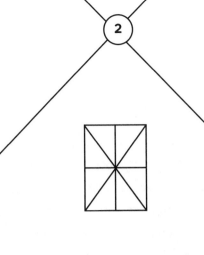

Our early steps into the horse world were haphazard and under-informed at best. That continued. It was probably unavoidable, because that's just how life is. I've often cautioned law students who come to me for career advice that they won't really be able to know whether they enjoy a certain type of practice until they're actually doing it. There's no way to replicate the demands that reality presents, and no way to predict how a given individual will respond to them. We've each got our own aptitudes and strengths, blind spots and weaknesses. Plenty of people who at first glance strike me as not well-suited to law practice in certain contexts end up thriving in them. Others who seem likely to be a perfect fit are not. There's no substitute for actually giving something a try. If you're lucky, you'll find a fit quickly.

Parenting provides an opening to a whole range of little worlds or communities or subcultures that might fit—and that mostly exist outside the notice of those in other phases of life. This first hit me when I visited some friends whose kids were a few years older than mine and who were in their early years of organized sports. I tagged along to a soccer game. The soccer was of the sort that mostly called to mind a swarm of insects following a ball, the action dominated by the one or two kids who had a slightly more advanced notion of what it was they were supposed to be doing and enough physical talent to carry through on it.

A large entourage of parents surrounded the field. Whether it was spring or fall I can't remember, but it was Minnesota, so there was a chill in the air. The parents wore jackets and hats and gloves and carried travel mugs that might have contained coffee or hot chocolate, or in some cases, something even a touch stronger. Some seemed to know each other well, but most interacted in the slightly formal way of people who have been assembled into a group from a collection of disparate parts.

I stood there as a visitor to this foreign land, watching the cars drive by on the adjacent streets, struck by the realization that I, too, had been in those cars. I had probably driven by hundreds of scenes like the one I was now a part of, each time not giving much thought at all to what was going on. But soon I, too, would be going to soccer games and standing somewhat uncomfortably among groups of not-quite strangers, driven not by my own desire to be there but by my kids' desire to be there.

The entry point to many of these little worlds defined by kids' interests is easy to find. In my youth you couldn't miss the paths to Little League and the 4-H club. Today's suburban family would have to be living under a rock to miss the chance to participate in youth soccer. Flyers come home from school, friends are doing it, it's often happening on a field adjacent to the playground. All three of our girls played soccer for a season or two, and no doubt there are pairs of tiny shin guards tucked away in some corner of our basement, a small part of the accumulated debris of three childhoods.

It takes a little more work when your kid's interest is off the beaten path. Things are certainly easier today, but in the early part of the 2000s, when the internet was not yet in full bloom, it was hard to figure out where to scratch an equestrian itch.

In retrospect I probably ought to have gathered more advice than I did. It's never been my instinct to do so, though. I would almost certainly not have ended up on the trajectory I did had I sought and then followed any readily available advice about where I should apply to college, for example. Early on in the process I told our high school guidance counselor, who was also the principal (because everybody's got to wear multiple hats in a small town) that I wanted to apply to MIT. His response was, "In California!" That's a tough spot for a seventeen-year-old, explaining to the person charged with giving him college-admission advice that MIT is an acronym for the *Massachusetts* Institute of Technology.

Our strengths and weaknesses are often just two sides of the same coin, however, and the instincts and strategies that worked well for me early in life have often been a hindrance in its later stages. I'm not temperamentally inclined to build networks or seek mentorship or advice, and those tendencies have not always served me well. Nor am I inclined to give advice except in the most hedged, "Your mileage may vary," sort of way. Indeed, I'm deeply suspicious of those who are too inclined to give advice to others. No doubt there are people who are good at it, who have an ability to look at another person's situation as a forest rather than a collection of trees, and who can suggest appropriate paths. Take advantage of those people when you find them. But often, I suspect, eager advice-givers are more in the nature of busybodies, people with a limited capacity for empathy, who, as a result, are unable to appreciate that others may have different priorities and perceptions than they do. Theirs is "one-size-fits-all" advice in a world in which one size most definitely *does not* fit all.

Still, I probably erred on the side of seeking *too little* advice. The result, in any case, was that Lea and I and the girls stumbled through the equestrian world a bit more than we might have. That's not to say that things didn't generally work out well. They did. But still, *my first piece of advice is to seek advice*, and not just from one person.

If you've ended up with this book in your hands because you've found yourself the parent of a child with a passion for horses and you're not quite sure what to do about it, then let me at least tell you not to run the other way. If your kid loves horses, and you can swing it, the experience can't be beat. But I also want to attempt to paint an accurate picture of the corners of equestrian sport I'm familiar with and to do so with the benefit of hindsight. Human nature is such that once we've made a decision we tend to focus on its positive aspects and minimize the negatives. Often, we'd prefer simply to ignore the negatives. Our family had a great experience, but it wasn't perfect. I'd do some things differently. And there are things I didn't know but wish I had.

n the early years it was enough for us simply to seek out horses. It didn't much matter whether they were carrying someone, pulling something, or standing in a field. The best songs were the ones with horses—not just "She'll Be Comin' Round the Mountain" but also "Rhinestone Cowboy." Books and videos were acceptable so long as there was a horse with a role in the story. Our satellite TV package included RFDTV, which would broadcast both horse racing and various sorts of horsemanship clinics. Ada was up for all of it. The combination of my rural background and our location in Oklahoma meant that most of what we encountered involved Western riding. We were vaguely aware that there were other forms, but as I imagined the future it involved Western saddles and a certain amount of "bling."

In the end, that's not the path we went down. Nearly all the riding my daughters would eventually do was the kind that took place in an English saddle and fell within the scope of the three equestrian sports that appear in the Olympics: show jumping, dressage, and eventing. Each, to a considerable degree, has roots in the military use of horses. I have considerably more familiarity with show jumping, and its broader umbrella known as "hunter/jumper," than the other two, seeing as my daughters have spent more time in that world. But I think I can manage a credible explanation of the basics of all three.

## HUNTER/JUMPER

Once in a Facebook post I used the phrase "hunter/jumper" without specifically linking it to horses. A friend left a comment in which he admitted that he didn't know what that was but envisioned some sort of activity combining guns and trampolines. No doubt the sport is often both exciting and dangerous. It's not quite *that* exciting and dangerous.

What ties the hunter/jumper world together is that each of its subdisciplines primarily involves riding horses over a course of jumps. Usually this takes place in a fenced-in arena, the surface of which is made up of sand or something sand-like. In their most basic form, the jumps consist of wooden poles (or "rails") held between two standards in such a way that they will fall if the horse hits them. There are three types of classes at hunter/jumper shows: hunter classes, in which the judging focuses on the horse; equitation classes, in which the judging focuses on the rider; and jumper classes, where what matters is getting around a course faster than the other horses while not knocking down any rails.

Several things happen as a rider advances through the sport. The jumps get higher. Poles on the ground become "cross-rails," which are simply pairs of poles set with one end on the ground and the other at a low setting on the standard, together forming an "X" in the middle. Then they become straight rails set about eighteen inches off the ground and move up at roughly six-inch increments from there (at least until the metric system gets involved at some of the higher levels). At the highest levels the rails stand over five feet off the ground. Also, additional types of jumps come into play. Some have different shapes; some add an element of width in addition to height. Some add water. The standards themselves become more colorful, distracting, and spooky. And finally, the jumps are placed in increasingly complex orders.

All of this comes together to create difficulty. As jumps become higher and wider, the margin of error for where the horse must take off in order to successfully clear a jump becomes smaller. Different sorts of jumps and combinations of jumps, short distances, and tight turns require different approaches and have different effects on the horse once he has landed. An error at one jump may not have obvious consequences until two or three jumps later.

Although there are, inevitably, elements of course design that regularly occur, courses are not the same from one show to the next, or even from one day at a show to the next. And they must be ridden on an animal that is genetically programmed to notice and run away from the unfamiliar.

What I've just described applies most directly to the jumper subset of the hunter/jumper world. As one of the Olympic disciplines, show jumping is scored in a way that's easily grasped by the outsider. So long as the horse and rider stay on the prescribed course, the only things that matter are the time on the clock, whether any of the rails fall, and whether the horse "refuses" a jump, either by stopping or running past it. Appearances and technique do not factor into the scoring. As long as he can clear the fences quickly, the ugliest horse in the world can be a champion.

The hunter divisions are considerably more opaque to the newcomer. They are "judged," rather than timed, with—as I've mentioned already—the focus on the horse rather than the rider. The origins of the hunters date back to English foxhunting, and in theory, at least, the criteria used to assess the horses are based on the factors that would make for a good foxhunting horse. Some of those concern the way the horse moves on the flat (that is, while moving about the ring other than while jumping) and how he jumps, while others relate to the horse's build, which is referred to as his "conformation." (Because these classes are all about appearances, the ugliest horse in the world *will not* fare well at all in hunter classes.) The jumping courses in hunter classes tend to be considerably less complicated than those in jumper classes, and the jumps tend to be less colorful and more likely to involve some sort of shrubbery. A single dropped rail or a refusal automatically lowers a score to an extent that winning becomes impossible. Time is not a factor. Indeed, a slow, even pace is desirable. The effect is hypnotic—which is a polite way of saying that those uninitiated in the discipline are likely to find it boring and inscrutable.

Which brings us to equitation—judged classes with the focus on the rider. The criteria relate to the rider's position, use of riding "aids" (meaning, in essence, the various cues that riders use to communicate with horses), and overall appearance, on the flat and over fences. The rider's skill is tested in other respects, too, as the courses become more complicated, with tighter turns and, as in the jumpers, combinations of jumps that have to be thought about and ridden in a way that takes into account how they relate to one another rather than simply as a sequence of individual jumps. One might imagine that the horse won't matter in an equitation class, but that's not the case. There is such a thing as an "equitation horse," and while some horses can perform credibly across multiple divisions, at the highest levels there tends to be quite a bit of specialization, all of which comes with a heavy price tag.

The outsider at a hunter/jumper show will easily be able to wrap his brain around jumper classes. The logic of a fast, clean round is easy to understand, and while shows tend not to play up the drama as much as they might, every rider goes into the ring knowing the time to beat to take the lead. Hunter and equitation classes, by contrast, will often seem arbitrary. Even when you reach the point, as I have, of knowing what you're supposed to be looking for, you won't always know whether you've seen it. For classes where scores are announced—which, puzzlingly, is not all of them—you will find your assessment diverging from the judge's on a regular basis. Or at least I have.

Another thing that will strike the outsider at a hunter/jumper show is that there's lots of waiting. So much waiting. Sometimes it seems like you're waiting for the opportunity to wait some more in a slightly different location. Hang around the beginner ring at a hunter/jumper show where the newcomer parents are likely to be and you're bound to find people who are both puzzled and irritated. Which is understandable for the simple reason that the waiting is usually both puzzling and irritating. Puzzling because it doesn't seem like it should be that hard to formulate and stick to a schedule (especially when you find out that the disciplines of dressage and eventing both manage to do just that). Irritating because each day and each show presents large swaths of seemingly wasted time. Often there are long intervals where there is absolutely nothing going on in a show ring, and no apparent reason why that's the case. Things will seem like they're starting to move quickly, then suddenly stop. Once my daughter Audrey was at a show and I was at home, about forty-five minutes away. She texted to let me know she had just found out she would be riding in about half an hour. That math didn't sound promising but still I ran to the car, drove to the showgrounds as fast as I could, then sprinted to the ring her classes were in, hoping I might be able to catch her last ride of the day. It was another hour before she went in the ring for the first time.

There's money to be made by someone who develops the software to help hunter/jumper shows run more efficiently. For everyone else I can offer only this: You get used to it. In roughly the same way, I'd guess, that residents of the Soviet Union got used to standing in line for toilet paper.

Something that might be less apparent to the outsider is the extent of the stratification, some of which turns on talent but much of which turns on wealth. This of course is certainly true to varying degrees throughout the horse world (and the world in general), but it's most pronounced, in my experience, in the realm of hunter/jumpers. Within the context of a given show, whether at the lowest level or the highest level, there will be a distinction between the nice horse and the merely adequate horse, and the average nice horse at a lower level will often be on the lower end of adequate at the highest levels. The nicest horses at the fanciest shows run well into the six figures.

It is—or at least can be—crazily expensive. But the market for horses is not, to use economist-speak, an "efficient market," meaning prices reflect all available information in an unbiased way. The price of a horse sometimes depends on who's selling, or who's buying, or what the horse will be used for. Whether the horse is likely to be successful at shows seems to matter only at the margins. There certainly are horses that are good enough to provide a strong chance of winning nearly every time out, at least when paired with a sufficiently talented rider. But those horses are rare, and they are extraordinarily expensive. (A million dollars is not out of the question, and may even be a bargain.) The mass of hunter and equitation horses instead seem to be what are called "Veblen goods" (after the economist and sociologist Thorstein Veblen, most famous for coming up with the notion of "conspicuous consumption")—things that become more desirable as they become more expensive based on their perceived exclusivity and value as a status symbol. Put differently, prices in this discipline make very little sense when viewed in terms of the results they produce, and instead are driven by appearance and perception. Someone will decide that a particular horse is, say, a mid-five-figures horse, and if it's the right sort of someone then that horse will be regarded as exactly that, even if his show record is (and will almost certainly continue to be) thoroughly undistinguished. Ease of riding also plays no necessary role. The most expensive horse our family has owned was, by a considerable margin, the one least likely to jump any given jump. The first horse we owned almost always tried to jump whatever he was pointed at. In my opinion he was the very best horse we owned, and we got him for five thousand dollars.

Now, it's entirely possible that I'm missing some things. My eye is not that sharp when it comes to distinguishing one horse from the next. No doubt some horses are nicer than others in the sense that some cars and clothes are perceived as nicer than others, even though they offer no real functional advantages apart from being more fun to drive or, I guess, to wear. I'm not one drawn to fanciness for its own sake in those contexts, either. But from the perspective of a parent asked to shell out money for a "better" horse, it can be a difficult expenditure to justify if it doesn't lead to improved results. If you're the sort of parent who thinks it important for your kid to have one of the nicest cars in the school parking lot, then none of this will trouble you. You can add "one of the nicest horses at the show" to your child's resume. But if that's not where you're at, then it's at least important for you to understand that these factors are at work.

The equine sales business is rife with questionable ethics as well: One routinely hears stories of sellers waiting to name their price for a horse until they know how much a potential buyer has to spend, and of the various professionals involved in a sale acting in ways that are more in the interests of their own commissions than in the interests of their clients. There are no formal ethical standards or even consistent norms that apply to these situations, and as in all corners of life, people are quite able to conjure up justifications that conveniently align with their self-interest. None of this is to suggest that every horse is overpriced or that everyone in the business is unethical. There are fair prices and even bargains to be had if you find the right people to deal with. We've been fortunate in finding a few of those people.

But appropriate caution is in order. To put the point a bit more sharply: There are a lot of people who stand to gain from convincing you (and themselves) that you should spend the money for that marginally nicer horse. A couple years back I read a pair of books at the same time. One was an autobiography of a famous horseperson, the other a biography of a less-famous musician. Both were sons of salesmen. The horseperson observed that his father was too honest to be more than mildly successful. The musician spoke of how his dad, who did not much like his job, would tell him, "There's larceny in every salesman's heart."

Bound up with all this is the hierarchy of the show world. At the bottom are "schooling shows." These are relatively low-dollar affairs, with a mix of horses that are less fancy or less experienced. There are ribbons and trophies awarded, but the focus is on learning and enjoyment. A rung above that are 4-H and local show circuits, which often involve a self-contained series of shows with placings and prizes as well as season-end awards. Up from that are shows that are within the ambit of the US Equestrian Federation. When we began showing these were denominated as B, A, and AA shows. They've since been rebranded as Local, Regional, National, and Premier, but everybody still uses the old "letter" designations.

Someone progressing through these levels will notice differences in terms of the "fanciness" of the horses, the quality of riding, and the nature of course design. The facilities at higher-rated shows are generally nicer, though the same showgrounds will often host shows at a variety of levels. The best horse-and-rider combinations are most likely to be at the highest-level shows, but that's a far cry from saying that everyone at the higher levels is more talented than those at lower levels. And plenty of the differences are simply cosmetic, with the exclusivity—or at least the appearance of exclusivity—itself being part of the appeal among a certain segment of the crowd that attends the shows. Use of the very same stall will often cost more at an A show than at a B show the following week. It's no accident that as one moves up through the levels there tends to be increasing use of grooms—people who are paid to do the work of caring for the horses and getting them saddled and otherwise ready for competition. The rider at a lower-level show is likely to have trailered her horse to the show, set up the stall, groomed her horse, tacked him up, and led him to the ring herself. The rider at the highest levels might have done some or occasionally even all of those things but is just as likely to meet her horse at the ring when it's her turn to show. There she'll be given a leg-up by the groom who did all the preparation, and then hop off and hand the reins back to her groom when her rounds are finished.

## DRESSAGE

The word "dressage," which is French for "training," gets used in two related but distinct ways. In one sense it refers somewhat generally to certain fundamental exercises and methods for training a horse. Hunter/jumper trainers and riders often resort to dressage in this sense as a form of cross-training, and my understanding is that other disciplines do likewise. The second sense refers to competitive dressage, which is a distinct discipline and one of the Olympic equestrian sports. As compared to hunter/jumper riding, the saddles and bridles are a bit different, the most desirable and effective riding position is a bit different, and the horses are different. Dressage is, to a more thorough degree than in any of the hunter/jumper subdisciplines, about precision. There are no jumps. Showing takes place in a somewhat smaller ring. Around the outside of the ring will be a set of letters, which might be on pylons or affixed to the rail or displayed in some other way. The array of the letters is consistently the same, and it follows no obvious logic whatsoever. (Nor is there one generally accepted explanation for why the letters are the way they are. By all appearances it is a random, confusing mess.) Letters also designate certain spots within the ring—"X" is the center, for at least one thing that makes intuitive sense—though those are unmarked.

Showing in dressage consists of performing a prescribed "test." The rider will, for example, enter the ring at point "A" and proceed to "X" at a prescribed gait. At "X" she will halt and salute the judge. From there she will complete a sequence of maneuvers, all performed with reference to the system of letters. At the most basic level this will include a series of circles as well as a few transitions between different gaits. The movements become increasingly complex as one advances, and the performances at the top of the sport are often compared to ballet.

The judge scores each movement within a test using a uniform rubric. These individual scores get written down and, because the judge has a scribe to take notes during each ride, so does a brief written explanation of the score, which in turn gets provided to the rider. (Notably, this does not happen in hunter and equitation classes, in which the rider often but not always gets an overall score, and never more than that.)

As with watching hunter or equitation classes, dressage for the spectator is an acquired taste. I find the difference between a well-ridden dressage test at a high level versus one at a lower level easier to see than the differences between high- and low-level hunter rounds. The movements in dressage are considerably more complex, and the upper-level dressage horse carries himself in a completely different way.

As befits a world in which precise riding is key, dressage shows differ from hunter/jumper shows in that each ride is scheduled down to the minute. Shows will sometimes get ahead of schedule—though no rider is required to ride before a scheduled time—and only rarely get behind schedule. You still do some waiting, and you might still end up spending your entire day at a show—the horse needs to be taken care of, after all, and rides might be scheduled hours apart—but there's considerably less uncertainty. You can plan when to eat, perhaps even to sneak away from the showgrounds for a bit. And your rider knows when she'll be riding.

Dressage offers an element of competition against oneself. A dressage test is the same at every dressage show—Third Level, Test One, for example, will be the same whether ridden at a show in New York, Oregon, or Iowa—and at least in theory is judged according to the same criteria. (There is undoubtedly some variation from one judge to the next in terms of the range of scores they are likely to give.) It allows for easier goal setting, in that a rider can focus on improving her scores over time on a given test, as well as on moving up through the levels of testing.

My family came to dressage shows relatively late in the game and so has been to fewer of them. I likely do not bring the same perspective to them that I bring to hunter/jumper events. I can't speak as confidently to the market for horses, though my impression is that it's much more common in dressage for a rider to find success on an inexpensive horse she has developed on her own. But I sense a different energy in the two contexts. The hunter/jumper scene, to me, has a vibe that is not so different from many other youth sports. (The other youth sport with which I have had the most involvement is figure skating, in both its individual and synchronized forms, and skating competitions are much more like hunter/jumper shows than dressage shows.) There's a focus on placings in classes, and on moving up, and on status relative to one's peers. All of this, perhaps, feeds into (or is a product of—it's not so clear which way the causation runs) the more general status obsession that seems to permeate the hunter/jumper world, especially at the elite levels.

Dressage shows, by contrast, seem to be more relaxed. The existence of and adherence to a schedule is no doubt part of it. It takes the edge off for everyone to have a near-exact idea of when they will ride. The extra adrenaline that's probably necessary to ride a course of jumps isn't required. And there's no need to learn a new course. The patterns are set, and up until the highest levels it's permissible to have a reader alongside the ring calling out the test to remind the rider what's next. Another reason is likely that the participants at dressage shows skew considerably more toward the adult. And it's not the adults of beer league softball or recreational hockey, who are often out in a futile attempt to recapture the lost glory of their youth. The sense I had walking through a recent dressage show was that it was a community of people who were there doing a thing that they love, and who will continue to do that thing into the foreseeable future. There wasn't the urgency that accompanies being a young hunter/jumper rider, no set of age ranges or dates on the calendar that marks a necessary progression through the ranks, no resulting need to have things happen—jumping bigger jumps, getting a "better" horse, and so on—according to some imposed schedule. People seem less concerned about who they might become and more at ease with who they are. When you're working with the horse you've got, and aren't as constrained by the passage of time, you can take a little bit of a longer view. And that's appropriate in dressage, where the relationship between horse and rider seems even more important, where the improvements are incremental, where the knowledge and skill involved is subtle and cumulative. As I've already mentioned, the competition becomes less clearly against others and more against oneself, and against the ideal. The satisfaction is less in "winning" versus one's peers and more in the process of working on a puzzle that grows increasingly complex the longer one works on it.

To capture the difference in another way: There seems to be a lot less crying at dressage shows.

## EVENTING

Eventing combines dressage and show jumping with a third phase called "cross-country." Cross-country involves jumping courses that are on grass outside of rings, considerably longer in terms of distance, and feature jumps that tend to be solid obstacles, ranging from tree trunks to various forms of wooden structures, and also including hedges, hills, ditches, and usually a trip or two through water. The phases occur in a specified order—dressage, followed by cross-country, and then show jumping—and each is scored separately. Events, sometimes called "horse trials," take place over a period from one to four days, depending in part on the level of competition.

I have considerably less familiarity with eventing than with hunter/jumper and dressage. Ada rode in one horse trial at about the midpoint of her career to date, and a couple years before that she and I made a trip to the Kentucky Horse Park to watch what was then called the Rolex Three-Day Event (it's now sponsored by Land Rover), which is the highest-level eventing competition in the United States. There's a t-shirt you can buy from vendors at horse trials that reads: "Red on right, white on left, insanity in the middle." The basic idea is this: the cross-country jumps have red flags on their right sides and white on their left (which tell the rider both what they're supposed to jump and in what direction), and the riders themselves, who must jump between those flags, are crazy.

Based on what I've witnessed, that seems about right. The cross-country jumps in Kentucky were some of the most imposing-looking things I've seen, and it was not difficult to imagine bad endings for horse, rider, or both if things went wrong. And things do go wrong, with bad endings as a result. Riders wear protective vests for cross-country that they do not typically wear in the other two phases. Even at the lower levels it's easy to see that riding cross-country provides a different sort of danger, and thus a different sort of adrenaline rush.

Eventing culture seems to differ from the other two disciplines I've described in at least a couple respects. One is that there's a more generally prevalent do-it-yourself ethos. Grooms are rare, as is the use of commercial horse transportation. Another concerns the horses. At least one of the riders competing in Kentucky the year Ada and I went to the event rode a Thoroughbred that she bought as a three-year-old when the horse's racing career came to an end. Another horse from perhaps the year before was famous for having been bought for $600. Both, remember, were competing at the highest possible level. That's not completely unheard of in the hunter/jumper world—indeed, for a couple years my daughter Audrey showed an off-the-track Thoroughbred (an OTTB, as they're called)—but they are not fashionable and are extraordinarily unlikely to do well in the judged divisions. In contrast, bringing one along in the eventing world seems to be a point of pride. Eventers, it seems to me, are the punk rockers of the equestrian scene. ❀

# 3

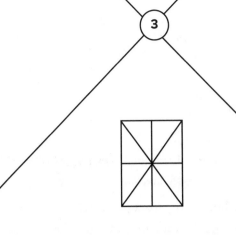

Rumor has it that there are barns where beginning riders start with a series of glorified pony rides that can stretch on for months. There may be a lesson or two where the new rider gets led around the ring, following which she advances to riding on a longe line (meaning that the instructor holds a rope attached to the horse's bridle, and the horse and rider travel in a circle around the instructor). That stage lasts a very long time. Eventually the *actual* riding begins.

I've never been able to tell just how much truth there is to that rumor, but it certainly was not the arrangement at Appy Orse. Beginners rode on their own right away, with the only concession being that they started out in

Western tack and the riders held the reins in one hand, leaving the other conveniently free to grab the saddle horn for security on an as-needed basis. But that was just a temporary stage. Most of the older riders rode in English tack, which, we quickly learned, was necessary for those who jumped. On a jumping horse—the front end of which comes quickly off the ground—a saddle horn can be a source of injury for reasons that don't require too much imagination to envision. A Western saddle also places the rider in a position that makes jumping more difficult for the horse. If you wanted to jump, you had to make the switch.

Ada's early lessons were all about the accumulation of basic skills. Getting a horse to go, getting him to stop, getting him to turn when and how Ada wanted him to. The challenge of making a turn to go across the ring was followed by the challenge of being able to weave in and out of a series of cones, first at a walk and then at a trot. She learned about not cutting corners, becoming aware of other horses in the ring, and working with other riders to stay out of one another's way. Looming above all this was the first big goal: to pass the test for getting to ride English, which was simply to canter (or, to use the term appropriate to Western riding, "lope") around the ring once without breaking stride.

The first horse she rode was Edgar. He was what's known as an Appendix Quarter Horse—meaning that he was mostly Quarter Horse but had some Thoroughbred mixed in. Barn lore was that he had been a very good jumper back in his day. Now he was a patient and forgiving teacher of beginners, the sort of horse that receives little of the glory but deserves all of it. For however many weekends in a row I watched from that same corner where Ada and I sat the first day, leaning in my chair the way one does when trying to steer a golf shot you've already hit as she worked to maneuver Edgar through the various challenges. Some lessons were great, and we left the barn on a high note, our drive home filled with talk of what happened and what would come next. Others went less well, and the trip home was somber and quiet.

The first big milestone Ada reached was one that nobody ever tries for. But anyone who gets on a horse enough times will eventually fall off. For all the parts of those early days that have receded into the fog of time, I can see, as vividly as if it happened yesterday, the moment she inadvertently gave Edgar the signal to lope. They were at the far end of the ring. He was moving a little too slowly for her taste, and she gave him a bit more of a kick than he was expecting. He switched gears and started to turn right. Ada did not start to turn right. Instead, she continued to go forward, disappearing over his left shoulder before showing up again, an eternity later, on the ground. I got about six steps into my sprint down the arena to her when Bernadette called out firmly that I should take my seat. (And when Bernadette tells you to take your seat, that is exactly what you do.) She then began to go through the routine with Ada: *Stay on the ground, make sure everything still works, walk down to the mounting block, and get back on.* Whatever it was that Ada had just been doing, I'm sure that the next thing that happened was that she did it again. And got it right.

Meanwhile, I started to wonder what this meant for the conversation on the ride home. Would this be devastating? What words did I need to have ready to make the best of the situation? Thankfully, a barn mom who was herself a rider came to my rescue. "You're not a real rider until you fall," she told Ada. "Now you're a real rider."

It wouldn't have worked coming from me. But now it was a badge of honor.

Most every lesson at Appy Orse was a group lesson. Set lesson times on Saturdays and Sundays were first-come, first-served, with signup sheets on a clipboard in the tack room. A roughly equivalent portion of the business model involved giving trail rides, and as a result the farm had a large herd of horses—perhaps sixty, perhaps more, only a small fraction of which were owned by boarders—all of whom lived outside year-round. Riders who had reached an appropriate age and experience level walked out into the herd to get their horses for lessons. Everyone, from the very first lesson, was responsible for grooming and tacking up. Because the horses lived outside in Wisconsin, this often meant having to deal with mud that had caked onto long winter coats. The barn wasn't heated apart from a small space heater in the tack room. It can get awfully cold in the depths of a Wisconsin winter, and hand- and toe-warmers help only so much. It was part of the deal, though, and a bit of suffering is a small price to pay to get to do a thing you love. The only complaints ever heard at Appy Orse were of the sort that build solidarity, subtle acknowledgement that "this is who we are." Nobody had to be there, everyone chose it.

One of the benefits of group lessons is, or at least can be, that they include riders of varying ages and skill levels. This gives beginner riders, in particular, the ability to watch and learn from the efforts and critiques of their more advanced counterparts. Ada rode with groups that were mostly filled with teenagers, but usually also included at least one other younger kid and an adult or two. In an hour-long lesson that makes for a lot of time in which it's other people who are doing the riding, and not every kid can avoid letting her mind wander while waiting her turn. Not a problem for Ada—she watched attentively throughout, soaking it all in. In the barn she often rejected offers of help, preferring to get her horse ready all by herself.

Although it seemed like a long journey at the time, it can't have taken all that long for Ada to make the transition out of the Western saddle. The fall startled her a little bit, and so things took somewhat longer than they otherwise might have. But the goal, and her resolve to reach it, remained. I'd hold my breath as she and Edgar would lope down the side of the ring, then not quite make it through the turn, or make it through the turn only to have him break down into a jog. Some days a full trip around the ring at the prescribed rocking-horse gait seemed a distant dream.

But the seasons hadn't yet changed enough for lessons to have moved to the outdoor ring when the breakthrough came. Ada and Edgar made it to the corner, then through the corner, then all the way around the ring—and they just kept going. I sat literally on the edge of my seat, my mind progressing from a simple state of hope that she would make it farther than she had before, to hope that she might actually pull off a full lap, to my first true appreciation of the notion of chest-bursting pride. I've experienced the sensation many times since, triggered each time by something that one of my daughters has done. Nothing I've ever accomplished for myself has felt anywhere near as good in the moment as that trip around the ring. Ada had set a goal for herself, and she had succeeded.

My sister was in town visiting us that weekend, and we stopped, as we often did, at a Dairy Queen a few miles from the farm. We ordered and took our seats in a play area that featured a small, three-horse carousel that Ada rode each visit. My daughter had a bite or two of ice cream, then paused to do a little dance while chanting, "I get to ride English!" over and over and over.

The next couple years included a lesson nearly every weekend. Ada moved from Edgar to Gary, the start of a series of transitions that would include horses named Max, Stroker, Sunny, Michael, and a few others who made only brief appearances in her riding career. I sat ringside for nearly every lesson, sometimes learning simply by paying attention, and other times helped by an adult rider or a parent a bit farther along in the journey who could explain things like diagonals and leads and why we pay attention to them. We gradually began to accumulate equipment—her own helmet, boots, and half chaps, then brushes and a lead rope and a bag in which to carry them—each item a quiet, hopeful step on the road to a horse of her own. Our trips to tack stores to add to our collection were in reality much larger adventures of exploration. We would wander the aisles, looking at and holding things that we had only read about in books, Ada picking up pieces of tack or equipment and explaining to me how they worked, the two of us speculating about the purposes of some item we'd never seen before. Together we were learning about this new world, and she took the lead as often as I did. At no point in my life have I had such a deep or encompassing interest in anything as she did in all of this. It was fascinating to watch and to be a part of, and impossible to resist encouraging.

The barn aisle at Appy Orse became the place where Ada began to learn the great many things that are better taught through showing rather than telling—how to brush, how to pick hooves, how to saddle and bridle a horse and how to check that you've done it right, how to work safely around a horse, what to do after a ride (you're unlikely to find a room with more sparkling clean bits than the tack room at Appy Orse), and so on. There are things to do and, as importantly, things not to do. (No wearing open-toed shoes or approaching a horse from behind without announcing your presence.) And there's a culture to learn, too—what things are called and when and how they're used, what sorts of things it's appropriate to complain about, what must simply be dealt with as part of life with horses, and what behavior's appropriate and what's not. This came in the barn aisle, along the paddock gate after lessons, and in the summer riding camps. Everyone's lived it in some form or another. One eye always on the older kids—and sometimes two, full-on staring, mouth open (if you think no one's watching), followed by emulation.

Ada and her friends would exchange news and opinions, and talk in knowing, sometimes reverent voices about the histories and tendencies of the various horses in the herd.

It was of course in the ring that Ada began to learn the subtleties of riding, the little things that are invisible to the casual observer—the importance of looking in the direction you want to go, of sending consistent messages to the horse, of almost undetectable changes in position and even, perhaps, in attitude that a horse can sense. Partly out of interest and partly because of Lea's allergies and what we'll call her relative discomfort around horses, I assumed primary horse-parenting duties, so I was present for all of this. I sat ringside for every lesson. I stood in the barn aisle before and after, sometimes lending a hand, but most of the time watching and listening and soaking in as much as I could. As often happens, the child's journey became the parent's journey as well. The progression played out in a familiar way, with large, quick gains followed by plateaus in which little seemed to happen, with occasional episodes of what seemed like backsliding before the next great advance came, seemingly out of nowhere.

Appy Orse occupies a unique and valuable niche in the equestrian world, and one that is severely underserved. As I've noted, a large part of the business model involves giving trail rides, and it is virtually the only place in greater Milwaukee that does so. That has a number of implications. One is that the horses mostly have to be able to perform two jobs, serving as jumpers for the lesson kids while also being the sort of animal that can be trusted to take a total neophyte through the woods. That sort of horse is necessarily tolerant of surprises and forgiving of mistakes, and thus well suited to beginner riders. Another is that it provides a young person interested in horses with a lot of additional chances to spend time around them. They may simply help get tack ready, or hold the horses before and after the rides, then graduate to grooming and tacking the horses, and finally to leading the trail rides themselves. All of this work gets exchanged, in a very informal way, for opportunity. At least some of the kids there would not have been able to afford to ride under any other sort of arrangement. (And as a family living on a single, academic's salary at the time, it certainly was the right place for us.)

Bernadette was (and is), without question, demanding, but more of effort than ability. The core message was to work hard, pay attention, and not whine. It's not an approach that all young people—not today, and probably not ever—take well to. Nor is it an approach that will consistently bring out the best in everyone. But those willing to make the effort get a chance to spend time around horses that might otherwise be out of reach. They get life lessons, too. Some of those lessons come cloaked in the garb of riding advice, such as Bernadette's consistent injunction to "be a rider and not a passenger" and her frequent reminder that "falls are never failures, they're learning experiences." Others more obviously apply to both riding and life, such as her emphasis on the need to "be a problem solver" and her prohibition on use of the words "I can't."

Another set of lessons comes via the example of Bernadette's strength of personality and will. One morning we got a call from one of the adult riders at the farm letting us know that there would be no lessons that weekend. A horse had bolted in the aisle the day before, knocking Bernadette over and leaving her with a seriously broken leg. We prepared Ada for the likelihood that there would be no lessons for weeks or possibly months. Bernadette had other ideas. She taught from a wheelchair a couple days later, and soon was walking and even riding on a timeline that was, shall we say, not consistent with her doctor's orders.

After I had been blogging for the equestrian magazine *The Chronicle of the Horse* for a while, I had an idea that I might write something about Appy Orse, and Bernadette, and what it all meant to the people who passed through her barn doors. I emailed a group that included individuals who had started riding there as kids, parents who didn't ride themselves but whose children had grown up riding there, and riders who found their way to Appy Orse as adults. The blog post didn't come together, but the responses were gold. Each was a testament to the profound effect one person can have on others' lives.

Most were variations on a theme: Bernadette was demanding but recognized hard work. A young woman who started riding there not long after Ada wrote of learning about leadership, responsibility, toughness, and "doing what needs to be done without being asked." Several mentioned how Bernadette pushed them out of their comfort zones and thereby taught them the value of trying and persisting. She was there for the kids suffering from the fallout of a nasty divorce or other bad situations at home—not in the sense of taking it easy on them, but in providing a place where they could prove themselves to be talented and valuable by being, as one mother characterized Bernadette's relationship with her daughter, "a good adult who honestly liked her and drove her to achieve." She was tough, one young woman wrote, "but she has such a heart of gold and she's an extremely giving person."

Audrey and Laura are two years younger than Ada, and so they have no memory of a world that did not feature horses. They were babies when we made that first tack-store trip in Oklahoma City, and they tagged along on many of the early equine-related adventures.

They likewise made early trips to Appy Orse to watch their big sister ride. And then, unsurprisingly, they wanted to ride, too. Audrey was most concerned that she begin riding at the same age that Ada had, and so she was first, starting out on a horse named Boogie Train, a gentle giant with whom she regularly teamed up for a "smallest rider on the largest horse" combination. Laura followed several months later. The twins, too, learned the lessons at the farm and soaked up the culture, doing so subject to all the advantages and disadvantages that accompany having an older sibling who has been at it for a while already.

There was a distinct rhythm to those early years. Most of the time, riding happened on the weekends, usually in the form of a single lesson. The girls and I would pile into our minivan and make the half-hour trip, timing it so we arrived well before their lesson began and there was enough time to groom and tack the horses and catch up with friends. I had, by this point, developed enough credibility to be allowed to help in appropriate ways, whether that meant getting horses in from the herd in the field when they had wandered far from the barn, helping groom an especially muddy horse, or simply lifting a saddle that young arms weren't quite ready to handle. Laura, who has a variety of allergies, would prepare her horse in the spot in the barn aisle nearest to the front door, which was usually open. Ada gradually moved farther back in the barn, which was the domain of the older kids, and Audrey did her best to get a spot near the back as well.

I stood in the middle, ready to assist as needed, but mostly just watching and listening and doing my best to stay out of the way. Occasionally Bernadette had a bigger job for me. There's always something that needs fixing at a horse farm, and often something that needs to be moved. Sometimes I had the skill to do the fixing, and usually I could find a way to move whatever it was. I learned to wear clothes that I didn't mind getting dirty, and I found that I had passed far enough into adulthood that the idea of doing farm work held a certain nostalgic appeal. One weekend I made a deep reacquaintance with bales of hay by spending most of my time at the farm dealing with a delivery that turned out to be not as dry as advertised. When hay is too wet, chemical reactions can cause enough heat for self-combustion to occur, and that's an especially bad situation when the hay is stored in an enclosed barn or shed, as the Appy Orse hay was. The bales needed to be spaced out and stacked in a way that allowed them to breathe, and I was just the man for the job. I ended up sweaty and dirty, with bits of hay having made their way to all the same places that sand ends up during a day at the beach. But it felt like my farm kid license was renewed, and I didn't mind at all.

In the summer, the wind down following a lesson happened slowly. The conversations in the aisle were more leisurely, the tack somehow took longer to clean, and if there was another lesson yet to come, the request "to stay and watch for just a little while" was almost inevitable. Every month there was a meeting of the Willow Hill Riding Club, a group consisting entirely of riders at the barn that did some riding and service work, often in combination, and that maintained a fund providing small scholarships to members who went on to college. Families took turns providing snacks for the meetings, which generally meant there would be soda and various other consumable goodies, in addition to yet another chance to spend some time talking about horses with friends.

For those first few years the biggest day on the calendar, always, was the Club's annual show, held on the Sunday of Memorial Day weekend. The excitement built over a several-month period. The run-up began with the formation of committees, some devoted to boring things like running the concession stand, but others to items like creating the list of classes and, most exciting of all, selecting the ribbons and trophies.

As soon as the weather allowed for it, the Club devoted a day to spring cleanup around the farm, a job that got revisited and refined in the few days before the show. There were weeds to pull, branches to trim, and jumps to retrieve from a storage shed on the far end of the farm. On the day before the show the riders squeezed in one more lesson, then turned their attention to grooming and other show prep. Parents and grandparents gathered to help with the annual ritual of final arrangements. Five or six heavy picnic tables had to be moved to viewing areas just outside the outdoor ring, and a camper that sat empty every winter needed cleaning in order to serve as the concession stand.

The biggest task was setting up temporary pens to hold horses during the show day. Most of these pens had spent the last year leaned against a wall in the hay barn, accumulating dust and bird poop. They were heavy, and the work was hard, but older, experienced hands guided the younger, newer ones. Bernadette moved about the farm, fielding questions and giving directions, then, after one last check in, finally giving the okay for riders and their families to head home.

The bedtime routine took a little longer the nights before the show. It wasn't that it was hard to get the girls ready for bed, of course. It was that it was hard to get them to fall asleep. The sense of anticipation was overwhelming.

But sleep was important. Show day began early. Being one of the first to arrive meant getting a pen in a good location and being able to get your horse bathed and ready without having to wait for access to the water. It meant getting checked in and set up. It meant being there, at a horse show, with your friends. So long as things went well, nothing could be better.

The arc of the day went like this: flat classes in the morning, costume class over the lunch break, jumping in the afternoon, all mostly divided into beginner, intermediate, advanced, and adult divisions. Often it would start with a chill in the air but end in sunlight and heat. There were some light showers during our years of participation, but never the truly bad weather that we heard talk of from those who'd been there before us.

The end of the show was not the end of the day. The picnic tables had to be moved back to their usual location at the front of the farm. The temporary pens had to be put away. There was nobody to do this work but the riders and their family members, and it was understood to be bad form to leave before the work was done. Sometimes we'd stop at a restaurant for a late dinner on the way home; sometimes we were too sweaty and dirty.

It was a long, long day.

Part of what's burned in my memory from those shows is simply what it was like to be there. Walking through the farmyard in the early morning light, wearing a jacket and gloves and sipping coffee to stay warm. Getting a pen for each horse and setting it up, making sure the appropriate grooming supplies were close at hand and properly arranged. Getting show numbers and a couple copies of the show program. Exchanging pleasantries with the other parents who had early-morning duty, maybe griping a little but all with the understanding that this was something we gladly did for our kids. Just standing by, waiting to do what was needed. Knowing that what was most often needed went unspoken—that I simply had to be there, trying to walk that always challenging line of providing support, encouragement, a calm presence, and the occasional push without being overbearing. Gradually the farm would come to life, and soon we were welcoming the guests—grandparents, cousins, neighbors, and friends.

So many of the moments from the Club show have receded into the great blur of personal history. Ada winning a high-point trophy in her first year of competition and the Club Youth Equitation Trophy in her last show at Appy Orse. Ada and the horse named Gary winning the trail class over a number of significantly older riders—even though she had never before ridden him in a Western saddle before—by deftly maneuvering through a series of tight obstacles, including a forward- and backward-pass over a blue tarp on the ground that many horses simply couldn't handle. Audrey, passing by where I was standing along the rail during the Simon Says class for younger riders and just after the field that had started with perhaps ten riders had been reduced to two. She looked me in the eye and gave me the sort of close-lipped smile that says, "I got this." And, indeed, she did. Audrey and Laura both telling me they wanted to skip their jumping classes because they weren't feeling well. I, having some familiarity with the temporary stomach illness that accompanies nervousness, suggested they just do the class, and do their best, and then they'd be done.

They both won.

Ribbons and trophies of course made the day fun, and we came away with plenty of those. And while it's easy to get fixated on them, it is both trite and true to say that other parts of the Club's show day were equally if not more important. There were all the lessons that youth sports teach: That you won't always win, and that sometimes you'll think you've done what's necessary to win but a judge will see things differently, and so you have to come up with a way to cope with disappointment. That something that goes well for you may not go well for your friend, or vice versa, and you have to figure out how to be a good friend in both sorts of situations. These aren't easy lessons to learn, and like most difficult things in life, some of us accept them more naturally and more quickly than others. Some of us always struggle with them, and some of us never quite seem to learn them at all.

After a couple years riding at Appy Orse, Ada got her first chance to show off the farm. It was a 4-H show held on the Ozaukee County Fairgrounds on the final day of the Ozaukee County Fair. This mattered for a couple reasons. It mattered first because the Appy Orse crew was showing out of a group of horse trailers, and finding convenient parking for several trucks and trailers quickly becomes a problem when there's a fair going on. The group's solution was to arrive very early in the day. That was fine, our family thought, because it gave us time to get acclimated, and to watch some of the halter classes before the riding part of the show began. We'd get to Appy Orse at daybreak so Ada could prepare her horse Max for the day, doing the necessary washing and grooming before loading onto the trailer. But that's what it meant to be part of a horse show. And the fair show, to us, was a big one, a "real" one. Her first chance to compete against riders from elsewhere and, as important, to wear a show coat.

Our group of trailers was nearly the first to the fairgrounds, so we got premium spots not far from the warm-up ring. The horses came out, the hay bags went up, and the second round of grooming began. The show schedule had a notation to the effect that the classes in which our riders were entered wouldn't begin any earlier than a certain specified time, and we imagined that that time would be more-or-less accurate. Surely, I thought, these show people have done this before and would only be a little wrong on their time estimates if they even turned out to be wrong at all.

I've seen many others fall into the same trap since.

As we discovered very early on, during our family trip to the show at the Oklahoma State Fairgrounds, halter classes hold interest for only so long. One supposes that the judge somehow sustains her interest. The judge at the Ozaukee County Fair seemed to, or at least feigned it well, taking her time walking around horse after horse after horse, staring intently from behind mirrored sunglasses at the various components of equine conformation, pausing occasionally to solemnly mark the paper on her clipboard. Meanwhile the sun beat down on the Appy Orse crew of riders and horses as their enthusiasm, patience, and energy level dissipated throughout the day. We played the "you really should eat something" game. At some point Max stepped on my foot.

It wasn't until the late afternoon that the jumping finally began. Not surprisingly, things did not go as planned. Somehow Ada hadn't yet learned about doing a courtesy circle upon entering the ring—she went in for her first class and headed straight for the jump, which was set along an outside line fairly close to the near end of the arena. She and Max had certainly come at jumps from an angle before, but in this case, the angle was such that Max was looking not only at the jump, but also at the fence surrounding the ring. His confusion and her nerves combined for the sort of run out that even a newbie dad can see coming from a mile away. Thankfully they got over the obstacle on the second try.

I'm sure some of the riders had a good show, but the younger riders, who like Ada were also at their first show, generally struggled. Time tends to lose meaning after you've spent most of the day in the sun, and somehow or other daylight began to disappear well before we had reached the end of the schedule. Having exhausted kids trying to jump horses in a poorly lit, unfamiliar ring was, in retrospect, not such a great idea. And remember: It was the last day of the fair. The show ring was right next to the hog barn, where, by this time, squealing pigs were being loaded onto trailers. Horse after horse made it to that end of the ring to find darkness and the unfamiliar sounds of animals who did not seem to be enjoying themselves. Bernadette's horses would put up with a lot, but this was a bridge too far. Our hopes for the day went unrealized.

We loaded the trailers in the dark, car headlights serving as the only source of illumination. Ada was tired, disappointed, and in one of those places where my options as a parent attempting to provide comfort ranged from the wrong thing to say to varying degrees of even worse things to say. But finally we were in our car, wanting to just go home but knowing that we still had a trip to the barn in front of us. We'd leave as soon as the last horse was loaded.

The problem was this: The last horse did not want to be loaded. He was a handsome and athletic dapple gray named Reggie who also happened to be a bit quirky. He hadn't been enthusiastic about getting in the trailer in the morning, and the long day apparently got to him as well. There was no getting him to connect the idea of getting in the trailer with being back in his familiar pasture. We sat, our headlights pointed at the trailer, and watched as Bernadette went through every trick in the book. Ada fell asleep. Time passed. It's a situation I've since lived through as one of the people trying to get the horse to load. You're tired, the horse is tired, there seem to be a thousand eyes on you, all of them, you suspect, sitting in silent judgment. Lose your temper and the task becomes even more difficult. You start to wonder about the possibility of just leaving the horse behind and coming back to try again in the morning—something that seems like an even better idea when all you want is a shower and an end to this day.

Finally, Reggie conceded. Had it taken thirty minutes? Had it taken an hour? Whatever the clock said, it had taken forever. But at least we were on the road. Twenty minutes later we reached Appy Orse. I woke Ada, and while she helped unload and put things away, I mucked out the trailers.

It was well after midnight when we left.

Jump ahead a couple years. Ada hadn't quite yet realized her dream of owning a horse, but she was (or we were) leasing one—a Paint horse named Sunny. Audrey laid claim to a POA (Pony of the Americas) named Ozzy as soon as he arrived at the farm, and soon she was leasing him. (Laura, meanwhile, had taken up figure skating, and while she still rode on a weekly basis, she was not quite so deeply into it.) With "horses of their own" to ride any time, we no longer went to the barn just once a week. A new routine took hold, especially in the months when darkness came early, as I would call Bernadette to let her know when the girls would be riding in the evenings. She would leave Sunny and Ozzy in a pen between the horse barn and the hay barn, and the girls and I would often have the farm to ourselves for the night.

Those nights were special. A place you've only ever experienced as busy takes on a different feel when you're the only ones there. Anything that needed figuring out was for us to figure out for ourselves. Usually it was fine, but some nights when wind was blowing hard or the horses seemed to sense things beyond our ability to perceive they'd get a little jittery. Sometimes we'd work through it. Other nights we'd cut things short. Better safe than sorry.

Once we got to the ring, I'd take my usual spectating spot and the girls would get to work. Ada had started watching riding videos at home, and she liked to work on things she absorbed from them in addition to what she learned in her lessons. Ozzy was young and green and some nights presented a challenge. Audrey sometimes accepted and sometimes resented her older sister's suggestions. Both were focused on their tasks. I had taken to bringing things to read, but I reminded myself to soak it in. To look around, to smell the air, to watch my daughters solving problems, to appreciate the moments that I knew would pass.

There was sometimes drama. One weekend afternoon the girls were riding in the outdoor ring. It was a somewhat busy day with a steady stream of riders coming and going. Someone left the gate open, and Ozzy, for reasons known only to him, decided he wanted out. He bolted, taking an unsuspecting Audrey out of the ring toward the barn.

Unexpected things are a part of parenthood, and you don't always have a scripted response that's any more developed than: *Freak out.* I took a second to freak out, then formulated a formal response, which was: *Run after them.* I was a few seconds behind the galloping Ozzy and not moving anywhere near as fast. The runaways turned the corner and went out of sight.

When I got around the hay barn, I found Audrey in the gravel perhaps eighty yards from the ring. It couldn't have been a soft landing. But for this I had a script. For me: *Stay calm.* For Audrey: *Stay down and make sure everything still works.*

She was a little startled and a little bruised but basically fine.

Ozzy was nowhere to be seen. When he finally turned up, I did not ask Audrey to get back on and do it again.

Another weekend the girls were in a lesson and Audrey fell off Ozzy after he stopped at a jump. Horses are surprisingly good about not stepping on riders they've just dumped, but in the confusion on this particular day, Ozzy clipped Audrey's elbow. This time it was immediately clear that she was *not* fine.

A parent who happened to be a nurse was there, and we went into Bernadette's house to take a look. It was not pretty. Audrey's elbow worked, but it was torn up pretty badly and filled with sand and whatever else ends up in arena footing. Audrey insisted through tears that she didn't need to go to the hospital.

We went to the hospital.

The wound was a mess, and it would take some work to get it clean. It didn't take long to figure out that that work would hurt too much to do without the help of a general anesthetic. An early morning surgery it would be. Audrey wouldn't let me take a picture even though I suggested that one day she'd wish she had one. (She now wishes she had one.) I spent the night with her in the hospital, where we were awakened far too frequently by an alarm connected to some sensor that kept falling out of proper adjustment. Eventually morning came and Audrey was wheeled off to surgery while I was relegated to a waiting area, the whole affair a metaphor for so much of parenthood: Things happen that are beyond your ability to fix. You provide the moral support you can, much of which consists simply of being there. And then you wait.

Though the nasty scar Audrey carries around to this day suggests otherwise, the surgery went well. Out of necessity, she spent a little time on the sidelines. She was not happy about it, especially because her injury meant that she had to miss a show that she had been especially looking forward to. When she returned to the saddle she was, understandably, a bit hesitant about jumping. But the important thing, the part of the story that matters most over the course of a lifetime, is this: She did not back away. To put it in terms of one of the mantras of our day: She had a nasty fall. Nevertheless, she persisted.

We didn't return to the Ozaukee County 4-H Show for a couple years, and then only after we learned that the organizers had mercifully moved all the halter classes to a different day. But there were other shows: A series of schooling shows put on by a pair of longtime members of the local horse community. A show put on by a different 4-H club.

(All seeming somewhat expensive at the time but looking like a bargain in light of what would come after.) Audrey joined Ada in the showing, and then Laura did. The good experiences and results outnumbered the bad. At the last show they all attended with Bernadette, my daughters finished first, second, and third in an equitation class.

Over this time a set of dreams started to grow. The internet keeps few secrets from the devoted seeker, and Ada discovered a larger world was out there. A pair of sisters at Appy Orse with substantial family resources bought comparatively fancy horses, and then began showing them with a different trainer. A couple of the older girls drifted away to ride elsewhere. They were all going to "rated" shows—the ones that fell under the competitive umbrella of the United States Equestrian Federation, and the next rung on the equestrian sports ladder—and we imagined what those might be like. It was the same dynamic as "small-town boy beckoned by the city," just with saddles and half-chaps. Lea's job situation had improved, making a barn move more feasible than it would have been before. The girls remained as committed to the sport as ever. We began to sense that a change might be in order.

That's the sort of thing that might be easy for some people. I've never found it easy. It's funny, because I'm often on the other side of the dynamic when students request letters of recommendation for their applications to transfer to other schools. I don't always think it's as good an idea as may first appear, and in those situations, I share my opinion. But I understand, as well, that there often *are* good reasons, whether in terms of geography, cost, or prestige, and that students have to do what's best for them. Still, they often struggle with the request, because it seems to them like a rejection, if not a betrayal, of both a place where they have experienced success and the people who have helped them while there. And that fear, that the message will be received as a form of ingratitude, is one I can relate to.

Not everybody who shares the fear handles it well. "Ghosting" often seems like the easy way out, especially compared to having what one might anticipate will be a hard conversation. But those conversations are usually easier than expected, while disappearing without a word of explanation almost always leaves someone feeling rejected and betrayed. ⑤

# 4

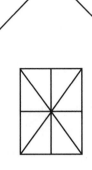

Just as we started to form thoughts of exploring riding options elsewhere, a good friend of mine reported that his sister-in-law had just bought a horse farm outside of Milwaukee. He was not a horse person himself and didn't really know much about what sort of barn it was going to be, but he was willing to make an introduction. Probably a waste of time, I imagined, but we'd take a look. And so it was that we found ourselves traveling beneath a canopy of trees as we made our way up the driveway of Hidden View Farm, pausing to let a deer cross in front of us. At the end of the drive sat a classic dairy barn, refurbished and repurposed as a horse barn, situated in a large yard featuring huge trees and, at the edge, paddocks with three-board fencing. A more picturesque scene would be hard to find. We met Kathy Happ, the new owner, and Kelly Doke, the barn manager, and got a tour. It was mildly dizzying in the way that such visits are, a series of "here's this" and "here's that" resulting in a vivid impression but not quite a strong sense of what it would be like to be a part of it. Even so, the verdict was unanimous and delivered as soon as the last car door closed for the drive home: Ada, Audrey, and Laura all wanted to take lessons there.

A week or so later Ada and I returned, this time to ride. This was, potentially, a big step, and we were each anxious in our own way. We met Charles Zwicky, the trainer, and Scotch, the horse she'd be riding. Charles and Ada worked together to get Scotch tacked up, and we all walked to the outdoor ring. I took a seat at a picnic table set on a small rise alongside the ring, and Charles got to work figuring out what he had, first on the flat, and then over jumps.

Looking back, two moments stand out.

The first came perhaps a third of the way into the lesson. Charles kept asking Ada to do things, and she kept doing them. First the basics—could she post on the correct diagonal, pick up the appropriate canter lead, and so forth—and then on to the slightly more advanced. He put a series of poles on the ground along the edge of the ring near where I sat and asked Ada to ride over them at a sitting trot. She did it flawlessly. As she made the turn at the end of the ring he shook his head a bit, turned to start making his way to whatever was coming next, and then, to himself but just loud enough that I could hear it, said, "Wow."

The second came at the end, when Charles pronounced his verdict. "Usually when a new rider comes to me there are things I have to fix. With you we'll just have to make adjustments." Somewhere along the line Kathy had mounted a horse and come into the ring, partly to ride and partly to watch. A couple years later she told me that Charles had walked near her after working with Ada a while and said, simply, "This girl can ride."

watched an unwise and probably unhealthy amount of television as a kid. Looking back, it seems that pretty much every series had an episode, or at least a drawn-out scene, in which some of the characters looked back with fondness to the early days, when it wasn't yet clear where the story of their lives would go. They were hungry, certainly figuratively and sometimes literally. Success or failure was all in the future, the present was nothing but anticipation, the plan to dream big and work hard. It's the impulse that keeps alums coming back to the colleges they attended, where they can follow the same paths they walked as younger, hopeful versions of themselves. There's something exhilarating about the prospect of something new, of having vague dreams become a little more specific, of having a sense that those dreams might be achievable.

Those first months at Hidden View were part of that stretch of early days. It was summer, and I had the flexibility to devote a weekday morning to driving Ada to the barn for her lesson. We'd stop for lunch on the drive home, talking about little things, sharing a mostly unspoken sense that this was heading somewhere exciting. As the summer drew to a close Kathy offered to let Ada ride her horse Luna at an upcoming show put on by the Wisconsin Hunter Jumper Association. Ada's first rated show. A big step.

There were no halter classes to endure at this show, and Ada got in the ring while the sun was still high in the sky, but the wait seemed long, nonetheless. Our whole family sat in the bleachers alongside what we didn't think of then as "the beginner ring," watching a series of classes we didn't yet understand. It's only with the benefit of the knowledge I gained in the following years that I can now say that the jumps were not high and the courses not complex. They seemed big enough and hard enough at the time. I may have been the most nervous member of our family, and not for the last time. It's a complex emotional calculus. It's not that I'd ever dreamed of having a child who was a successful equestrian. And even if I had I'm not sure I'd have felt so invested if it were only my dreams she was riding for. It meant a lot to me simply because it meant so much to *her*.

This all happened in the days when we didn't all carry cameras around in our pockets. There are no recordings of the rounds. And while I can't tell you with any specificity what went right or what might have gone better, I could take you to the showgrounds and show you the exact spot where I stood along the rail to watch Ada's class. I could show you where the Hidden View team stood, about twenty feet away, providing enthusiastic support. And I could show you a photo that would tell you much of what you would need to know to fill in the blanks in the story. It shows Ada standing next to Luna. On Luna's bridle is a huge blue ribbon. On Ada's face is a smile as large and genuine as they come.

A successful first step leads to a second step, which in this case was a big step. We would have to find a horse to call our own. We came up with our budget, and Charles went to work. By all indications it was work he loved, a search for a hidden gem. From time to time he'd show me a picture of a horse he'd identified as potentially a good fit and was going to go try. A few of those came and went. Not what we were looking for. Then one day he said he'd found one worth having the girls ride.

A few days later Ada, Audrey, and I met Charles at the barn and piled into a pickup truck to go take a look. Before he even started the engine, he passed on some wisdom: "You shouldn't buy the first horse you try." Especially when it's the first horse you'll ever own. There's too much excitement, too much of a tendency to confuse that excitement for love at first sight, too much risk. He did not add that all of this goes double when "you" is a pair of preteen girls, but I took the point. He pointed out that there was no trailer behind the truck. This process could take a while.

It was a forty-minute drive to our destination, and we talked horses the whole ride. We learned about his experiences and accomplishments as a young rider, about how as the son of a trainer he'd often ended up having to ride the difficult horses, about how he always hoped the judge would ask the riders to switch horses with one another during the work-off portion of an equitation class because he inevitably had a horse the other riders would likely struggle with, about how his path had intersected with those of riders who had gone on to some prominence in the horse world, about the person who was selling the horse.

When we first met Cash, he was standing in cross-ties getting a last bit of brushing before he got saddled up. He was a bay with a shiny coat. As Ada later recalled it, he seemed big and fancy. We walked out to a ring. Charles rode him for a bit, then Ada, then Audrey. It went well. We talked about it on the drive back, then Charles and I talked more back at Hidden View. I discussed it with Lea. A couple days later Cash was at Hidden View for a more extended trial and then a prepurchase exam by a veterinarian—a general assessment of his health and overall condition.

A week or so after that I was walking from my office to my car when I got a call from Charles. "We own a horse," he said.

"Good news," I replied. (There's no exclamation point there, you'll notice. I'm pretty sure there was no exclamation point in my voice, either. I thought it probably was good news. But I'm cautious by nature.)

"I think it is," he responded. (No exclamation point there, either. Just hopefulness tempered by realism.)

We bought the first horse we tried.

Cash was an Iowa-bred Appendix Quarter Horse. His formal name when we bought him was "Speed Thru Traffic," and his barn name no doubt arose out of his lineage. He was a great grandson of Dash For Cash, and a grandson of First Down Dash, both of whom were Quarter Horse racing greats and members of the American Quarter Horse Hall of Fame. Cash's performance at the track never lived up to his bloodline, though. He raced eighteen times and won exactly once. After that, so far as we could tell, he'd spent a few years under the radar in Illinois.

It wasn't immediately clear that he was going to be the horse we imagined, and there were moments when we faced what seemed like it might be a cautionary tale about love at first sight. He was too strong sometimes, with the occasional buck, especially on days when the weather left him less able to burn off energy during turnout. This was a change from Bernadette's bombproof trail horses. As before, most of our trips to the barn during the week were at night, and often we were the only ones there. More than once we cut our visit short because Cash was more horse than we felt comfortable handling on our own.

And so, Charles taught us how to longe Cash—have him trot and canter in a circle around us, while we held a long rope attached to his bridle—which was one way to burn off some of his energy. But our favorite technique, on nights when no one else was around, was to lead Cash to the indoor ring and simply turn him loose. He would sprint from one end of the ring to the other, often adding a buck or a kick that he'd punctuate with a squeal. After a few minutes of this he would usually pause to roll, then get up, ready to be an agreeable ride. We'd walk him back to the barn, tack him up, and go about the routine.

It was an approach we'd later put to use with other horses.

We had a problem in those early days, in that we had three daughters who rode and only one horse. Often it was simply a matter of division. We'd plan to devote an hour to riding, with each girl getting twenty minutes. I'm not sure how many times it actually was all four of us, but the sharing went better than one might anticipate. That's not to say there weren't moments of bickering over what the order would be or how much time someone actually got to ride. There were. There was some excitement, too, such as the time when Laura was riding and Cash decided that he had one more burst of sprinting and bucking to go. I happened to be recording, and the video shows them traveling down the long side of the ring, across and away from the corner in which I was standing. Laura looks increasingly like a rag doll until the video ends at the moment I realized what was going on. I don't need video to have a clear picture of what happened next, which was a fall that ended with her landing flat on her back. She and I spent some time alone in a darkened room after that making sure that she didn't have a concussion.

Cash never became a perfect horse. He loved the left lead but not the right. It's not that he did poorly at the first couple shows we took him to, but something seemed to remind him of the racetrack—it was a challenge to keep him calm and a necessity to keep him clear of other horses. But soon time and training began to work their magic. He never loved to change from his left lead to his right, but he would do it. As a jumper he was as honest as they come—I always said he'd try to jump the moon if someone pointed him at it—which allowed the girls to focus on other things. Trainers from other barns started to make unsolicited comments about what a nice horse he was. He was a hit at home, too, getting along with anyone in turnout and charming the humans by smacking his lips repeatedly when he got a little bored.

Not long after Cash's arrival Charles walked down the barn aisle as all three of my daughters were grooming the horse's bay coat. Charles paused, leaned in, gave Cash a pat on the nose, and said to him, "Son, you've hit the jackpot."

But it turned out that it was we who had hit the jackpot. (Charles, I came to understand, had a gifted eye, including the ability to uncover talented horses in unlikely places.) Ada, Audrey, and Laura each had a chance to show Cash the first summer we had him, and he won blue ribbons and championships for each of them, from ground poles to jumps as high as 2'3". A summer later Ada showed him at 3'6".

There were, of course, bumps in the road. He never completely got over throwing in the occasional buck. A handful of times he refused in competition, and in particular he seemed to have something against jumps featuring sailboat-themed standards. He once refused a tricky fence in a medal finals (a pretty important class at a show), and then, at the end of what had already been a very long day, spent what I'll quantify as *a really long time* refusing to get on the trailer to go home.

This wasn't an entirely new situation for us; years before, we'd had to wait for Reggie to load at the end of that very long day at the Ozaukee County Fairgrounds. But it's one thing to watch *somebody else's* horse refuse to load and another thing entirely when it's *your* horse. The first is an inconvenience, the second is extraordinarily awkward and uncomfortable. At first other people pause to watch for a bit. Then they start to offer suggestions. Somewhere along the line you begin to sweat profusely. You struggle to maintain your cool because you know that getting angry will only make it worse. The people who first offered their thoughts drift away and others take their place. Eventually somebody says that maybe if you let her try, she can get it done. You let her try. She doesn't get it done. Someone from the first set of bystanders returns and helpfully lets you know that you're still there. Another person tells you that she's got a horse that loads really easily and maybe if you put that one in the trailer first your horse will get in. Normally, you'd question whether that's a good idea given that you've got a slant-load trailer and it's not clear how you'll get the first horse back out. But at this point you'll try anything. Your safety-related concerns turn out to be entirely unwarranted for the simple reason that Cash doesn't care whether another horse gets on before he does. You're pretty sure you're never leaving.

And then, suddenly and for no apparent reason, he steps right in.

We all have our bad days and our bad moments, and his were rare. Most of the time he was—and here's the part where you have to conjure up your best "talking to a gelding" voice—a good boy. He wasn't a perfect horse, but he was *the best horse*.

I find it hard to capture my affection for Cash. I never rode him, so I can't claim to have developed that sort of bond. The rest of it sounds trite. Was it the way that he always seemed to take a step or two forward when he saw me coming? The way he'd smack his lips? How he seemed to enjoy it when I'd sneak into his stall at shows to hang out for a bit? The fact that he was an underdog and outsider, a horse who on paper had little business doing the things he did in the places he did them? No doubt part of it was his role at an early stage of my daughters' journey, when everything still stretched ahead, when most of what seemed to exist was possibility. And then how he, and Charles, helped to turn possibility into reality. It was all this and more, plus that undefinable whatever-it-is that makes some people, and animals, especially suitable companions.

As things progressed Laura began to devote more of her time to her figure skating. That meant lots of nights where it was me, Ada, and Audrey, and sometimes just me and Ada. The nights I remember best were the ones in winter. We'd arrive in darkness, often with snow on the ground and, when it got especially cold, frost coating the barn door. Cash's stall was near the front entrance to the barn, close to the wash stall and tack room, and we needed only to turn on the first set of lights, leaving the back of the barn dark. The effect was to make us feel alone in the world, just us, the horses, and the barn cats tucked away in the lower level of the old dairy barn. Once the grooming and tacking up were far enough along, I'd make the short walk outside to the indoor arena to turn on the lights so they had time to warm up, then return to the barn to help throw a cooler over Cash for the walk outside.

We carried over much of our routine from Appy Orse. There were chairs in a corner of the ring. Sometimes I'd bring a book, sometimes I'd just scroll through my phone. Always, though, I'd also make sure to just watch and enjoy the moment. The sand footing tended to pile up against the walls, and often to pass the time I'd grab a rake and work my way along the side of the ring, filling in the track that had worn into a shallow ditch. (This work went from optional to mandatory in the coldest months for the simple reason that it was a way to keep myself warm.) If I got all four sides done with time to spare, I'd rake patterns into the arena footing, a highly temporary way to mark the territory.

Often Ada would put me to work. She'd managed to watch a reality series that originally aired on Animal Planet called *Horse Power: Road to the Maclay*, which was focused on Junior equitation riders in a pair of New York barns. There were no copies available for sale that I could ever find, but someone had uploaded a poor-quality version to YouTube. (Ada had once resisted watching anything not filmed in high-definition. For this, though, she was willing to put up with much worse.) It was her—and therefore my—introduction to the world known as "Big Eq." The term referred both to certain classes at horse shows—equitation classes run at fence heights of 3'6" for riders who are still "Juniors" (roughly, eighteen and under) —and to a set of prestigious national finals, one of which was the Maclay Finals, featuring what were arguably the best Junior riders in the country.

One of the trainers featured in the series was Frank Madden, who was based out of the greater New York City area and had trained several highly successful Junior riders. Ada and I had gone to see a clinic he gave at a barn north of Chicago. (At which, through a combination of strategic table selection and sheer luck, we had ended up sitting next to him at lunch.) Some of the exercises he had given the riders at the clinic involved riding from different approach points over a series of ground poles, and these exercises became part of Ada's routine. My job was to move the poles, mark off the appropriate distance between them, and provide feedback to the extent I was able. Ada and Cash would adjust their pace, change their approach, and work things from both directions.

The goals motivating these drills went largely unmentioned but were present, nonetheless. The Maclay Finals, Big Eq, the events that were enough of a big deal for someone to make a TV series about them. At the end of more than a few of those nights Ada would ask me to set the poles on one of the jumps to 3'6"—not so that she could jump it (unsupervised jumping was not allowed), but just so that she could ride past it, see what it looked like from Cash's back, imagine the day when they would clear it, and beyond.

Audrey once again found her way to ponies. She rode two during our time at Hidden View: a green Haflinger named Heilig, and a small Welsh named Rosie. Each was headstrong in her own way. Of the two it was Rosie who really captured Audrey's heart. By the time we had been at Hidden View for perhaps a year, Audrey was itching to have a horse of her own to ride. The girls were still sharing Cash, and from time to time she got to hack some of the other horses at the barn during the week, but none of that is quite the same as getting to have a pony of your own. That wasn't ever quite the reality with Rosie, but for a while it was close enough.

The Rosie story began as a possibility: *There might be a pony coming.* It was a pony that had been ridden by one of Charles's former students, and now she was living in Michigan, but her owners were considering sending her to Hidden View for a while. "Might" come soon turned into "will" come, with the question then turning into, "When?" Kids, of course, work on a different time frame. "Soon" for Audrey often seemed like "forever," and occasionally, even "never." "I don't think there even is a pony," she proclaimed at one moment of peak impatience. "I think everyone just made it up."

But eventually Rosie arrived.

Ponies, as a category, seem to have evolved to be just cute enough to get away with things. Without exception, people adored Rosie. She seemed to sense this and used it to her advantage. One of Rosie's tricks was to decide that she was happy in her paddock, thank you very much, and did not want to be caught because that meant going to work. She seemed to turn it into a game, letting her pursuer get just so close before trotting off to a safe distance. Sometimes clipping a lead rope to the halter of her turnout companion and starting toward the barn was enough to bring Rosie to the gate. Other times it took a bucket of grain. Once or twice nothing but waiting her out would do.

Rosie had a lead change in one direction but not the other, so Audrey learned to use an opening rein over the jumps to get her to land on the correct lead. The pony also possessed a selective willingness to jump. She understood that there were two ways to get to the other side of a jump, and to her way of thinking simply *going around* often worked just as well as going over. Once, at a show, she stopped in especially abrupt fashion at a jump that featured a large wooden box as its base. It happened toward the far end of the ring, and Audrey appeared to fall directly into the jump, an appearance that was intensified by a loud thud. My daughter rose from the box, gathered her pony's reins, and made her way slowly out of the ring, where she and I went to an out-of-the-way corner so she could collect herself. The onsite medic rushed over, assuming that Audrey was hurt. But the thud had been from her boot hitting the wooden box just right. The rest of her had just hit the ground. Her injuries, such as they were, were to her pride.

There were also times when Rosie would assume a different persona, entering the ring with a head full of steam and a heart full of exuberance. Her signature moment of this sort came during one edition of the Wisconsin Hunter Jumper Association Fall Finals. The class was in the "big ring" and featured many more horses than ponies. The fences didn't get any higher than 3' at those shows, and these were set lower than that. Whatever the precise measurement, they were plenty big for a small pony, and Rosie gathered momentum as she and Audrey made their way around the ring. Somewhere in the middle of the course they turned toward a diagonal line featuring a pair of jumps that were, for a horse, two canter strides apart. For Rosie they should have been three strides apart. She wanted no part of what "they" said she should or shouldn't do. She flew down the line, easily making the two strides. Not the best performance for the moment, because it was a judged class. But that was Rosie, and it was certainly a learning experience for Audrey.

And that, to her great credit, was how Audrey treated her riding career. She consistently rode the difficult mounts with good cheer. There were moments of disappointment, for sure, but she persisted through it all, buoyed both by the praise she got for doing it and by the sense that the experience would serve her well in the long run. And, indeed, she and Rosie reached enough of an understanding that they won some year-end awards. The difficult moments, and the work of getting past them, led to some very good results.

Heilig the Haflinger was a part of our story only briefly, but she provides a highlight. She was not naturally inclined to jump things, and once opted to destroy a small box jump by crashing through it rather than simply lifting first her front and then her rear feet to get over it. But Audrey worked at it and got the pony to the point where she would get around courses at home and made us all comfortable with the idea of giving a show a try.

The show was in July at Ledges Sporting Horses in Roscoe, Illinois. The main show rings at Ledges are along the western edge of the property. The warm-up rings are adjacent to the show rings and are separated from the nearest portion of the barn by a gravel parking lot. The entrance to the indoor show ring—at least if you are not going through the barn—is some distance away, behind the barn and more toward the south of the property. It's neither a short trip nor a straight trip from any of the outdoor rings.

You can perhaps see where this is headed.

Charles, who was in a walking cast at the time, was in the warm-up ring with Audrey and Heilig. I had been sent back to the barn to get something, and I returned to the warm-up area to find he and Audrey and Heilig were no longer there. I hadn't been gone that long, so the show ring was the next logical place to check. Maybe things were running ahead of schedule and she'd already gone in. Not there either. I lingered, not quite sure where to look next.

My search ended when Audrey and Heilig, led by a hobbling Charles, reentered the warm-up ring from the far side. Heilig, apparently drawing on the same pony logic that had driven Ozzy out of the ring a couple years earlier, had bolted. Charles followed behind as quickly as he could, eventually finding Audrey and her pony in the indoor ring (curiously), a bit shaken but otherwise intact. Audrey's riding resume had a second entry for its "bolting pony" section, and this time she had stayed in the saddle.

Audrey and Heilig put together a few nice rounds that day, but it was clear that the job was not one that Heilig enjoyed. We needed to explore other options.

Horses and ponies are, of course, only a part of the story. A large part of the equestrian experience involves the people you meet along the way. We were fortunate to have a group of especially suitable companions in the Hidden View family. The barn itself was a welcoming, relaxed place, with plenty of just hanging out in addition to riding, cake on people's birthdays, and pizza that would sometimes show up just because. The riders spanned the range of ages, and it was at Hidden View that I first began to recognize one of the under-appreciated benefits of riding—namely that it's often a context in which there's considerably less segregation by age than there is in most of the world, which means that kids get to spend a lot of time with adults who serve as a unique blend of role models and peers. It's nothing like I ever experienced as a kid. Nor was it replicated in the other youth sports my daughters participated in, where the competitors were all kids, the spectators were mostly adults, and the two groups generally did not interact.

There was a core group of six riders—Heidi Modesto, Debbie Knuth, Reilly Fardy, Kathy Happ, and my daughters—that traveled with Charles to "B" shows across Wisconsin and into Illinois. That was three adults, one high-schooler, and a pair still in elementary school, accompanied by Heidi's husband Nick, me, and occasionally others. This group went to four or five multi-day shows a year, spaced from May to early October, all within a couple hours' drive from the barn. We had a routine. Charles would set a time for departure, and it was our job to be ready to leave on time (which we always did). We'd head out once the last horse was in the trailer, traveling as a caravan. We'd pull up at the showgrounds and get to work in near-militaristic fashion. There was an understood plan: Locate the stalls, get shavings down, get the horses settled with hay and water. Then unload and move equipment and tack, set up fans in the stalls if the weather was hot, and so forth, before finally heading to the show office to get show numbers, fill out any missing paperwork, and take care of whatever other business needed to be taken care of. All of this as a team, with everyone pitching in and no one complaining or sloughing off. None of it done by grooms.

Show days had a distinct rhythm. The entire group would arrive at the grounds at roughly the same time in the morning and get to work. There were water buckets to fill and stalls to muck out. Horses needed to be groomed and grazed and often to have their manes braided. If you weren't showing you were watching other members of the Hidden View team show, and if you weren't doing either of those you were sitting around killing time, sometimes with a book, and sometimes just taking part in the sort of group goofing around that you had to be there to fully appreciate. Everyone stayed until everything was done at the end of the day—the horses fed and watered, the tack cleaned, the aisle swept. Then it was off to the hotel for a quick shower and a change of clothes before meeting up with the same people for dinner. You've got to like people to want to spend that much time with them several days in a row. We liked them all, and shared a certain sensibility that was product of a combination of factors, including not just compatible personalities, but also the niche in the show world that we were a part of and how we felt about it. It's a remarkable thing to be a part of such a cohesive group, especially when it's made up of people from a range of ages and backgrounds, and I don't know of any other sport where that sort of mix occurs regularly.

There was a purity to that stage of life in the horse world. For my part, it's clear only now that we have long since passed out of it that it was a distinct stage. In the moment, it seemed to be just how things would be for the foreseeable future. Continued improvement, moving through the ranks, milestones starting as distant points on the horizon, then slowly coming into view and eventually moving to the rearview mirror before receding into the world of used-to-be. It wasn't a fully logical appreciation of the situation, and a moment's thought would have of course revealed that it couldn't always continue to be that way, because nothing ever lasts forever. Time, as the saying has it, is undefeated. All things—good, bad, and in between—must end.

It's been my experience as a parent that I tend to see the world through my children's eyes, especially when it comes to parts of the world that are new to me, like its equestrian corners were during this time. That no doubt helped drive my assessment of those early show days, when what I might now think of as the "main ring" at a show was a foreign land, a "maybe someday" sort of place filled with giant jumps and otherworldly horses.

At most rated shows there are at least two rings in which the action takes place. At the larger shows there will be several, some of which are devoted entirely to one type of class or another. There's always one ring featuring the highest-level classes, and another where the lower-level classes take place. That ring, the "beginner ring," was our home in those days. It was a ring populated mostly by riders who were, to a great degree, simply thrilled to be there. And it was a place where even an observer who was only moderately informed about the sport could have a good sense of how things were going. It didn't take long, sitting there, to see all the things that could go wrong during a trip around a show ring. Stops, swaps, and bad distances. The wrong lead or the wrong diagonal. Ponies that just weren't having it. The pure heartbreak of the occasional young rider who ended up in the dirt and wasn't quite able to hold herself together long enough to make it out of the ring without bursting into tears.

But all of this was punctuated by moments of perfection. Maybe just for a couple lines, maybe for an entire course. A parent who'd been paying attention would be able to recognize it, though. The turns would be good, the distances close enough to ideal given the size of the jumps, the lead changes as smooth as could be. The horse staying straight and going over the middle of the jumps. Those were the moments that kept people coming back. "I've put it all together before," riders can say to themselves after a round or two like that. "No reason I can't do it again."

Success in the beginner ring comes in its most basic form: making it around the jumps with no obvious problems. The trainers might themselves be a little jaded about all of this, having seen it a thousand times before, but they mostly hide it. They offer effusive praise for the things that went well, and gentle suggestions about what might have been done just a little bit differently. Some clearly share in the joy.

The parents at this ring are often not jaded at all, especially if it is still a new world to them. The ones for whom the show is a foreign land are fresh-faced and nervous and not always entirely sure where they should be. Sometimes there will be grandparents in tow. When things go well, the pride is palpable and mixed with that combination of relief and joy that appears whenever one's child succeeds at something so important to her. (Of course, the emotions can run just as strongly in the other direction when things do not go well. But let's leave that aside for now.) The hopes and dreams are fresh and large, the future seems unbounded. The "main ring," the place where the really big classes take place, seems a little bit closer.

Growth happens incrementally at this stage, but as is the case with youth in general, it happens fast enough to be noticeable. The young rider ends the show season jumping bigger jumps than when the season began. She emerges from what seemed like a long, dark, boring winter without competition to find that all those drills she did, all those lessons in which she never once jumped an entire course but rather did drill after drill after drill, made her a considerably better rider. She rides other horses every chance she gets, mostly because it's fun, but also because she understands that it will help her improve.

Ada and Audrey both made that progression over the course of their time at Hidden View. What for Ada began with Luna on a basic course with tiny jumps ended on Cash over equitation and jumper courses featuring the biggest jumps available on the Wisconsin and Illinois B Circuit. What for Audrey started on Cash ended on ponies and entailed its own form of success. The rounds certainly weren't all perfect, and not every judge saw things the same way as those of us sitting in the stands. But plenty did go well. And since progression and movement and growth seemed simply like how things happened, the familiar questions appeared again: *What's next? What's it like at the next level? How far can we go?*

Here we reached a point where Ada and Audrey's paths diverged for a year. Audrey, you will soon see, got a chance to live the "pony kid's dream." For Ada, an opportunity arose toward the end of our last summer at Hidden View. One of the more energetic and engaged trainers in

Southeastern Wisconsin, a woman named Courtney Hayden-Fromm, regularly put on the Wisconsin Equine Derby. The centerpiece of the weekend was of course the competition, consisting of a day of hunter derbies on Saturday and of jumper derbies on Sunday. But for our purposes the action came on the Friday before the show, when clinics for the riders were offered, typically involving well-established clinicians.

The clinician for the jumper riders that year was Diane Carney, a prominent trainer based in the Chicago area. She had been the judge at the Wisconsin Hunter Jumper Association's Fall Finals show the year before, where Ada had done especially well in equitation classes, and she and I had exchanged a couple brief emails after I had sought her input, but we had not really connected. Ada was excited for the chance to ride in front of her again; it seemed like a good opportunity.

The riders in the clinic were grouped roughly according to the height they would be jumping in the derby on Sunday. Ada's group, for the riders competing over the highest fences, was large, and the ring was crowded. (This turned out to be one of, but hardly the only, times that starting out in group lessons at Appy Orse proved to have been a valuable experience. Crowded rings have never been a problem for my daughters.) It was difficult to keep track of which rider was which, and not only for someone like me who doesn't have a great eye when it comes to telling horses apart. I watched next to a local trainer who also was confused, despite knowing many of the horses and riders. The riders moved through a series of exercises, one after another, and the clinic necessarily had something of an "assembly line" feel. I tried, of course, to gauge Ada's performance, doing my best to follow both Ada and Diane's eyes at the key moments. The trainer was clearly watching Ada and Cash at times, but none of her commentary suggested anything remarkable. My impression was that Ada did well but hardly stood out.

The clinic came to a close, the riders left the ring, and I made a snap decision. Since we had exchanged emails, I thought, I'd introduce myself to Diane and thank her for the clinic. It would be a moment of pleasantries and then I'd head back into the barn to hold Cash while Ada hosed him down.

That's not quite how things unfolded. I introduced myself. Diane asked which rider was my daughter, and somehow we got from "she was on a bay horse" to the specific bay horse she was on. Diane's verdict was clear: Ada had ridden very well and I should go get Ada (who reported through a smile that on her way out of the ring Diane had called her "a future Grand Prix rider") so we could have a conversation. The details of the discussion that followed have escaped me, but the upshot was this: We would contact Diane's protege Serah Vogus. Ada could set up lessons with her, and we would see where things went from there. ❦

5

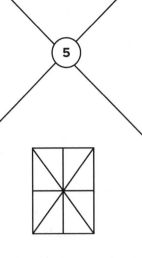

I t's an idea I've already mentioned, that there's a gap between how you imagine parenthood is going to go and how it actually turns out. There was a stretch in my early twenties, when parenthood was all very hypothetical, in which I was convinced that I would have hockey-playing children. It was an idea that made *some* sense, given that I grew up in Minnesota, but not as much as you might expect, since playing hockey wasn't even an option in a small town in the southern part of the state. But it appealed to me somehow. And so I'd have kids who played. How? Well, I'd just influence their tastes in obvious (to me) and heavy-handed ways. They would be miniature versions of me, carefully crafted to minimize or avoid my own shortcomings. And they would play hockey. I'd do all the things I wished my parents had been able to do for me, and then some.

The optimism and idealism of youth collides with the hard edge of reality in all sorts of ways, and this is one of them. Kids, you discover pretty quickly, come with their own ideas. They're not always drawn to the same things you are. Sometimes, as they age, the fact that you like something might be reason enough for them not to like it. Their talents and inclinations may fall well outside your family's expected range. An acquaintance who grew up in a family of avid golfers has no talent for the game at all and went to college to become an opera singer. My dad certainly did not anticipate a bookish son drawn to the abstract and theoretical rather than the tangible implements of the farm. Most apples fall close to the tree. A few somehow end up a good distance away, at least in some respects. So, what, as a parent, do you do about it?

One approach is to force things. We're all familiar with the overbearing parent, the one who insists on setting a path and requires the child to follow it. The classic example is the parent whose own dreams of athletic greatness never quite came to fruition despite a fierceness of desire and intensity of effort. The parent redirects this intensity to his children's lives, shaping and restricting and pushing achievement at the highest possible levels. The child becomes a proxy warrior in the fight for the parent's dreams, a second shot at glory.

A different subset of these parents consists of those who perhaps just find themselves adrift in the early-middle stages of adulthood, living a life that is no longer entirely about them, working a job that's not fulfilling, in need of an outlet for their energy, which then gets directed to the micromanaging of their child's pursuits. I'm sure there are other stories as well, each unique in its way, all leading to the same place: A child who's doing something because a parent wants her to. Or who is doing it at a level well beyond what she otherwise would. The reward is the parent's approval, or the avoidance of the parent's disapproval, rather than anything intrinsic to the activity itself. I've got no first-hand experience with it, but I've got to believe the long-term effects of such a tactic are, shall we say, not entirely positive.

Our approach was different. Let the girls try pretty much anything they wanted to try and not push too hard on any of it. The desire to continue, and to improve, would have to come from them. If they found their way to something they wanted to be passionate about—and each of them did—we'd support it to the best of our abilities. Coaches, camps, the whole apparatus of middle-class investment, aided by the good fortune of having jobs with flexible enough schedules to allow us to work in trips to gyms, soccer fields, music teachers' homes, ice rinks, and horse farms. My personal investment in "the hockey plan, " it turned out, was not all that significant. There was one day early in our years of taking Laura to the skating rink, where a hockey team of girls about her age was practicing on an adjacent rink at the same time as her synchronized skating team. I suggested that maybe she'd be interested in trying that. She wasn't. And that was the end of that portion of my parenting master plan.

This approach wasn't so much a product of conscious choice as it was a replication of both my and Lea's childhood. We both were expected to go to college—or at least, in my case, my mom made it clear that she would like it very much if I were to do that. But there were no expectations of especially high achievement, or that we'd end up going to law school. And for me, "no expectations" was pretty much the general rule. Growing up and getting some sort of job would be doing my part. I meandered through my youth. I played high school sports, but never at a level that approached individual glory. I was also in plays and in the band and otherwise involved in most every extracurricular activity available at my very small school. But I can't say that I was passionate about any of it. No single thing ever gripped hold of my imagination and kept my attention, and I did virtually nothing to develop whatever talents and potential I might have had. There weren't any readily available models for doing so, and in a world that predated the internet and in a place that was a long way from a decent library or bookstore, discovering what was available to me was spotty at best.

That's not to say I didn't form some big dreams, but they were vague and undefined, and I had no real idea how to go about achieving them. Fortunately for me, I had one clear natural talent: I was very, very good at taking standardized tests. The first thing that got me was an invitation to spend a portion of the summer between my junior and senior years of high school taking part in a new program at the University of Minnesota called the Summer Honors College. The idea was to provide a taste of the college experience—a chance to spend some time in residence on the Minneapolis campus while taking a pair of intensive classes. This put me, for the first time, in the city as something other than a day-tripper. Perhaps most importantly, it meant I got to spend time among a group of other academically inclined kids, to get a taste of what it would be like to be part of a community whose members were driven to achieve. I loved it.

I had taken the SAT in late spring of that year, and it turned out that my scores arrived while I was at the Summer Honors College. The only phones we had access to were pay phones in the lobby of Frontier Hall, the dorm where we were staying, and it was there that I stood when my mom relayed the results. I had only a general sense of their significance, made more concrete when I mentioned them to my roommate, who was from one of the wealthier Minneapolis suburbs. He didn't hesitate in his reaction. "You can go to college wherever you want."

It's just as well that I didn't know enough at the time to question his judgment. I wouldn't have appeared anywhere near the top of a list of the most accomplished member of the class of 1986, because while I had done many things, I hadn't done any of them well. But I had good test scores and came from a family of decidedly modest means in a tiny town with a funny name (both the town's and mine). So when my handwritten, deeply unsophisticated application to Harvard arrived the admissions committee's reaction must have been mostly in the nature of, "Why not give it a shot?" Whatever the nature of their discussion, they let me in.

I mention all this because my arrival in Cambridge, Massachusetts, for college marked a significant inflection point in my life. It was educationally significant, of course, and it got me a fancy line for my resume, but that's not all that happened. A college experience is only partly about what happens in the classroom. Much of the learning takes place in the dorm room and around the dinner table. And in those places, one of the things I noticed almost immediately was that the people I was now spending all my time around looked at the world in a fundamentally different way. I'd grown up amongst farmers and factory workers, people who rightly understood themselves to be at the mercy of forces they couldn't control. There's nothing to be done about the weather, and there's nothing to be done about decisions made in some distant corporate office to shut down a facility or lay a bunch of people off. My classmates, by contrast, generally did not have working-class backgrounds. They clearly felt a sense of agency with respect to their own lives that was foreign to me. I was conditioned to see what would happen; they insisted on making something happen. And they tended, as well, to be internally motivated to achieve at a high level. In my professional life, at least, I've spent my all my days since largely around that sort of person.

The point I've been wandering toward is this: context matters. It's harder to develop your own talents when nobody around you is doing much to develop theirs. We calibrate ourselves to those around us. If I'm with a group of high achievers, I'm going to be motivated to try to keep up. It doesn't matter if their achievements are physical, intellectual, or something else entirely. This hit me again during the peak period of Laura's time as a skater. For several years she and I would wake up before 5:00 a.m. so that she could be at the rink for the 5:45 slot, sometimes for a lesson, but usually just for her to skate on her own. It wasn't an easy thing to do, but it would have been harder if there hadn't consistently been other kids there doing the same thing. But there were, and because there were it felt more natural, and it felt like there was a little bit of an obligation to be there. Not that anyone would be upset if Laura missed a day, or that it would necessarily impact anything. But people would notice, and if more than a day or so went by without her presence, they might ask where she had been, and even something as small as that can be a source of motivation.

One more example: I did much of the work of writing this book during the COVID-19 lockdown days of 2020. Another thing I did during that time was a lot of running. I had been a casual runner for most of my adult life, and to that point had run three marathons, perhaps a dozen races between a half-marathon and twenty miles, and an assortment of shorter races. I'd often felt that I'd like to do more, but the press of daily life made it difficult until, suddenly, I no longer had to devote time to things like commuting to my office. Even so, I hadn't planned on ramping things up in any dramatic way. Then I came across a Facebook post by a man named Gary Cantrell, who in the person of his alter ego Lazarus Lake has attained something of a larger-than-life role in the running world, mostly for putting on a series of extraordinarily difficult and unconventional races.

Because in-person races were being cancelled, he had decided to put on a virtual race across his home state of Tennessee, expecting perhaps a few hundred people to participate. I signed up immediately and was the two hundred and twenty-third person to do so. It grew quickly from there. What Laz imagined would draw a couple hundred people ended up drawing nearly 20,000, all committed to attempting to log 635 miles between the first of May and the last day of August.

This would require running more than I had in a long time, and at the outset I wasn't sure I'd be able to maintain the necessary pace. But then group dynamics started to work their magic. In addition to creating the race, Laz created a Facebook group for participants. That group became incredibly active. By the time the race started, I knew that I was in the company of some extraordinarily dedicated runners. One person made her first virtual crossing of Tennessee in eleven days. Many others put up similarly impossible-seeming daily totals. I began not only to read the Facebook posts, but also to watch documentaries about ultramarathoners and to listen to running-related podcasts while I ran. My entry into this subculture, even though it was entirely virtual, changed my perspective. Racking up miles at perhaps the greatest rate in my life started to seem normal. Rather than taking four months to get across Tennessee, I completed the trip in sixty-eight days. I did the work, but I wouldn't have had I not found my way to the group.

Horse barns tend to come with some of this built in. Even at Appy Orse Acres, which had lots of people who would try riding for a bit but not stick with it, there were people who seemed like they were always at the barn. The effect was magnified at each of the subsequent barns we spent time at. When a barn reaches a critical mass of boarders— people who own or lease horses—it takes on a different character. There's almost always someone around, and that someone is generally happy to talk about horses. Where things differ is as to the nature of those discussions. The barn filled with adults who are mostly interested in trail rides will have a different culture than a barn oriented toward showing. A "B"-show barn will have a different vibe than an "A"-show barn, and there are undoubtedly subcategories within those as well. Whatever the culture is, it will shape the expectations of the young rider growing up within it.

In the past, this culture likely also placed boundaries on the expectations of the young rider. I arrived at college to find that many of my classmates had done extraordinary things that I didn't even know were possible. There had been no way to find out. Life is no longer that way. The sort of information that was inaccessible in my youth now exists in abundance and only a tap on the phone away. A kid with interest and motivation is able not only to absorb the culture in person at the barn, but to supplement her learning by reading and watching a limitless supply of content. She can easily form dreams that extend well beyond her immediate horizons. She can learn about the Maclay Finals.

Ideally parents could anticipate this. They could get a sense of what's involved at the various levels, both in terms of personal and monetary commitment. They could form a realistic assessment of where the true horizons are likely to be and set expectations accordingly. It's all easier said than done, especially for parents who are newcomers to a world and who have multiple kids drawn to a sport, each of whom is very much her own person with her own motivations, talents, and needs. Parents of multiple children face basic questions of equal treatment all the time and quickly recognize that rigidly treating kids the same is not the same as treating them equally. Different personalities react differently to praise, criticism, and adversity, and getting the best out of multiple children can entail very different approaches. That's not always an easy sell to the child who thinks she's getting the short end of the stick at any given moment. Mistakes and bad moments are inevitable, and there are days when your goal is simply to minimize the consequences of your own misjudgment.

There was value for me in having grown up with no real expectations. If nothing else, it left me space to have a variety of experiences, and it required me to cope with boredom, to figure out what to do with large chunks of unscheduled time. And it meant that whatever I did would be a product of my own choices, coupled with whatever luck came my way. (And I've been the beneficiary of considerable amounts of luck.) Still, I can't help but wonder what the alternatives might have looked like. What if my childhood had included role models who were the sorts of people I'd end up spending my adult life around? What if someone had pushed me a bit more? I mean to cast no aspersions, or to suggest that anyone was doing anything other than their best under the circumstances. And I certainly believe that the environment in which I grew up was vastly superior to many of the alternatives, because it was a place and a people that openly valued education. But I began college at a distinct disadvantage relative to my peers.

As we've tried to navigate a path between the poles of too much and too little, I find myself thinking back to two dads I remember from my days as a clueless teen. Both stories involve high school wrestling, which was one of my sports. I wasn't an especially good wrestler, and part of the reason why I became a wrestler had to do with the fact that I was an even worse basketball player. Still, it was something that I started doing during elementary school.

There was always a two-week period during the year when the high school team held practices for kids who were interested in trying it out. That culminated in a tournament in the high school gym, and at least a couple times a group of kids traveled to other schools that hosted larger tournaments. We could practice with the high school team starting in seventh grade, and so for six years, my winters revolved around wrestling. Unless we had a meet, we had practice after school.

The first dad I think of had a son who was really into wrestling. Problem was, the school in the nearby small town they lived in didn't have a wrestling team. So he jumped through whatever hoops were necessary to get the two school districts to agree to allow his son to be a part of our team. And then every day during the season he drove his son to our school for practice, which he would then sit and watch. Our wrestling room was in what we called the "old gym," which also served as the cafeteria. A small section of bleachers remained, and that's where he'd be, day after day, in a room smelling of sweat, cleaning fluid, and the lingering odors of that day's lunch, watching and (worse) listening to a bunch of teenage boys wrestle.

It makes perfect sense to me now, but it wasn't the sort of thing you saw parents doing in that time and place. And he was in no way over-the-top about it. I recall him as pleasant and soft-spoken, always there, staying out of the coaches' way, never drawing much attention to himself. If he did any of what we'd now call "helicopter parenting," I missed it. His kid wanted to wrestle, and he did what he had to do to make it happen. I was, to be honest, a little mystified by it all.

The second dad who comes to mind I saw only once, at the postseason district tournament. It was one of those "win and advance to the regional tournament or lose and your season's over" kind of affairs. His son was wrestling against a much better opponent and losing by a substantial amount. The match was winding down, and it was clear the son had given up and was simply looking to run out the clock.

I did not know the kid, and I did not know his dad, and I can tell you nothing of the history leading up to the moment. But the moment itself remains clear. The dad paced back and forth alongside the mat like a caged animal. He shouted in a voice that could easily have been the model for comedian Chris Farley's "van down by the river" character on *Saturday Night Live*. "You wrestle to *win*!" he commanded. Over and over again. "You wrestle to *win*!"

Oblivious as my teenage self might generally have been, even I recognized that an entire gymnasium full of people felt very uncomfortable. And more than a little bit sorry for the kid. I detected no sympathy for the dad. We all wanted it to be over. None of us wanted to think about what might transpire between the two later that night.

Over the years I've come to understand completely where Dad Number One was coming from. His son had a passion, and he did what he could to allow his son to pursue it. I get that. I spent many of the years leading up to the writing of this book regularly making even longer drives so that I could sit in an indoor arena watching riding lessons. I won't say that I never complained about it, and I certainly won't claim there were no moments where I felt deserving of slightly more gratitude than I got. But on the whole I did it eagerly. I had daughters who wanted to ride, to continue to develop their talents, and to take advantage of the opportunities that came along. I did what I could to make it happen.

And over the years I've softened a little on Dad Number Two. Or at least come to understand that there might be a version of the story in which he was not the villain that he appeared to be. Maybe. That's not to say that I'd ever behave like that or condone that sort of thing from anyone else. It'd still be an awfully uncomfortable moment to watch. And yet...

Certainly, the story might have been the thoroughly unhappy one we all imagined. Perhaps the dad still carried his own unfulfilled dreams, and the son wrestled mostly because it seemed like his old man really wanted him to. It might have been the dad's dreams that were dying—again—as the seconds ticked off the clock. Maybe the dad was just an angry person. There are lots of scenarios leading to the conclusions those of us in the crowd drew that night: "I feel sorry for that kid," and "I'm glad that's not my dad."

But, having now spent time as a dad, I can't help but imagine the possibility that there's a better version of the story. It would go something like this: Dad Number Two found himself in the same boat as Dad Number One. His kid loved wrestling. Nobody could really say why. The boy just had a taste for it and some talent to match. And so, the dad took his son to practices and clinics. He cleared out the basement and put in a wrestling mat and a weight set. He went to all the meets and paced around during his son's matches because who can bear to sit for something like that? He got wrapped up in it because that was his kid out there, and he knew how much all of it meant to his son, and when something means that much to your child, you do what you have to do.

That version of Dad Number Two was watching a dream die. The hurt he felt for his kid was like nothing he'd ever felt before. It was unbearable. All he could do was try to coax a miracle out of the situation. And for that to happen the son was going to have to do *something,* and there was only one way to let him know that *he had to do something.* The dad had to yell. It was the only way he might possibly keep his son's dreams alive. Desperate times, desperate measures.

That's probably not the story. But if it were? I don't have to condone it to be able to relate to it.

I've thought a lot about both of these dads over the last fifteen years. I've tried my best to be Dad Number One. The passion, it seems to me, has to come from the kid. But I have to admit there have been moments where I've felt a bit of Dad Number Two—the version I imagine, anyway—sneaking out. It's hard to invest your time and your money without investing your heart. That's your kid out there. If it means a lot to her, it means a lot to you. You want to help. You *really* want to help. You don't always know how to do it. Sometimes you reach out to the prominent trainer who, as a judge, liked your daughter's riding. Sometimes you do what you wouldn't ordinarily do and approach that trainer after a clinic. It *seems* like the right thing to do in the moment. But then, so, too, did some of the things you may end up wishing you hadn't done, the words that came out wrong, the ones that you wish you hadn't said at all.

It's hard to chart the right course as a parent and impossible to have every step be the perfect one. How do you know when the best thing is just to be there, when all you should offer is your presence or a hug? Or when it's time to give a gentle, and occasionally not-so-gentle, nudge? How do you pick the right words to say? When should you let that little piece of Dad Number Two, sympathetic version, slip out? What do you do with the fact that watching your kid experience disappointment often stings a lot more than any of your own disappointments ever did?

There's no way to know for sure, no way to avoid sometimes ending up thinking that you shouldn't have said that thing that you said, or at least not in the specific way you said it. Or that you misread what was really a time for a hug as a time for a nudge.

There are tears in every childhood. Some from pain, some from disappointment, some from frustration. There are bursts of anger for the same reasons. My family wasn't immune to those moments, though I'm sure we'd prefer to forget them. As the parent you try to be the wise one, the one who knows just what to say. But sometimes you're tired, or disappointed, or frustrated, and it affects your judgment. Sometimes it's just not clear what to do. You do your best. You just hope to get it wrong as little as possible. And you hope that the times you got it wrong aren't the times that your kids carry with them for the rest of their lives.

Because you're pretty sure you got it right a lot of the time. And because there have been so many good times along the way. Big moments and little ones and pauses in between. Those early trips to tack stores, where it was a thrill just to figure out what everything was and how it might be used, and to imagine that one, far-off day there would be a real horse to ride and groom. The times when it was enough just to stand and watch horses, any horses, for twenty or thirty minutes. The quest for more Breyer horses. The lessons and the trail rides and those early shows that were by far the most important days of the year.

For a while it all unfolds slowly. You're looking ahead, thinking about what comes next and about what you hope might come after that, and what the road from here to there might look like. You're a necessary part of the team, providing the transportation and the ice cream cones afterward, helping with grooming and tacking and cleaning the bridle at the end so you can get home more quickly. But they get taller and stronger and more knowledgeable. You become more of an accessory than a necessity. One day they get a license to drive. You've been focused on the road ahead, trying to anticipate what's coming next, but now find yourself more often looking in the rearview mirror. The role of "dad" becomes an ever-more-minor character in the production.

All three of our daughters are now in college. Some of those same friends who prepared me for the early parts of the parenting journey let me know how difficult this stage would be. One of my closest friends, someone you'd never imagine this to be true of, reportedly cried himself to sleep the night before he dropped his daughter off at school. And then did it the night after, too.

As a kid, I was oblivious to how things felt from my parents' side. I couldn't wait to get to college and begin the process of finding out what life held in store for me. The idea that anyone from home might miss me didn't really register.

When I left for Harvard, I flew by myself. It was still possible then for pretty much anyone to get to the airport gates, and so my parents waited with me until it was time to board. I took a quick look back before entering the jetway to the plane that would take me to Boston. My mom was crying. I figured it was just one of those things, and that she'd be fine by the time they got home. I'm quite certain now that I was wrong about that.

Sorry, Mom. ✸

6

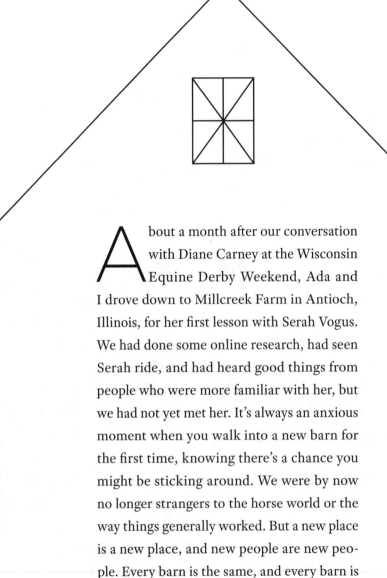

About a month after our conversation with Diane Carney at the Wisconsin Equine Derby Weekend, Ada and I drove down to Millcreek Farm in Antioch, Illinois, for her first lesson with Serah Vogus. We had done some online research, had seen Serah ride, and had heard good things from people who were more familiar with her, but we had not yet met her. It's always an anxious moment when you walk into a new barn for the first time, knowing there's a chance you might be sticking around. We were by now no longer strangers to the horse world or the way things generally worked. But a new place is a new place, and new people are new people. Every barn is the same, and every barn is

——— CHAPTER 6 ———

different. There are horses and saddles and stalls. But the bedding in the stalls might be straw, or wood shavings, or pellets. You clean bridles this way at one barn and that way at another. Each one has its own smell, some rich with the sweeter notes of hay, others more ambiguously the accumulated result of hundreds of horses and dozens of years.

Serah gave us a brief tour; Ada and I exchanged a few meaningful glances. Millcreek, too, was the same. But in important-seeming respects, it was different. And then it was time to ride.

Those early lessons were exhilarating. Part of it was the sense that things were happening, and a whole new world of possibility was opening. Part of it was riding for someone new, who brought a fresh pair of eyes that noticed different things and offered different corrections. Improvement tends to come quickly, or at least to be more noticeable, after a change. Part of it was getting to ride a new group of horses, which happened as well to include some that were fairly fancy and accomplished. A lot of it was that Serah was an extraordinarily charismatic person. Ada fell in her first two lessons. Serah later told her, "You got right back on, and your dad didn't move an inch, so I knew this would work."

At first it was a once-a-week affair. Saturdays at 9:00 a.m. at Millcreek, lesson for roughly an hour, then, if we could, hang around for a while to watch some of the following lessons. It's time well-spent, that sort of hanging out. You can get only so much of a feel for a place by just showing up for a lesson and then leaving. There's lots to be gained from seeing the mistakes that others make and how they fix them, from seeing the trainer-student interaction, from seeing how the other students interact with each other. As a parent, it allows you to get a sense of the other families. Are these people who seem to have and model the right sort of values? Are they people you'll enjoy spending large chunks of horse-show downtime with? You choose a barn to shape a rider, but you're also shaping a human. No place is perfect, of course, and there's at least one in every crowd (you'll have to answer the "one of what?" question in your own way). But Millcreek seemed to check all the boxes.

Cash remained at Hidden View, and Ada continued her Sunday lessons with Charles. None of "the change" happened in secret. I was always as open as I could be with all our trainers at these moments of transition. It is, as I've already noted, an uncomfortable topic to broach and the conversations are never easy, but so far as I can tell they're always appreciated. For the most part people understand that young riders move on, and for the most part they don't, and shouldn't, take it personally.

When winter break arrived, we trailered Cash down to Millcreek so that Serah could work directly with him and Ada. He stepped almost literally off the trailer and into a group lesson, a mass of new horses and new people in a ring he had never seen. He performed like the old pro he had become, unperturbed and doing what he was asked to do. The plan was that he would be there for a few weeks, then return to Hidden View, although we understood that there was a good chance that things wouldn't work out that way.

And, indeed, they didn't. Ada caught some sort of bug early on and got sick enough that she was unable to ride as often as we anticipated. By the time break was over, we had made the drive enough times to get to that counterintuitive point where familiarity made the trip seem shorter than it initially did. It was going well. So Cash stayed.

Cash and Ada made their "A"-circuit debut that March at the Lake St. Louis Winter Festival. It was an exhilarating set of firsts. There was the simple thrill of having reached a destination. Just a few years earlier even "B" shows had seemed like a distant, other world and "A" shows the stuff of fantasy. This was a major milestone. It was also Ada's first show with a new trainer and new group of barn mates, our first visit to a new-to-us facility, first indoor show, first time seeing a live Grand Prix class.

Our biggest obstacles were navigational. Google Maps initially led us to a vacant lot across the street from an auto parts store. Then it took a while to get a handle on the layout of the facility. (It's hard to escape the feeling that indoor horse show facilities are just scaled-up hamster habi-tats.) But Cash and Ada did their part. Their first round was a "blue-rib-bon class," so-named because that's what a clean round will get you, and that's what they had. From there things generally went according to plan, and together Cash and Ada brought home a solid set of ribbons, including a blue in an equitation class.

The trend continued. Not two months later, Ada and I drove to Lex-ington to meet Cash, Serah, and crew at the Kentucky Horse Park. Here, undoubtedly, was a dream come true. An "A" show was one thing. An "A" show at the Horse Park was something else entirely. This was a venue that only a couple years earlier had seemed impossibly distant, a place about which you say "maybe someday" in the sort of way where "but probably not" is unstated but understood. Cash got a new name as part of the preparation—Speed Thru Traffic transformed into the Cash-related Walk the Line. I brought the nice camera and documented all of it—the moment Ada first mounted Cash, the trip up the path to the Murphy Ring for their first ride, a ride in the double warm-up ring with Rolex Stadium looming in the background, a series of photos over a line of or-nately decorated jumps in the Stonelea Ring. On one of the afternoons, I accompanied Ada as she and Cash walked around the cross-country course where a couple years earlier, she and I had watched some of the top eventing riders and horses in the world. They approached some of the more impressive obstacles just so Ada could see how they looked from the back of a horse. I've got photos of that, too.

The story inside the ring had only a tiny element of fairy tale. This was high-level competition, and many of the names casually announced as "now entering the ring" were names that even I had heard. While I haven't checked the records, I feel confident in saying that there were no other Iowa-bred Quarter Horses taking part. By nearly every measure of fanciness, Cash was a gatecrasher, and we understood that this was a show where the goal was experience rather than glory. And, indeed, the show record shows a number of DNPs ("did not place"). But it also shows this: that in *Class No. 256, Low Working Hunter*, Ada and Walk the Line took home the blue ribbon. (The record shows that it was Serah who rode him in that class, but in that respect the record is wrong.) The gatecrasher snagged one glass of champagne.

There comes a moment, for each of us, when things are as good as they'll ever get. That's probably true in an all-in, single-best-moment-of-your-life sense, although that may be hard to pin down. It's definitely true when it comes to athletic competition. I have long since run the fastest 800 meters of my life. And while the marathon I ran at forty-three was faster than the one I ran a decade earlier, the pace of my longer runs these days suggests to me that I've hit the downward slope, and that my personal bests are fixed entities.

For better or worse we don't know we're in those moments when we live them. When I crossed the finish line my fastest races were only my fastest races *so far*. I ran that 800 about halfway through my senior season in high school and had every reason to expect faster ones to come.

The forty-three-year-old who ran faster than the thirty-something had no reason to believe that he couldn't, and therefore wouldn't, train just a little bit harder and turn in a stronger effort the following year. And to be honest I'm still not quite ready to concede that my best effort is in the past. I write this in my early fifties, which somehow to my mind is younger than my late thirties. And while I know that I'll never again be as fast over a short distance as I was at eighteen, I can't shake the sense that if I were to train hard, to be systematic about it for once, I just might be able to beat my best marathon time. The mind doesn't want to let go. I recently read an article about a running coach who mentioned having a client several years older than me who is attempting to top the fastest mile he ran as a high school track athlete. Whether he succeeds or not is less important than the fact that he *might*. Not knowing isn't all of what keeps us going, but the possibility of improvement, the idea that there's still a little magic left, provides another reason to get out of bed, a nice incentive to keep moving forward on days when it would be easier just to rest.

It's similar with writing. One of these times I just might put the right words in exactly the right order, and then everyone will take notice. One of these times. You never know until you try.

One of the blessings of equestrian life is that it's more like distance running than track and field when it comes to knowing whether you've reached your peak. I ran my last 800-meter race as a senior in high school, toward the end of a six-month period in which I also played my last football game, wrestled my last match, and played my last baseball game. I walked away from each of those knowing I was done. The closest I've come to competing in the same way since is by being a part of several slow-pitch softball teams. Future athletic competition for me, if there was to be any, would have to come in some other way. It's not the same in the equestrian world. It's not unusual to have Olympians in their fifties, and

I know riders in their sixties who regularly compete successfully against riders less than half their age. A rider's peak is not so clearly confined to the early part of life, and the fact that the sport depends so much on an accumulated sense of feel rather than simply pure physical ability makes it likely that any given rider's best years come well into adulthood, at least if she remains dedicated to the sport.

Ada's best rides, then, remain in the future. But for Ada and Cash as a team the best rides may have come at their third show on the "A"-circuit. It was week one of a show called Spring Spectacular, held at the Lamplight Equestrian Center in Wayne, Illinois. Lamplight is a truly beautiful facility, short on parking but not on trees. Most everything takes place against a nice backdrop, and the layout of the facility makes sense. At least once you get to know it.

The show did not start off well. We had not been to Lamplight before and had no feel for the grounds. Due to a miscommunication, we were still at the barn when Ada's first class was starting. This presented two immediate problems. The first was that the barn, which in reality was a large tent with temporary stabling, was about as far from the ring as it was possible to be while still being on the showgrounds. The second was that we had no idea where the ring was. Our instructions were to follow a path until it ended. That, we were assured, would lead us straight to the ring. I jogged alongside as Ada and Cash trotted. We followed the path. But what nobody had accounted for was that there was a fork in the path. The left fork traveled alongside the Grand Prix ring. The right fork looked, or at least it did in the moment, more path-like, and since our instructions were to follow the *path* to the end, that was the fork we took. And for perhaps fifty yards or more that route had the feel of a nice horse show path, lined with trees on both sides and edged by a block wall. But then the vibe started to change and there was an abrupt transition.

We found ourselves making our way through an area filled with equipment, clusters of jump standards, and piles of poles. We kept going, though, even as our surroundings seemed less and less like where we were supposed to be. We traveled through a parking lot on the backside of what we didn't yet know was the show office, along a short path next to a house, and suddenly—to the great surprise of all the people who were looking for us to come from a completely different direction—emerged exactly where we were supposed to be. (I've since walked the route again, and can only conclude that it was pure luck that brought us to the right place. But that was where the luck ended.)

It was a flat class, and all the other riders were already in the ring. There was no time for a warm-up, no time for Ada to collect her thoughts, no time to wipe off the dirt that was surely on her boots. She went in, the gate closed, and the announcer informed the riders that they were now being judged.

Not surprisingly, that class didn't go so well.

But things came together quickly after that. The highlight came when Ada and Cash won two of their three medal classes and placed second in the third. But it's not the ribbons that stand out in my memory. Instead, it was their confidence. I recall standing near the in-gate, which just a day before we had rushed to find, listening to Ada conferring with Serah before her rides. So often those conversations between a trainer and rider involve reviewing the course, together with a healthy portion of "remember the basics," "stay calm," "breathe," and the like. It's an exercise in calming nerves. That's often valuable, but here it was unnecessary. The basics would happen. That was understood. They were beyond that. There are times when you're "in the zone," where you know, with as much certainty as one can know anything, that it's going to be good, and the only question is how good. It's happened to me enough—sometimes in athletic competition, but mostly in professional contexts—to be able to recognize it. And that's where they were. Any nervous energy was the productive kind. The conversation was not just about how to do it, but how to do it with the most style. An attentive bystander who knew nothing about the horse or rider beyond having heard these conversations would know to watch for a strong ride. They knew they would do well, and they did.

It was like that in lessons, too. Raise the jumps, make the turns tighter, it didn't much matter. They would do whatever they were asked, and they would do it well. The partnership had advanced and solidified. It was a joy to watch.

But for as good a team as they were, the situation created a problem. It's natural to want to pull for the underdog. And it's easy to imagine that the storybook ending can be *your* ending, that maybe, just maybe, there's room for a horse plucked from obscurity—for *your* horse plucked from obscurity—to shine on the big stage. I'm sure Ada and Cash never left the ring after any class thinking they'd just been as good as they were ever going to be together. But it nonetheless seemed clear that they were nearing their limits. In important ways the dreams were all starting to seem possible. Riding in a show at the Kentucky Horse Park had become a reality, which made it seem that adding just a few words, so that the phrase was "riding at the Kentucky Horse Park in the Maclay Finals," might be possible as well. If one could happen, why not the other?

The problem, of course, was that Cash simply didn't fit the bill. One could say, and I would guess that the words probably crossed my lips on one or more occasions, that he wasn't a nice enough horse. But that, I now think, is to bring an unwarranted snobbishness into the picture. He wasn't the right sort of horse, where what counts as the right sort is, to a degree, a product of fashion. A rider might once have been competitive at a national level on a Thoroughbred or even an Appendix Quarter Horse. But hunter/jumper shows are the domain of Warmbloods now. Cash didn't fit the picture. A gatecrasher might get into the dance, but only in movies will he win any prizes. The dreams would require a different horse. Our budget, comparatively speaking, was not large. But you do what you can do as a parent, and we would support this next step. We gave the okay for Serah to start a search for a new horse.

Somewhere along the line I had started reading *The Chronicle of the Horse*. It is, for the most part, the place to go for coverage of the higher reaches of the hunter/jumper, dressage, and eventing worlds. Its online forums provide an equal mix of gossip and good information, and its website and Facebook pages feature the work of a mix of bloggers writing about their experiences in the horse world. It's primarily a group of trainers and riders, and I had the thought, as someone who's naturally inclined to ponder things, that I might have something to add. Of course, I have a lot of ideas, and most of them don't make it out of my daydreams. But this time I found myself with a long solo drive back home from Lexington, which gave me time to listen to satellite radio and think about things like the possibility of writing about my experiences. Somewhere north of Indianapolis the DJ spent a little extra time introducing the song he was about to play. He described hearing it the first time as a transformational experience. I figured I'd better listen closely. The song was "Peggy Sang the Blues" by Frank Turner. The chorus includes the line "no one gets remembered for the things they didn't do."

We can each draw our own conclusions about whether that was any kind of sign. It was certainly the prod I needed to follow through on the idea. I put together a pitch and hit "send." A few weeks later I followed up. Not long after that I made my debut on the *Chronicle*'s website. Some of what you've read and will read in these pages began as those posts. As I write now I'm looking back. As I wrote then, I was looking forward. It's useful to convey that perspective.

Here's how I opened my very first contribution to the *Chronicle*:

> *Legend has it that blues musician Robert Johnson couldn't play all that well. At least not until just before midnight one evening when he got himself to a crossroads outside Clarksdale, Mississippi. There he met the devil, and in exchange for Johnson's soul the devil gave him the ability to play guitar like no one had played before.*
>
> *Lately I've been thinking about heading down to Clarksdale to see what the going rate might be for a couple of nice equitation horses.*
>
> *You wanna know what's giving me the most pause? I'm a little bit afraid my soul might not be worth that much.*

One might think, given that the Maclay Finals and the other events that Ada had set her eye on are based on equitation—in other words, the judging is to be based on the rider's performance and ability rather than the horse's—that the horse doesn't matter that much. As a naive outsider, one might even think that an Iowa-bred Appendix Quarter Horse would do the trick. So long as the horse could jump the jumps, the reasoning would go, a judge would be able to factor that into her expert assessment. She would of course know that some horses are easier to ride than others and would have the ability to tell where along that spectrum a given horse falls—and could make an all-in judgment about which rider in a class did the best job of riding. There'd be imperfection, sure. That's inevitable. Even if it were somehow possible for every competitor to ride a course on the same horse, there would be small variations from one trip to the next, and the differences between riders would often be so small as to make those relative judgments a product of something other than the quality of riding—the judge happens not to be focused on Rider One's hands at the moment of a small mistake but does see it when Rider Two makes the same error. It's an inherently imprecise undertaking no matter what. An effort to account for the talent level of the horse might increase the imprecision, but it wouldn't change the nature of the inquiry.

One might think all of those things, and one would be wrong. No doubt judges often disregard errors during a round if they conclude the mistake was the horse's rather than the rider's. But I've never heard a judge, or anyone else deep into the horse show culture for that matter, suggest that there's any kind of general accounting for the talent of the horse. As far as I've been able to discern it's often not apparent even to an informed observer that a given horse is difficult to ride. Instead, it's understood that there's such a thing as an equitation horse, and that the best ones are the kind that enable a rider to make it look easy. The phrases that get tossed around are revealing—"push-button" and "made" horses that allow riders to "pose" rather than ride. There aren't a lot of those horses, and when supply meets demand, the prices get out of hand. The sort of horse that allows a rider merely to compete in a high-level equitation class without feeling like she's the one who showed up to a formal event in a t-shirt and jeans runs well into the five figures. The top of the market touches the low seven figures.

Cash and Ada had their final rides together about a month after their successful outing at Lamplight. The setting was a regional session of the US Hunter Jumper Association's Emerging Athletes Program (EAP), held at Ledges Sporting Horses in Roscoe, Illinois. The EAP, which

I'll discuss more extensively in a later chapter, is a well-intentioned effort by the sport's governing body to provide the highest-level instruction to talented riders who might not otherwise have access to it, and to enable some of those riders to get opportunities within the sport that they otherwise might not get. Riders must apply and be selected in order to participate. As a fourteen-year-old, Ada was one of the youngest riders at the week-long session. The clinician was Chris Kappler, winner of, among other things, individual silver and team gold medals at the 2004 Olympics.

The week or so before we had somewhat hurriedly agreed to purchase a new horse for Ada, and exchanging Cash was part of that deal. So, we knew from the beginning that the clinic would be the conclusion of their partnership. That knowledge certainly didn't make the week any easier. Cash perhaps sensed it as well, since he misbehaved as much over those five days as he had for quite some time. Still, they had a good week, and Kappler's comments in the ring and written evaluation at the conclusion included strong praise for Ada's riding. The highlight came in their second-to-last ride, which was over a full course of jumps at the conclusion of the last session of instruction for the week. Ada and Cash had a strong ride, and afterward Kappler praised Ada's "natural feel" and encouraged her to continue to accumulate time in the saddle as the way to further refine and build on it.

On the last day of an EAP session, each rider gets one chance at a final ride. The participants walk the course as a group at the start of the day, then ride in an order prescribed by the clinician. A small number from each regional group gets selected to advance to a national session, and at none of the sessions I've been to is it completely clear who's in the running for those spots. As a result, there's a strong nervous energy in the air prior to the final ride.

It had rained heavily overnight, and large puddles dotted the ring. An especially large pool—more than a puddle, slightly less than a flood—stood at the end of the arena near the in-gate. Cash had never been a fan of going through water, so this wasn't a recipe for a flawless round. Still, things went well—as long as you're willing to overlook the string of bucks he added as they traversed the water near the in-gate. Ada rode through it like a champ and completed the round. It certainly wasn't a fairy-tale ending, but it was the end.

I met them right after they left the ring, and together we walked toward the barn. It had been a long week, featuring both late nights and early mornings. Ada was exhausted and ready to get home. I patted Cash and let him know he was a good boy, doing my best not to make a big deal out of what I understood to be a significant moment. Parents had been excluded from the barn during the week—the kids were to do all the work themselves—but now that the session was over, I could help Ada get her things ready to load.

We knew that one more challenge awaited. The last time we had been at Ledges, you'll remember, it took an eternity to get Cash loaded. We feared a repeat performance. I pulled our trailer into position. We brought out Ada's tack, trunk, and other equipment. We had the prime loading spot, and a line of other trailers formed behind us, some picking up horses from the EAP, others bringing horses in for the show that would take place over the weekend. Cash was hot and tired, too, and so we mentally prepared for the worst. Soon there would be a ring of haulers and show-goers standing around watching us, arms folded and toes tapping impatiently, their contempt palpable. We went to get Cash. Who, of course, loaded like a perfect gentleman.

We drove back to Millcreek, unloaded, checked in with Serah, and headed home. We expected Cash to remain there for a while, as the details of his next destination got sorted out, and so did not realize that that day's goodbyes would be our last goodbyes. But they were.

When we returned a couple days later, he was gone.

When we got Cash, I imagined that we would always have him. For a while our plan was to find a house on a few acres of land, perhaps even with a small barn already in place, so we'd have a place for him when he retired. There would be times, I imagined, when I'd join him in his paddock. We'd stand together for a while, he and I, enjoying the moment and one another's company, looking back on the journey and maybe even congratulating one another for the role we played in helping to raise three independent young women.

That's not how things turned out. We've seen him only once since the last day of the EAP, in the warm-up ring at a show where he played the role of "practice horse" rather than "show horse" for a young woman who was gearing up for her last shot at the Maclay and other equitation finals. A different rider showed him one or two times, but not at a level near where he and Ada left off. So far as I know he remains in a good situation. But still, there are many days when I feel like I didn't hold up my end of the bargain. He did his part, and then some, and then we just let him go. The pursuit of achievement often entails tradeoffs, of course. Parting with him was just such a thing, and it left me with a lingering feeling of unease. It's always struck me as a discordant feature of the horse world that many people who are deeply attached to their dogs and cats will nonetheless part with horses without seeming to give the matter much thought or regret. In the higher levels of the sport, in particular, horses tend to be viewed as commodities rather than companions.

It's not everyone, of course, who comes to that view, and there are no doubt differences in the nature of the relationships between humans and various sorts of animals that make the issue a complicated one. I'll offer no firm conclusions beyond the observation that I've come to admire the people I know who regard horse ownership as a lifetime commitment.

As for Cash, we're left with ribbons, photographs, and memories. I think often of him, and of the wonderful period in our lives marked by his time with us. So many images come to mind, but in the one that most fully captures his spirit he is mid-course, just coming out of the turn at the far end of the ring on his favored left lead. It's a perfect summer day somewhere at a show in Wisconsin, this ride is going well, and the future is bright and limitless. His manner is one of yeoman-like determination, his rhythmic puffing reminiscent of an old John Deere tractor making its way across a field. He is handsome but not pretty, solid but not flashy, the perfect embodiment of his Iowa roots. He has a job to do, and he will complete it to the best of his ability.

Cash had come out of obscurity to exceed our expectations. Ada's next horse had a very different biography. D'Lovely K—simply "K" in the barn—came to Millcreek from a moderately prominent barn in New Jersey. She had shown in some notable venues, and now found herself at Millcreek as a sale horse. She'd been there for several weeks. Ada had ridden her a few times, but not really with the idea that this could be her new horse. Still, one Saturday morning the idea to make an offer came quickly together and we gave the okay. The offer was accepted, and the purchase completed during the week of EAP.

There's a saying you often hear in the horse world: You ask a stallion, tell a gelding, and negotiate with a mare. We commenced negotiations. One sunny afternoon a few weeks in I found myself in charge of K as she munched on grass alongside a show ring. Even now I don't have the words to describe the ways in which it felt different from grazing Cash, but it clearly did. And I had never worried about stepping into the stall with Cash. Sometimes I'd join him just to hang out for a minute or two. K did not like having visitors to her stall. She would turn away, threatening to kick anyone who entered.

There was another sense in which K presented us with a problem unique to mares. She started to become noticeably larger not long after she became ours. And it wasn't just an illusion. The girths that had once been large enough to hold her saddle in place no longer were. It wasn't a lack of work. Adjustments to her feed didn't help. Could it be possible, we asked—at first jokingly, but then with increasing seriousness—that she was pregnant?

It wasn't entirely out of the realm of possibility. The barn she had come from insisted there was no chance. But other people told us stories. Things can happen when a gate doesn't get completely secured. Sometimes the person who discovers the open gate and its aftermath is the person who left the gate open, and sometimes they decide to deal with the situation by not telling anyone and hoping for the best. We had serious discussions about what we'd do if we found ourselves with an unexpected foal. We waited until a vet came to the barn on other business, then sheepishly requested a pregnancy test.

It was negative.

Experience has taught me to always prefer a text message from my daughters' trainers over a phone call. A text typically brings news that falls with a certain range between "pretty good" and "not-too-bad."

Sometimes it will even make you laugh out loud. Phone calls, on the other hand, mean you're about to spend money. Often there's a vet involved. Even on those rare occasions when the first thing you hear is, "Great news!" when you answer, the trainer's name on the caller ID signals a good chance the checkbook's coming out.

But, of course, every rule has its exceptions.

It was nearing noon on the Thursday of the Illinois Hunter Jumper Association "A" Finals at Lamplight. I was in my office, about to leave to pick up Ada from school so we could head to the show.

This wasn't an ordinary show trip. It was Ada's first "A" Finals, and so perhaps a big enough deal in its own right, including some first trips in the grand prix ring at Lamplight. But there was more. Ada's first show on K had not gone well. But they had made some adjustments and a had great schooling session at the showgrounds earlier in the week. We were hopeful they had turned a corner.

That's where it all stood when my phone buzzed. A text from Serah. No doubt the expected update on how quickly things were moving and when we needed to be there. Except no.

*Sit down I have bad news.*

K appeared to have popped a splint (meaning, basically, there was an inflammation of the lower leg, which was later confirmed, and possibly connected to the disappointment of the first show) and was on a trailer headed home. There would be no show for her.

This was bad news, indeed. We had purchased K in a rush, spending more than I ever would have imagined paying for a horse. And yet it was also a gamble, because she was not, in the context of the Big Eq world, an expensive horse. Still, her lineage was respectable, her show record included some positive signs, and she came to us from a well-known barn. This latter fact, in particular, we convinced ourselves was a good thing.

It's a strange situation to be in. On the one hand, our ability to take even this step was the product of good fortune. When our journey began, we were operating on a single salary. Over time Lea restarted her legal career and began to progress in her role, which enabled us to get a bit deeper in. We knew plenty of kids from Appy Orse who had all the passion, talent, and discipline to succeed in the "A"-show world but not the resources to make that happen, and so we understood that we were among the lucky ones. Yet the human tendency is to gaze upward, and to focus on what others have that you don't. There's always somebody with more, and they aren't hard to find in the horse world. What results is a natural pressure to stretch one's resources.

No sane retirement planner would have recommended our purchase of K. It was easy to wonder why we were chasing these dreams. Many of the players in the game had access to practically infinite resources, and they could afford the sorts of mistakes and mishaps that would be devastating to us. There would be no string of horses in our future, and our daughters showed when we could afford it rather than whenever their trainer went to a show. To pull this off would certainly be to thread a needle under suboptimal conditions. There were competing voices in my head. One told me that this was a fool's errand, that those 4-H and "B" shows were plenty enjoyable, and that we ought not have left that world behind. The other proclaimed the virtues of aiming high, working hard, and taking your shot.

The first voice was most vocal in the middle of the night. It worried about how treacherous the path ahead might be. It worried about the prospect of conversations that begin, "Sit down I have bad news."

The second voice reminded me of things like the 2004 Boston Red Sox, a team that hadn't won a World Series in eighty-six years. They wore shirts that read, "Why not us?" Then they won the World Series. And so, the second voice asked the same question. "Why not us?" The only way to ensure failure is not to try at all. The things most worth trying are the things where failure is a real possibility. It might not work out, but then maybe it will. Life is short. Take the chance.

We took the chance, and now we were about to depart for a show at which there would be no horse waiting for Ada to ride.

Fortunately, Serah came up with a Plan B. And fortunately, we had found in Millcreek another barn family that was generous and supportive. Kate Wilson graciously offered to share Bonfeuer, who she would be showing in the Junior hunters and equitation. Ada had never so much as sat on Bon but agreed to give it a whirl. A "catch ride," as they call it when a rider shows a horse she doesn't own or train, it would be. She had two days to figure him out before the medal finals on Sunday.

Friday and Saturday's rounds were solid but not quite perfect. Bon certainly held up his end of the deal. One round was shaping up beautifully—good pace, good distances, nice turns, timely lead changes, and all that—until Ada momentarily and uncharacteristically confused the course she was on with the next one. The graceful and stylish circle that she worked in as a result turned out not to be the sort of innovation that this judge was quite ready to embrace.

So it goes.

And Sunday? I'd love to give you the Hollywood ending. And for a moment following her medal round, I thought I might have that chance. The only problem was that I forgot to watch all four of Bon's legs for lead changes, and I missed a couple cross-canters, which are all it takes to be out of the ribbons in a thirty-rider class.

So it also goes.

Viewed from one angle, it was a lost weekend. The plan had been to show up and put in a set of solid rounds on K and get their relationship on the right track. That didn't happen.

But there's value in a catch ride, and in the knowledge that you can get on a new horse and lay down some solid trips. And more than that, there was this: a smile after coming out of the ring, every single time, and professions of love for Bon as we walked back to the barn. It wasn't the plan, and it wasn't a fairy tale. It was something more important. It was fun. ✿

# 7

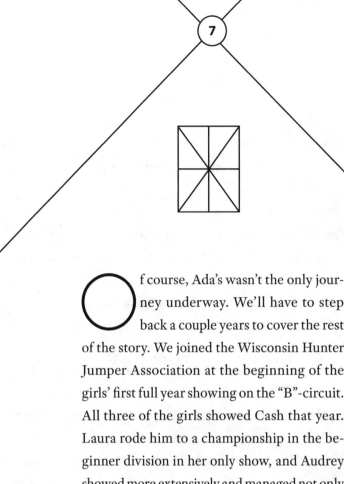

Of course, Ada's wasn't the only journey underway. We'll have to step back a couple years to cover the rest of the story. We joined the Wisconsin Hunter Jumper Association at the beginning of the girls' first full year showing on the "B"-circuit. All three of the girls showed Cash that year. Laura rode him to a championship in the beginner division in her only show, and Audrey showed more extensively and managed not only successful shows but some year-end awards, including a trophy that was almost as large as she was. Photos taken at the Association's annual awards banquet show Ada, Audrey, and Laura, together with Charles, around a table heaped with trophies, ribbons, and other prizes.

CHAPTER 7

It seemed that we'd be deep into this world for quite some time, which in turn made it seem like a good idea to get more involved. We decided to attend the annual members meeting of the Wisconsin Hunter Jumper Association. The emails to the membership created the impression (in me, anyway) that it would be a somewhat significant event. I expected a good-sized crowd. The location was a restaurant in suburban Milwaukee, and I assumed we must have arrived early when we got to the designated room only to find it mostly empty. A group of people sat along a table at the front, facing a series of tables that at the moment seated three or four others. The people at the front were the current members of the board. We introduced ourselves and took a seat.

Several others arrived, but the room did not fill. I remember little about the meeting itself, other than that there almost certainly ended up being more pizzas than people in attendance. That, and that there was discussion of an upcoming election to fill a couple of impending vacancies on the board. Someone asked me if I'd be interested. The next thing I knew I was writing a candidate statement for distribution to the membership, and not long after that I was at a table at a different restaurant attending my first board meeting.

There's a steep learning curve involved in stepping into something like a board position as an outsider. There's a difference, it turns out, between knowing one's way around a "B" show and knowing enough to make a meaningful contribution to the operation of the organization that oversees them. And, of course, there are longstanding tensions the new person is completely oblivious to. People tried with varying degrees of effectiveness to explain the divides to me. The conversations often involved names I didn't recognize and events that were recent history for everyone except the person who hadn't been around for any of it. Some of the tensions arose out of these past events, others were products of the presence of people whose personalities clashed.

I tend not to have a lot of patience for petty disagreement, and so I'm not sure I ever wrapped my brain completely around what all the feuds and sources of division were about. But some of the disputes were legit. One group wanted to make sure the organization had money for a rainy day, and another seemed confident the sun would shine forever. And while there were no pro-doping advocates, there was a camp concerned about organizational changes that would make doping and other mistreatment of horses too easy to get away with and a camp that pointed out that nobody was enforcing the rules that existed anyway. Underneath it all were the echoes of longstanding grievances involving people who were no longer on the scene. (I later got enticed to join a similar board connected to Laura's figure-skating team. If my two experiences are representative, all these boards are in some sense the same.)

Although not without its moments, volunteering for the board was, on the whole, an enjoyable and worthwhile experience. I was deeply involved in an effort to update the Association's rules, which in turn required me to become familiar with the rules of the sport more generally. The Association itself put on its annual Fall Finals, and so I learned about organizing and running a show from the earliest stages of planning to the nitty-gritty of setting jumps, dragging rings, and emptying garbage cans.

I also got to know a lot of the people in the Wisconsin horse community. Understand that I'm not one of those people who easily adds to his large network of friends wherever he goes. I'm generally bad with names and faces and often lost in my own thoughts. Which is why I remember so well an afternoon a couple years later during a show at Ledges in Illinois. I'm not sure whether I was going to or coming from the bleachers overlooking the main ring. Whichever it was, it began with the intent to go on a simple Point A to Point B journey. Then I ran into someone I knew and stopped to chat. A bit later someone else I knew joined us. I stood there—maybe it was for forty-five minutes, maybe it was an hour—at the center as this conversation with a continually shifting group of people continued. Two years earlier I had known none of them. Unremarkable for a certain sort of people person, unheard of for me. It was striking.

My time on the board mattered as well because the president at the time was Emily Elek. Emily, through her business Stonewall Farm, was one of the premier pony people in the United States. From breeding, to training, to sales and leasing, with lots of showing along the way, she lived the life that countless young barn rats dream of, with a barn and fields filled with ponies (and the occasional horse) and a trailer that was always ready for the next show. "Pony Island," she called her place. And it just so happened that we could be helpful to her. Ponies need riding to stay in shape, and I had pony-sized daughters who could ride.

"Would they like to come out sometime to ride ponies?" Emily asked, not long after I had joined the board, knowing full well what the answer would be.

I cleared it with Charles, and we made the drive out to Ixonia, Wisconsin. There was no direct route from our house to Stonewall Farm, and that day we took a route that was mostly freeway, but with a good ten minutes' worth of winding, "How much longer?" roads at the end. Audrey by this point had ridden and shown three ponies—Ozzy, Heilig, and Rosie—and knew quite well how headstrong and difficult they could be. We came over a rise and spotted the fields dotted with ponies. It took a minute or two to make our way to and then up the driveway. Even so, the first thing Emily heard when we got out of the car was Audrey, still bursting with delight.

One trip led to another, and eventually we worked our way to an arrangement where on one day each week I would pick the girls up from school and we'd head to Ixonia. We'd often stop on the way to pick up Lexi Miller, Emily's main pony jockey, and from there wind through back roads. I'd occasionally join in a round or two of the Pony Guessing Game, a twenty-questions-like game in which one person would think of a pony—usually, but not always, one of Emily's—which the others had to try to figure out. The questions would progress through a roughly standard order: *Small, medium, or large? Green? Have I ridden him? Have you ridden him?* And so on. (The fact that a single round could occasionally go on for a while provides a sense of the scope of Emily's enterprise.)

Then it was time to ride. Usually, each girl got three ponies, which meant three rounds of grooming, tacking, and riding, with Emily watching over and providing instruction the whole while. Much of this happened on cold winter nights. You might imagine that barns in our part of the world would consistently feature heated viewing areas overlooking their indoor rings. Many, maybe even most, do. Just not most of the ones where I've found myself spending time. Stonewall was the main exception. I would sit at a table in front of a window to the ring prepping for my class the next day while keeping an eye on the riding. I'd sometimes pop out between ponies to help, but otherwise usually managed a productive evening. If there was time when the riding was done, we'd stop in the Ixonia Pub for a late bar-food dinner, always including an order of sour-cream-and-chive fries. (I realize, as I write this, that a pub might strike some readers as an unusual dinner destination given the age of the other members of my party. All I can say is: This is Wisconsin. A pub is a family restaurant here.)

I t was a time of transition. Ada was devoting her time and attention to Millcreek. While experience with Heilig had not panned out for Audrey, the chance to ride with Emily provided an alternative, and she showed one of Emily's ponies at that year's WHJA Fall Finals.

Charles and Hidden View parted ways a short time later, but Laura continued to take lessons there with Heidi Modesto, who had transitioned into a training role. For a while we were dividing our time between three barns. It was unsustainable.

For the following year, Audrey became a full-fledged citizen of Pony Island. She rode as often as she could, and she got the chance to show Celtic Melody, a medium green Welsh pony. The goal was simple: qualify for, and then ride at, US Pony Finals.

I can't say precisely when I first heard about Pony Finals. Likely Ada first discovered it via one of the many books we had, or through the copious online reading she did, or through conversation at the barn. But I can still picture a scene at one of the early "B" shows. We were killing time between rides when Ada gestured in a way that said, "Don't be too obvious when you're doing it, but look over there."

"That pony," she said, with just enough reverence in her voice, "has been to Pony Finals."

I'm not sure how she knew this piece of information, and in retrospect, I would bet that it had been one of Emily's ponies. But we made a point to watch the round, just to see what *that* kind of pony looked like in the ring.

As its name suggests, Pony Finals is kind of a national-level pony Olympics. It's held at the Kentucky Horse Park, and a pony has to qualify in order to enter. Because it's primarily a pony hunter show, it's technically the pony rather than the rider being judged, and hence it's the pony rather than the rider that must qualify. And the rider who shows a qualified pony at Pony Finals need not be the rider who rode the pony when he qualified, which in turn means there's a market for qualified ponies, which is certainly one of the niches that Emily fills. Qualification is straightforward: a pony must have been champion or reserve champion in his division at an "A"- or "AA"-rated show during the preceding year.

Melody, it's fair to say, was not a pony for whom qualifying was a given. Most weeks Audrey had only one chance to ride her, and there were only so many shows we could afford to attend. One of her lead changes tended to be sticky, and for various reasons, many of their rounds were, as we came to put it, "one fence from glory." Sometimes it was Audrey's mistake, other times it was Melody's. Once in Lake St. Louis they were heading down the far side of the ring—the one on which there are no spectators—when a show worker decided to bolt up from a chair hidden by the fence around the ring. His timing was unfortunately uncanny. He popped up just as they approached a jump next to where he was now standing. Melody, of course, took that as her cue to make a dramatic cut toward the center of the ring.

There were moments and there were rounds where it all came together. But neither a moment nor even a round of brilliance is enough to finish as champion or reserve. The rounds have to be consistently good. There might be room for mistakes, but only if they're small. One fence from glory is both a short distance and a very long way.

The incident in Lake St. Louis occurred during the first of two weeks that Emily was scheduled to be at the show. Our plan had been for Audrey to show only during the first week; I wasn't able to stick around longer. But someone—and I'm not sure I ever learned exactly who came up with the idea—proposed that perhaps Audrey could stay for the second week, too. You know how the dance goes: Casually float the idea to plant the seed and get an initial reaction. Return to it a while later to see if the seed has taken. Exploit the opening if it's there. I'm usually a pretty easy mark. It wasn't a problem that I wasn't able to stay at the show, they explained, because Audrey could just stay in Emily's room. Audrey and Melody were making progress. A second week in a row of showing might be just the thing to get them where they needed to be.

I talked to Emily to make sure she knew that, among other things, her hotel room was offered up as part of the package. Then I talked to Lea and we rationalized our way to agreeing to the plan. I wished Audrey luck, gave Melody a pep talk, and drove home alone.

It wasn't quite as easy then to follow show results online. If they were available at all it tended to be at the end of the day. Audrey's not one to provide a detailed play-by-play, so we mostly went about our business with occasional pauses to hope for the best. And then, finally, we got a text accompanied by a photo of Audrey, Melody, and a reserve champion ribbon. They had done it. A day or so later I drove to Emily's to fetch Audrey. She was exhausted, but glowing with a sense of accomplishment.

That show took place in March. It was just their third show together. The plan had called for another one or two, but then it was Melody's turn to pop a splint. Not ideal. We continued to make the weekly trips to Ixonia to get in time on the ponies, with weekend days mixed in whenever Emily was at home. It wasn't the same as riding in competition, of course, and I'm sure the numbers would reveal that when Audrey and Melody arrived at the Kentucky Horse Park for Pony Finals in August, they had something close to the least amount of combined show experience in the preceding year, and certainly in the preceding months.

We were fortunate, at least, to be in the hands of one of the best in the business. Emily's plan called for spending the week prior to Pony Finals at the Kentucky Summer Classic, which provides ponies and riders a chance to get comfortable with their surroundings before the big event begins. She was responsible for some twenty ponies during this time, many of which were ridden by kids whose trainers had turned them over to Emily just for those two weeks because of her expertise.

For us, it provided instant credibility. We often found ourselves being asked who Audrey's trainer was as we made our way around the grounds. "Ah, the pony lady," went the typical reaction to our response, generally accompanied by a nod of recognition.

The week of Kentucky Summer was a recapitulation of the shows before. There were twenty ponies in the medium green division. Melody managed a seventh in the under-saddle class but was shut out of the ribbons over fences. The lead change was still a problem. If it wasn't that, there was always one line where the strides didn't quite fit, leaving the pair, as ever, one fence from glory. The planets did not seem to be aligning. Still, Pony Finals was around the corner, and that was cause enough for excitement.

I'll admit that I had some preconceived notions about Pony Finals. I expected to find an unholy mixture of people named Muffy and Chip together with folks whose psychological profile would not be out of place on a show like *Toddlers & Tiaras*. During the week of the Kentucky Summer show one of the long-term vendors at the Horse Park fed my preconceptions, making it clear that this was the calm before the storm and warning me that "some of those pony moms are a little bit over the top."

The Horse Park's Walnut Ring was transformed in a way that seemed to confirm these impressions. A VIP tent filled most of two sides of the arena, with reserved tables and a setup for buffet meals. The shelter between the Claiborne and Stonelea Rings, usually the habitat of judges and the occasional dad who hopes to overhear things he can later write about, became a place for the stressed pony parent to get some wine and a massage.

Now, I'll admit to often walking around in a haze of mild obliviousness, not always noticing what's going on around me. So, it's likely that I missed some things. I stood for a while next to a couple who certainly looked like they'd have answered to Muffy and Chip, or at least would have been able to tell me where I could find them. And there was definitely one parent of a somewhat prominent rider whose behavior was, shall we say, overexuberant. But that was about it. Maybe it was because we were surrounded by the good people of Team Stonewall, or maybe it was because things just aren't so bad if you're not viewing the spectacle through the eyes of a vendor. On the whole, both parents and riders seemed to me to have the right attitude.

One of the phases of the competition is the "model," in which the rider leads the untacked pony into the ring to be judged both while moving and standing. There's an art to this, of course, and Emily recommended that all her inexperienced riders attend one of the modeling clinics offered in the early part of the week. Audrey got one of the last slots, in the earliest session of the day. It was still dark when we, very much behind our planned schedule, jogged for most of the trip from the barn to the covered arena, worried that we would be scolded for our late arrival. We weren't, and the clinic was worth the trouble. I don't remember all the tricks of the trade, but I do know this: A crinkly peppermint wrapper is your best friend if you want to get a pony's attention as part of your effort to get him to stand in exactly the right way.

Among the adjectives that describe Audrey are these: focused, determined, and tenacious. She loves a challenge, so it's no coincidence that she also came to love ponies, and it's no surprise that she had transformed that passion into an opportunity. I'm sure the thought, "What if we win it all?" crossed her mind, but Audrey's goal was more realistic. They give ribbons to twenty places overall at Pony Finals, and to ten in the individual classes. What she hoped for was this: a ribbon. Just one. Something to hang on the wall to remind her that it had happened, that this particular dream had come true.

There were seventy-nine ponies in the medium greens. That's way too many ponies to have in the ring at once, of course, and so the judging took place in subgroups. Audrey and Melody were in one of the early sections to model and hack. We made our way to the Walnut Ring under a gray sky, the day working its way into shape by alternating mist and drizzle. We worried that the splint Melody had popped in the summer might be a significant problem in the model. The splint might not have been ideal, but it wasn't fatal. They placed twenty-third.

The under-saddle went even better. The drizzle had turned into an intense rain. The cardboard numbers the riders wore, attached to strings around their torsos, turned to mush. One rider's number had completely detached, and she struggled to hold both it and her reins. The hack had consistently been Melody's strong suit, though, and she and Audrey rose to the occasion, finishing second in their section, with a good enough score that a top ten finish was not out of the question. We found shelter in the covered arena and waited. I refreshed my phone every few minutes to check the updated results. The pair ended up sixteenth under saddle and stood in seventeenth place overall after the first two phases. They were in a good position. A strong round over fences would bring home a ribbon.

But a strong round over fences was far from a sure thing. The Walnut Ring is large and irregularly shaped. The course was longer than any they had ridden before. And while they had been in the ring together multiple times, it would be different performing in front of a crowd. It would be different because this was *Pony Finals*. This was the moment Audrey had dreamed of.

The warm-up process at Pony Finals is more controlled than at most horse shows. It's not a first-come, first-served free-for-all with trainers jockeying for open jumps and riders nearly colliding. Instead, it's a limited-access, ticketed affair, held in a ring set with an entire course of jumps rather than a row of single jumps in the center. Emily had Audrey and Melody in the warm-up ring multiple times over the course of the week.

They had worked and worked and worked. They were closer, but not quite there. And then, finally, in their very last session, minutes before it was time to show, the lead change came. They did it once, then they did it again. Enough repetitions to prove it wasn't luck. The jumps looked good. They were as ready as they would have the chance to be, because it was time to make the walk over to the Walnut Ring.

We all understood that this was likely to be Audrey's one shot at Pony Finals, and that whatever happened next would define this singular life experience. As was my custom, I stayed near but not too close as we walked up the ramp to the ring on the way to the in-gate. Time has different properties in situations like that. Surely, we had to wait for at least one rider to complete a round, and probably more. But I remember it seeming instantaneous, like we got to the top of the ramp, and they went straight into the ring. I found what seemed like a lucky-looking spot along the rail, ran through my standard superstitious rituals, and hoped for a happy ending.

The late writer Christopher Hitchens held all sorts of controversial opinions, but he stood on pretty solid ground when he wrote this about parenthood: "Nothing can make one so happily exhilarated or so frightened: it's a solid lesson in the limitations of self to realize that your heart is running around inside someone else's body."

I can find no fault with those words. My heart was about to enter the Walnut Ring, and all I could do was watch. I've never taken the time to formulate the authoritative list of "times in my life I've been most nervous," but this certainly made the top ten.

I watched from about twenty feet down from the in-gate. Normally I would have had a camera or tried to capture the action with my phone. Not this time. You need steady hands for that.

Audrey and Melody entered the ring and began their trip.

My eye for hunter rounds is only partly developed. I've got a long way to go to have a sense of what distinguishes good form over a fence. But I can generally catch whether the distance was good, and I've got a handle on leads and lead changes. I'm better at telling when something has gone wrong, I suppose, than at telling when a round has gone especially well.

Nothing was going wrong. Perhaps a hair deep to Fence 3. But Melody was landing her leads or changing when asked. They kept a consistent pace. It was a blur, but a pleasant one. Before I knew it, they were turning for the last line.

I had a somewhat obstructed view of the last fence, but I could see that Audrey and Melody cleared it in stride. The pony nailed the lead change on the other side. They circled. I exhaled.

They had done it.

Here, of course, is the part where the celebration should go, where the scoreboard shows that my daughter is in fifth place or better with fifteen ponies to go, where she's guaranteed a ribbon and the only question is what color it will be.

That's how it looked to me. I was sure that was how it had gone.

Not quite. My obstructed view kept me from seeing that the distance to the last fence was not ideal. We've since debated whether it was a chip or just a very deep distance. Whichever it was, it was enough to void the guarantee.

One fence from glory, one more time.

They were in fourteenth place with fifteen ponies left to go. I stayed with Melody in the shade of a tree beneath the Walnut Ring as Audrey stood along the rail with a friend she had made that week who was in thirteenth place. Together the two watched themselves slowly slide off the leaderboard.

Audrey and Melody ended up twenty-third. There would be no ribbon.

The disappointment was real. It was real enough that I explored one other avenue. The Welsh Pony and Cob Society of America gave out ribbons for the highest-placing Welsh Ponies in each division. Melody was a Welsh Pony, and her score should have earned her a ribbon. Parenthood leads a person to do all sorts of things he'd never do on his own behalf. This was one of those times. I walked back to the ring and found the WPCSA tent. Had there been a mistake?

The answer was yes. But not in a way that would help.

Melody's breeder (who was not Emily) had not completed the necessary paperwork to have the mare officially listed with the association. They were very sorry, but if I were to take the right steps, she'd be eligible next year.

But I knew there would be no next year.

It didn't take long for Audrey's disappointment to give way to something more substantial. Stages don't get much bigger for twelve-year-olds, and she had risen to the occasion. It wasn't quite perfection, but given the journey to get there, it was a performance to be proud of. She had made new friends and new memories. She had been able to do something that most pony-crazy kids don't get the chance to do at all. There's no ribbon on her wall, but there's a photo above her desk. She and Melody are mid-jump, both of them looking ahead to what comes next. The scoreboard in the background leaves no doubt as to what is going on. It is the US Pony Finals. Entry number 880, Celtic Melody, ridden by Audrey Oldfather.

Her dream did, in fact, come true. ✹

8

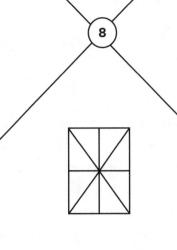

By late 2015, Ada had had her last rides on Cash at the EAP, her first disappointing show on K, and a catch ride on Bon when K got injured. Audrey, meanwhile, had realized the dream of showing at Pony Finals, but fell just short of getting the ribbon she had hoped to win. Things had not gone perfectly, but they had gone well enough overall.

Not long after Pony Finals Audrey started to ride more often at Millcreek with Ada, and our weekdays took on a new routine once again. I'd pick them up from school, and we'd make the trip just into Illinois.

We'd long since become used to spending time in the car together. In the Appy Orse and Hidden View days, we had always allowed a half-hour for travel. Stonewall Farm was forty-five minutes away, so long as there was no traffic—but there was always traffic. The trip to Millcreek was yet another turn of the ratchet. Much depended on the vagaries of rush hour, timing, and just plain luck. If any one thing didn't break in our direction, it would easily be an hour-long journey.

Nobody was ill-mannered enough to tell me to my face that it was a crazy thing to do as often as we did it, but I'm sure the thought crossed many minds and lips, including my own. There were certainly days when it was a burden for all of us. On some of those days I may have noted my frustration a little too openly, and there were moments when I questioned whether it was worth it.

But most of the time then, and especially now that I'm looking at it in the rearview mirror, I considered it time well spent. Oddly enough, it was a story about a hockey player that crystallized my thinking. It is, I'll warn you, a tragic tale.

Derek Boogaard was what's called an "enforcer," the sort of player whose role in the National Hockey League involves a lot of fighting. It was, in a sense, his job to get on the ice and push around players on the other team, with the idea being that his presence would deter the other team from treating his team's more skilled players too roughly. It's a role that led to injuries throughout his career, which in turn led to the use of the painkillers that ultimately contributed to his untimely death.

A number of years ago the *New York Times* ran a three-part series on Boogaard. The articles covered his entire life, beginning with his childhood in Saskatchewan. The first piece outlined the extensive travel involved in youth hockey, which the *Times* describes as "a perpetual series of long drives across dark and icy landscapes." Boogaard had kept a journal, discovered after his death, and the *Times* story included some excerpts. Here, for me, was the payoff: "I think the best part of playing hockey from ages three until sixteen," Boogaard wrote, "was the little road trips with Dad."

This was a kid who was chasing a dream and who eventually caught it. He looked back on it all, and what did he conclude? Spending time with his dad was the *best part*.

It's easy to imagine that the sport is the thing that matters. That the driving is a chore, a necessary step on the road to the next thing, something to be tolerated. But what seems in the moment like the main event might well not be. Both Derek Boogaard and his dad would probably have answered a question about what they were doing in the same way: "Driving to a hockey game." If you ran into me on a late afternoon in those years, I'd have told you I was driving my daughters to a riding lesson. That's what it seemed to me I was doing. That's probably what it seemed to anyone else I was doing. And now that all my daughters are adults and my services are less in demand, it's all that time together in the car that I miss. We were focused on the destination. It was the journey that mattered.

Taken one by one many of those drives were far from the best part of anything. Sometimes, I confess, I was not in the greatest mood. Occasionally—and you'll just have to trust me on this—one of my passengers wasn't having the best day. There were days when none of us felt like saying much of anything. On those days we'd just drive along listening to the radio. Invariably music if Ada was in the car, baseball if it was summer and happened to be just Audrey and me. Every so often we'd turn the radio off and have our soundtrack be nothing more than the sound of wheels whirring over pavement. We're mostly not a group made uncomfortable by silence. There can be something reassuring about simply being in one another's presence.

Other days were clearly good days, not so much because of anything extraordinary that happened, but because they were a part of the routine, part of the glue that held (and holds) us together, the sort of thing we'll think back to decades from now when we're playing "remember when." We'd talk, but not about much of anything at all, stuff like the mundane happenings at the barn or school. We'd get into the habit of stopping at certain restaurants, sometimes becoming regulars. There was a Taco Bell that we'd stop at on our way home from Hidden View, and for a time there was a container of mints next to the sauces. It was a situation that called for a customer to take one or two, just enough to cover up the aftertaste. Once Audrey decided to grab a handful on her way out to the car. Which, she discovered, ended up being over twenty mints. It's not a great story to tell at parties, or one that has any sort of broad appeal no matter how well told. But it's a part of our story, a "you had to be there" where we were all there, a small moment that we shared and every so often bring out to relive.

And then there were those days when the stars aligned, when we were all in a good mood and somebody had something bigger on her mind. The right sort of question led to the right sort of answer and suddenly we found ourselves deep in conversation. It might have been about college, it might have been about careers, it might have been about something that came up at school. Whatever it was, we were all engaged. We were thinking, we were listening to one another, and there's a very good chance that I used some variation of the phrase, "I don't know," an awful lot. (This was mostly because I often don't know, and also part of an effort to model the idea that anyone who claims to have all the answers, or speaks as if he does, is not to be trusted.) On those days, before we knew it, we had arrived at the barn. Mostly it was just understood, but sometimes one of us would say it out loud: "That was a good conversation."

I'm not alone in finding that time in cars will sometimes create this sort of magic. I've spoken to lots of parents who have experienced the same thing. There's something about being together in an enclosed space with nowhere else to go, about facing in the same direction rather than toward one another, about whatever else it might be that fosters meaningful conversation. In the tightrope walk that is parenthood—where words don't always come out the way you'd like, and what you meant to say is not always what gets heard—it's nice to have a space where talking *just happens* rather than being forced. Ours may not have been a family that spent a lot of time together around the dinner table, but we got the same sort of connection while traveling down the highway.

In her early days of transitioning to Millcreek, Audrey rode any horse that was available. But she was drawn in particular to one called Legado—once named Aerospeed and known as "Alex" in the barn. He was an off-the-track Thoroughbred, foaled in Michigan in 2002 and raced seven times over the summer of 2005. Alex had more than a couple drops of famed racehorse Native Dancer's blood, but neither the results nor the racing charts suggested that the racetrack was where he belonged. His temperament, though, suggested that the racetrack taught him what he understood to be one of life's great lessons. That lesson was that there is a single solution to any problem the world might send your way: *Go faster.*

He had been sold off the track for $450 and eventually made his way to Millcreek. His owner was a young woman named Emma Alhalel. She had lots of stories about Alex, two of which I'll share to give you a feel for his personality.

Not long after getting Alex, Emma rode him in a lesson in the outdoor ring (which does not have a fence around it). After jumping a course, Serah asked her to halt him at the end of the ring. She tried. And eventually he stopped. But not until he was in the parking lot, a good seventy-five yards away.

"That," she said, "was one of the first times I remember riding him thinking '[some words we won't include here].'"

The second story was when another rider from the barn showed Alex in a jumper class. He had two refusals, "but they were flying around so fast they still ended with nothing even close to a time fault."

All of this was like catnip to Audrey. She felt a kinship with the Thoroughbred since she was also born in 2002. And she always liked a challenge. For her, in those early days at Appy Orse, Bernadette's ban on saying, "I can't," was simply a reminder. I often think of a moment from when she was very little. I was working on the computer and she was on the floor next to me, playing with some sort of bag or backpack. It had a strap that fastened with one of those plastic buckles that snaps together but requires pushing on both sides to take apart. She snapped it together, and I took it apart.

We repeated this a few times until she decided to try to get it apart without me. She worked on it for a while, then got frustrated and started to hand it to me, but then snatched it away before I could complete the job. She wanted to do it herself, and after not too long, she figured it out.

A few years later she used a similar method—try, fail, try again—to teach herself how to ride a bike. It wasn't long before she was riding up and down our block singing a song she'd made up at the top of her lungs.

So, Audrey was not the sort to back away. That was doubly true where horses were involved. She'd ridden through runouts and refusals, dramatic falls, and as I've already shared, two different ponies bolting out of a ring with her in the saddle, as well as a night in the hospital after a fall. She had never hesitated to get back on.

So it's no surprise she was drawn to Alex. I once asked her why she liked him so much. "Speed," she immediately said with a laugh and a sly smile, then paused for a moment and added, "That's actually probably true. Speed, and he looked fun to ride."

She rode him a few times in lessons. They'd get a couple jumps into a course, and he'd start to accelerate. The only thing that kept them out of the parking lot was the fact that it was winter, and they were riding indoors. (There are videos of this that I show to close friends only.)

Like most horse-crazy kids, Audrey wanted to ride *all* the horses, and I admit that I didn't immediately pick up on her attraction to Alex. But then he was leased by another rider with an option to buy, and Audrey posted a love letter of sorts to him beneath a picture of them together on Instagram. "Riding him I felt like I could do anything. Words cannot say how much I love and miss this horse."

Whoever had leased Alex decided not to buy. He came back to Millcreek, and in November 2015, he became Audrey's.

When February 2016 rolled around things seemed to be getting back on track. K had recovered from her injury, and Audrey and Alex had spent a couple months working together intensively. We went with a group from Millcreek to a show at the World Equestrian Center in Ohio. It was our first time there, and as it probably true for most newcomers, it initially presented as a maze. This was winter, of course, and the entire operation took place in a sprawling indoor facility. As seemed to often be the case, our barn was perhaps the one farthest from the rings. Still, the show got off to a good start. For a moment.

It was early Friday morning, and the first class of the day. You know how that is: the coffee still hasn't fully taken hold, and the minor aches of an unfamiliar bed haven't yet worked themselves free. But Ada and K had already completed their warm-up and moved to the in-gate. They were fourth in the order, and we stood together and watched the first three riders go.

There were other people near the in-gate, too. Riders, trainers, some grooms, maybe even a few parents. Among them was a woman whose long, dark hair was braided into a ponytail and who otherwise had the look of someone who had been to many horse shows before. Beyond that I could only speculate. She was probably a trainer. Maybe her show was already off to a bad start. Maybe she'd just had to endure the rantings of some parent whose desire to see a child do well had morphed into something toxic. Maybe she wasn't feeling well and had a horrible night of sleep and not enough coffee. Maybe years of competitive pressure had left their mark. I will never know.

But what I do know is that she also stood near the in-gate while the first three riders went. And while she was standing there, she noticed something.

Ada's turn came. She and K walked into the ring, picked up the canter, and went to work. Jumps one and two were nice. It was a promising start. It was the start they needed after a rocky first show and a long layoff during K's recovery. They had a nice, forward pace. Things looked good. Ada eyed up the third jump and began the turn. And then came the double buzzer.

We who were watching were puzzled. Nothing seemed to have gone wrong. No refusals, no going off course.

Then came the announcement: "We have an equipment violation."

Here is what the woman at the in-gate had noticed: K had on a standing martingale. In that first class—the USHJA Jumping Seat Medal—only running martingales were allowed. She had waited until Ada entered the ring, and then immediately reported the violation. Then the judge, who other judges have told me has discretion in such a situation to let a rider finish a round, elected to immediately buzz Ada out.

It was not a good way to start the day, and it did not turn out to be a good way to start the show. Ada and K did not find a rhythm after that, and the result was a second show that did not go well.

My immediate reaction to the incident was to be angry at the woman by the in-gate. And as I write this, years later, I find that it's still my reaction. (To the point where I'm now going to start referring to her as "the villain.") Of course, rules are rules, and this was a situation in which a rule wasn't followed. For a certain sort of person, that's all that matters. That sort of person is not my sort of person and is almost certainly neither a fellow law professor nor anyone else who has given real thought to the nature of rules or of competition. Whatever the right answer is—if indeed there is one—the path to it is nowhere near so simple.

Because there's still the question of what the villain of our story *should* have done. Having noticed a minor compliance issue, it seems to me that she had three options.

Option 1: She could have politely let Ada and Serah know that somebody had overlooked something in the early morning hours on the first day of a show. "Excuse me," she might have said. "I hate to interfere, but I thought you'd want to know that standing martingales aren't allowed in this class. It's an easy thing to overlook, especially for a class that hasn't been in existence all that long. And especially before you've had any coffee."

Option 2: She could have said nothing. "Not my job," she might have thought to herself. "Maybe the judge will notice it, maybe not." (I suspect any judge you asked would say, "I'd notice it." Color me skeptical of that claim, though. Judges are human, too.)

Option 3: She could do exactly what she did.

To me it's a no-brainer. The best option is Option 1, and the best example of sportsmanship in a situation like that would be to let the competitor know. Certainly, it's most consistent with the Golden Rule—by which I don't mean the one I first encountered as a young lawyer trying to negotiate against banks ("He who has the gold make the rules") but rather the one I learned in kindergarten ("Treat others the way you want to be treated"). And it's most consistent with the whole point of competition. Let's assume Ada's round would have continued the way it started. Worst-case scenario for the villain is that Ada places ahead of her clients. What she gets out of intervening is that her clients moved up one place in the ribbons. Why? Not because they had a better ride. Because their trainer happened to notice a rule violation that—and this is key to the whole analysis and so worth emphasizing—conferred no competitive advantage. There's a difference, it seems to me, between violating the rules with the intent of achieving an unfair edge (as, for example, by doping) versus failing to follow the rules without meaning to do so and where that failure to follow the rules doesn't provide any sort of advantage. While I'm hardly an expert on the matter, nobody yet has suggested to me that one type of martingale provides a competitive advantage over another in a 3'3" equitation class. This was self-evidently not an effort to gain an edge, nor was it a mistake that provided one.

I come to this not simply as an aggrieved parent, although I am undoubtedly also that. I've long recognized that sports serve as their own self-contained legal systems, involving many of the same features and presenting many of the same problems as the formal legal system that I teach and study. Marquette University Law School—where I teach—has the country's preeminent Sports Law program, and as part of it I teach a seminar called The Jurisprudence of Sport that explores this overlap. The goal is to enable students to better appreciate the legal system by thinking about legal problems through the lens of sport, and also to be able to approach problems in sport by thinking about them as analogous to law. (I mention all this just to underscore the point that I've thought a lot about these sorts of things.)

One of our topics in the seminar is sportsmanship, and on that topic I'm persuaded by the analysis of my fellow law professor Mitch Berman. His take is that true sportsmanship arises where a competitor does something that reduces her chances of winning in a situation where doing so allows the skills the sport is designed to test to be the thing that determines the outcome. Applied here, the question concerns which of two scenarios would be the one in which the results of the class best reflected the skills of the riders involved: the one with a rider eliminated for a technical violation, or the one without. On this view the key question is whether the equipment violation provided an advantage. Again, I've yet to find the person who thinks that it could have.

So where does that leave us? As a result of her reporting the violation the villain's clients gained a better placing, and perhaps even a victory. But either that would have been the result anyway, in which case reporting did not benefit her at all, or it happened partly as a result of something unrelated to the skill being tested in competition. It's a hollow victory, grounded in a technicality coupled with poor sportsmanship.

Note that my target here is the villain and her behavior. I certainly understand that horse showing, like most sports, has its nit-picky technical rules, and I have no quarrel with the idea that a failure to comply with those rules is legitimate grounds for some sort of penalty. (There's certainly a good argument to be made that disqualification is too harsh a sanction in this case.) I'd likely also regard the situation differently were the only thing that happened was that the judge noticed the problem. I'd still question the decision not to allow Ada to complete the course, but the problematic sportsmanship would be out of the picture. In other words, I can concede those points and still have reason to believe the villain acted wrongly.

No doubt part of why I remain upset about the incident is that it couldn't have come at a worse moment. For Ada and K, this was the show to get back on track, to find some common ground, to begin to establish the necessary confidence in one another. Success breeds success, and a strong first round would have been a positive step.

Small things can have huge effects. I've seen professional baseball players go from the top of the sport to struggling for no apparent reason. They've suffered no injury and made no conscious changes to their approach. And yet something has changed. Sometimes it takes months of watching video of past performances to discover the one, small thing they inadvertently started to do differently. Sometimes the mystery's never solved. Tiny adjustments can work in the other direction as well. A coach suggests gripping the ball just a bit differently, or making a slight adjustment to how a player holds the bat, and suddenly the game opens up for him. Mediocrity morphs into stardom. Luck often seems to play as great a role as talent. If only the right coach had made the right suggestion at the right time, the guy who's an assistant coach for the high school team in his hometown would be a household name. The one who became a star could just as easily have remained another face in the crowd.

There's a psychological dimension as well. Its most extreme manifestation comes in the form of "the yips"—a term that originated with the Scottish golfer Tommy Armour to describe what he called a "brain spasm that impairs the short game," but which can affect all athletes. For example, a baseball player who's been throwing a ball with great accuracy for his entire life will make a couple bad throws in a row and suddenly start to question himself. He starts to think about what he had always done unconsciously and suddenly he can't do it anymore. A pitcher can no longer throw strikes. A second baseman can't make the short throw to first. A catcher has to make an underhanded toss back to the pitcher, because otherwise the ball will end up in the outfield. Careers have ended because of the yips. But it extends well beyond these dramatic cases. You start to think about the things you've long done automatically, and you find you can't do them quite as well anymore.

This wasn't the yips, but whatever it was, something small wasn't quite right. And so, I have wondered whether things might have gone differently had the villain not intervened. What would have happened if that round had continued to go as solidly as it started? Whether they'd placed high or not, it would have been their first hiccup-free round in competition. It would have been the right start to a weekend of showing. It might have been the first step toward developing the sort of feel for one another that Ada and K never managed to find. That feel didn't emerge over the course of the rest of the show. The villain's role in all this was, in a sense, small. No doubt she's never thought of the incident again and would barely remember it if asked. But a ripple can become a wave.

Audrey and Alex's show that week had a different storyline but a similar conclusion. They'd been making progress in lessons, Alex slowly working his way toward an understanding that steadiness was the goal, and that Audrey would trust him if he trusted her. He wasn't always ready to deliver, but he was trying.

Alex remained a fundamentally high-strung horse, and the show environment brought out that side of his personality. Somewhere along the line his alter ego got a name: "The Dark Lord of Show Jumping." A little grandiose, perhaps, because it suggested a string of accomplishments he didn't have. But accurate in capturing the place he went to, an otherwise amiable and even goofy character turned uncontrollable. Audrey had to work to keep him from turning the warm-up ring into a bumper car ride. In the show ring he'd give her two or three calm jumps before trying to relive his days on the track. On the first day there were a couple classes where Alex might have run past more jumps than he went over (or so it seemed). No change in approach or change in bit got the desired results. It was not the stuff of dreams. But still, at the end of the day Audrey posted a photo of her and Alex on Instagram, along with this: "Today may have been a bit rough (to say the least) but we stuck with it and didn't give up…. Tomorrow's always another chance to improve!"

Goals change to fit circumstances, and the girl who not long before was striving for a ribbon at Pony Finals found herself aspiring to get Alex to complete a course without being disqualified for runouts. In one class they were perhaps halfway around the course, having a good round and coming down a line toward the in-gate. He jumped her out of the tack, but she didn't fall off. They came to a stop along the rail next to the gate, Audrey dangling from her horse's neck. Determined to make it around the course, she held firm and began the struggle to get back in the saddle without touching the ground, methodically working herself back up Alex's body toward a spot where a final oomph would find her back in place. It was only a matter of time before she recovered. The small victory of a clear round remained within reach. The crowd began to cheer her on.

But then Serah, no doubt exercising good judgment, ordered Audrey to dismount. Once wasn't enough, of course. Whether Audrey didn't hear or simply didn't want to hear, the first orders went unfollowed. Serah persisted, and finally, Audrey relented.

It's a moment they relive from time to time. The concern, as Serah explained it later, was that Alex would decide to take off, which was both something that he might have decided to do and something that would not have made for a good situation if it happened while Audrey still had only one foot in a stirrup. But when Audrey came out of the ring that day, as the retelling goes, she was as upset with Serah as she has ever been.

Alex and Audrey returned for the second week of the show and made progress. They made it around courses and earned a couple ribbons. But plenty of work remained to be done.

Audrey, conditioned as she was by all the naughty ponies in her past, embraced the challenge. The months that followed featured hard work, gradual improvement, and what seemed to be a thousand different bit and bridle combinations. There was a long stretch where I could barely walk down the hall without imagining that Serah was just out of the picture imploring me to keep my hands up and my heels down.

Improvement came. Week by week, lesson by lesson, and show by show. At an outing in late August, Audrey and Alex were reserve champions in the low children's jumpers and made their debut in the high children's jumpers with a pair of double-clear rounds. He was a perfect gentleman—though the sort with a definite spring in his step.

That's not to say that Alex completely calmed down. He was always high strung, The Dark Lord always one unexpected development away from emerging. It was routine for people to ask me if I got scared watching her ride him. The question always took me a little bit by surprise. And made me wonder whether I was doing my job as a parent correctly. Because the answer was always no. I didn't get scared.

Why? Partly because I grew up around large animals and had by that time spent more than a decade around jumping horses. The risks had become familiar and so probably less fearsome-seeming.

Partly because I never detected a hint of malice in Alex's antics. He wasn't out to lose his riders and was in general about as benevolent and big-hearted as they come. Mostly because Audrey never seemed to be having anything but fun. If she wasn't scared, I wasn't scared.

Magic can happen when a rider, a trainer, and a horse all believe in one another. I had seen it before, and it seemed like I might be seeing it again.

But, of course, we often see what we want to see.

That September took us to the Kentucky National Horse Show. For us, a trip to the Kentucky Horse Park was always kind of a big deal. It was Kentucky, for one thing. The first place you think about when you think about horses. And it was the place where the largest number of the sport's "cool kids" were likely to be, where you'd most likely hear a name casually announced and think to yourself, "Hey, I've read about that person."

It wasn't just a return to the Horse Park, but a return to the Walnut Ring. For Audrey, it was a return to the site of mixed emotions, the place where she and Melody had put it all together just in time to turn in a solid round at Pony Finals, but also the place where she had come up just short of the ribbon she had so hoped for.

As I've already mentioned, the Walnut Ring was distinctive in a couple respects. It was large and irregularly shaped, and only partially bordered by a low fence. It sat well above the warm-up ring; horses had to walk perhaps fifty yards up a relatively narrow fenced ramp to get to it. Looking up from the bottom, it was hard to know where that ramp led, and the grandstands of the Rolex Arena, perhaps only a hundred yards behind the ring, loom large in one's view. It's possible, if you had spent the first part of your life as a racehorse, that you'd look up that ramp, see the grandstands, and imagine that you were on the track.

There's no way to know whether that theory is correct, but this much was clear: somewhere along the line, Alex concluded that all was definitely not cool with the Walnut Ring. When at the Horse Park with his previous owner, Emma, things started to go poorly in the warm-up. "We were having trouble, and I mean a lot of trouble," Emma told us before we left for the show. "We stopped going straight and forward, and we were leaping and going sideways. And then a group of Amish people visiting the Horse Park came down to watch and they were pointing and laughing and clapping because I'm pretty sure they thought I was doing 'cool tricks.'"

Apparently, the trip up the ramp from there was an adventure. Alex ran forward and then he ran backward. He spun in circles and reared. Show organizers stopped everything, cleared the ramp, and finally, after a drawn-out struggle, he and Emma went in.

Given this history, Serah rode Alex the first two days of the show. It was, shall we say, not so easy to get him in the ring, and for a moment or two it looked like jumping the rail into the ring would be easier than walking through the gate. But things went well once she had him inside. He'd have been champion in the Take 2 Thoroughbred Jumper division if they had awarded it (there were only two classes and there have to be at least three for a champion to be crowned). His other trips were solid. There was reason for hope.

And then it was Audrey's turn. Their first class was in the Claiborne Ring, which is a more traditional, rectangular ring, with an adjacent warm-up ring. The plan was to play it by ear. If it went well, they could move up to the 1.10-meter jumpers in the Walnut Ring. It went well. Alex maintained his calm and they had a drama-free, clean round. It was time for the next step.

Showing in the Walnut Ring required getting into the Walnut Ring, which was going to require some coordination. There was a plan: Someone would stand near the in-gate and give a signal when the horse before Alex entered the ring. Then there would be a clearing of the ramp, followed by clucking and chasing and possibly some waving of arms and shaking of blankets to help Alex reach the conclusion that there was only one way to go. All done in the most dignified fashion, naturally.

The plan didn't quite work to perfection. There were two places you could go when you got to the top of the ramp. One was the ring. The other was an area just behind the bleachers. That was the intended destination. There, maybe, Alex would regain his composure and be reasonably calm at the start of their round.

Runaway horses aren't an uncommon thing at showgrounds. You might not see one every single show, but neither would you ever be surprised to come around a corner and find yourself facing a fully tacked but agitated and sometimes riderless horse. It had happened with Audrey and Heilig, and more recently a young woman who rode with Emily found herself atop a horse giving her an express tour of the Horse Park, politely calling out, "Excuse us!" to the people nearly in harm's way as she struggled to regain control. It happens often enough that anyone who's spent time around horses knows exactly what to do: Stand with your feet wide and your arms stretched as far to the side as you can. The idea is to make it appear to the horse that he can't get past you. He might slow down, he might stop, he might turn around and go back the way he came from. Whatever happens, the hope is that he will be at least slightly less of a runaway than he was before.

That small digression was necessary to give you a sense of how Audrey and Alex looked coming up the ramp. They were moving fast, with Serah and barn manager Lauren Carter running behind. A woman who was standing at the entrance to the area behind the bleachers read the situation as "runaway horse" and assumed the position. That left Alex with one place to go: the ring.

It was what they call a dramatic entrance. Audrey's greatest disappointment for the whole show was that I didn't get it on video.

All of this would have been fine, except for the fact that the horse two ahead of them was still on course. Which meant that now there were three horses in the ring. Leaving was not an option, because leaving would require getting back in, and that seemed unlikely to be easier the next time around. With the judge's permission they lingered along the edge of the ring as the horse and rider before them completed their round (which was, fortunately, clean).

Suffice it to say that the trip that followed had some hiccups. In the meantime, Audrey and The Dark Lord had become a little bit famous. "That was *you*?" asked a young woman who later overheard Audrey re-telling the story.

By the end of the day, it was clear that Alex had not left his alter ego at home. And so, because a dad's gotta do what a dad's gotta do, and because I flattered myself with the idea that Alex and I had developed a certain rapport, I felt it was time for an intervention. While the other members of the Millcreek Farm contingent were elsewhere, I slipped into Alex's stall.

I'll openly admit to being one of those people who talks to his dogs. Lots of our "conversations" are standard fare, with me both asking and answering the very important question, "Who's a good girl?" But often there's a real exchange. "Time for a walk?" almost always gets an enthusiastic "Yes!" "Do you want to go outside?" only sometimes does. We manage to say quite a bit to one another even though only one of us uses words.

I'm far from being one of those folks who claims to be able to read animals' minds in some deep way. But I think I can at least sometimes convey something important, and often the most important message for an animal is not so different from what's frequently the best thing for a child to hear from a parent. It's this: "Remain calm. I'm not freaking out, so you shouldn't be freaking out either. We'll figure it out."

I oriented myself to Alex in much the same way that Midwestern farmers do when they converse, at an angle so that we were both looking out into the same middle distance, with no chance of a threatening posture or the dreaded eye contact. Tone matters much more than words in a situation like this, but I told Alex what I was thinking anyway.

"I get it, friend. You're The Dark Lord. Or something just doesn't look right about the path to the Walnut Ring. Maybe the grandstand reminds you too much of the racetrack. For all I know you're feeling insecure because you're a Michigan-born Thoroughbred in an ocean of fancy Warmbloods. But here's the thing: You're with familiar people. People who you can trust. Audrey has been good to you, and this show is a big deal for her. It's fine. You're fine. You can do this."

Did I actually believe it would work? Sort of. I certainly think that humans can effectively convey a sense of calm to animals. I also think the human brain consistently tricks us into seeing an illusion of cause and effect. But more than anything my gamble was that it *might* work, and that it couldn't hurt, and that as a result it made sense under the circumstances as one of those things a dad's gotta do.

I'm much better at imagining the dramatic happy ending than I am at bringing it about. What followed was not a blizzard of double-clear rounds, blue ribbons, and so much prize money that they wrote a check *to me* at the end of the show. Still, the show was a success in the sense that Alex was great in the Claiborne Ring, and each trip into the Walnut Ring was a little bit calmer than the last. His second entrance involved a gallop from the bottom of the ramp all the way into the ring. That gallop turned into a trot the next time, which, on their last trip, became a spirited walk. Maybe, I humored myself, I had gotten through to him.

It was progress. In the ring he and Audrey faced the biggest, most difficult courses they had yet seen. And they learned. They studied the pieces of the puzzle, examined their shape, and felt their contours. All that remained was to put them together. ❧

9

While Audrey and Alex worked to figure things out, Ada's run of bad luck continued. She'd been dealing with progressively intense back pain, and after another tough show and some ineffective chiropractic treatments a doctor diagnosed an injury that required several months off. It was, by far, the longest she had been out of the saddle since she first started riding. That sort of opportunity to reset can, of course, be valuable over the long run. But in the moment, it can be difficult medicine to swallow.

It's a funny thing to say, given the nature of the book you're now reading, but we tend toward stoicism in our family, and so I can't provide you with a detailed accounting of how the layoff felt from Ada's perspective. Some relief, perhaps, because finally a nagging injury would start to improve, and because it provided time away from a situation that was not going according to plan. And no doubt some frustration, because things had not gone as planned, and because she was denied what had been one of the constants in her life.

It certainly brought change for me. I still made regular trips to the barn, but for the first time in over a decade, I made them without Ada. Audrey and I were of course able to have a perfectly fine time by ourselves, putting our own spin on the habits and routines we had accumulated over the years. For one thing, as I've already mentioned, the two of us represented the family combination most likely to conclude that listening to a baseball game while driving was a good idea, even if it didn't involve any of the teams we followed. There's a soothing rhythm to a baseball broadcast, even if it's simply serving as background, and satellite radio makes games easy to find. The fact that the sportscast is on the radio places you in a certain part of the year, and the experienced ear can locate itself even more precisely in time based on the combination of crowd noise and announcer cadence. The relaxed pace and low murmur of the crowd in the early part of the season gives way to manufactured enthusiasm for teams whose seasons have not gone well, or to tension and loud, engaged crowds for teams still in the running later on. Of course, the scene outside your own car matters, too. Where is the sun? Is there a sun? Is that the air conditioner or the heater you have turned on? Sometimes a game just happened to be on while Audrey and I talked about something else. Sometimes I listened while Audrey rested. Occasionally we'd catch a game we were both interested in, in which case we'd listen intently, speaking only to discuss the game or some other important matter, such as where we'd be stopping to get dinner. We more than made it work, and there's a lot to be said for one-on-one time.

This change unfolded against a bittersweet backdrop. Ada had just earned her learner's permit, which meant a driver's license was not far off. I had long understood that my primary day-to-day contribution was to serve as a source of transportation, and that one day I would no longer be an essential part of the mix, but the idea had been an abstraction. Just as my own adulthood seemed far enough off to be incomprehensible when I was a kid, so too had my daughters' eventual adulthood seemed a distant enough thing that it would never actually happen. But now that day loomed ever closer. Ada, Audrey, and Laura would start to create their own sets of driving memories. And as much as I understood that that was how it should be, and that a part of me would welcome the extra time, I also knew that I would miss it. I would miss the conversations, and I would miss the simple, comforting fact of having a daughter in the passenger seat.

Ada has always liked music, and from the earliest days of our trips together to Appy Orse Acres we'd spend our drives listening to a playlist that I put together. Its early versions included lots of songs that involved horses, and over time it changed as the group grew tired of some songs and I found others that seemed to fit while being appropriate to the phase of childhood they were in at the time. Somewhere along the line I discovered a band called Old Crow Medicine Show, and a song called "Wagon Wheel." It's a song built around some discarded Bob Dylan lyrics, which were themselves rooted in 1940s blues, and it was later made popular by singer Darius Rucker. It has nothing to do with horses, but a lot to do with traveling, and it somehow just seemed to fit. I don't remember the specific moment of introducing other songs to our playlist, but the way we added "Wagon Wheel" stuck with me. One day on our drive to the barn I played it for Ada, noting it was a song I thought she might like. Then we listened to it again on the drive home.

A few things happened over time. One was that "Wagon Wheel" became a mainstay of the playlist. Another was that the playlist itself had to share time with the radio as Ada developed musical tastes of her own. A third was that, somewhere between the first and the second developments, we settled on a particular playlist for horse-show mornings. It was a good-luck ritual. We'd make our way to the car, not quite awake, usually at a time when we'd normally still be in bed. If we were away from home, I'd have a cup of hotel coffee. The girls would be carrying a muffin or a banana grabbed from the breakfast area in a half-hearted effort to appease my request that they eat something. We all understood that there was a good chance I'd later be throwing away a muffin or banana with a single bite taken out of it. We also understood that I'd be the one pressing "play," partly because that was the routine and partly because I was the only one with enough energy to do it. I won't share the secrets of our entire playlist, but I will tell you that it always started with "Wagon Wheel."

So, it wouldn't be wrong to say that "Wagon Wheel" is our song. For me it has come to signify our family's entire experience in the horse world, and thus not a small part of my life. If anybody cares to honor my request, they'll play it at my funeral.

There eventually came a point where Ada was able to join us again on a weeknight trip to the barn, the first since she'd been ordered to rest. We were all in a good mood, and there was very much a "We've got the band back together!" vibe in the air as we pulled out of the driveway. Probably because we were once again doing something we'd done together for a long time, I got the approval to play our music.

On non-horse show days that meant dipping into a different playlist, one that had well over a hundred songs on it. So I pulled it up. I plugged in my phone and hit "shuffle."

It's worth saying that last part again. *I hit "shuffle."* This wasn't planned, and it wasn't the case that the list was playing from the start, which would have led to a different result anyway. I hit "shuffle." As in, "play the tracks in this playlist in a random order." As in, there was a less than one percent chance that any one song from the playlist would be first to play.

Of course, you know exactly what's coming next. The first song? A live version of "Wagon Wheel."

Our song.

If you've never seen a grown man struggle to fight back tears made of sentimentality and nostalgia and just plain old happiness to be alive and able to experience a moment, well, you missed a chance.

Audrey rode in her lesson, and Serah, knowing exactly what the occasion called for, summoned Ada to join her in the ring as assistant trainer. Afterward, as we often did on Wednesday nights, a group from the barn went out for dinner. It was a good dinner. Not because anything special happened, but because it didn't. We were back to the routine. This was what we did, and now we were doing it again. We talked, we ate, we took a respectable number of mints from the bowl on our way out the door.

When we got in the car to head home, I plugged in my phone and hit play so we could pick up where we had left off. Still shuffling, still a less than one percent chance that any one song would be next. There were a few seconds left in the song that had been playing when we arrived at the farm.

We pulled out of the parking lot onto the road. The song ended, and there was a pause. And then: a strumming guitar, followed a few bars later by a fiddle. You might know the song I'm talking about. The album version of "Wagon Wheel." The one that kicked off our horse-show play-list. Our song. Again. Lightning striking twice. A sign, perhaps, that things would be returning to how they were.

And that's what we wanted, of course. That's what *I* wanted. A sign that things were back on track, that the struggles were in the past, that we'd settle back into the habits and perspectives of a year or so before. Some form of cosmic reassurance that order would be restored.

In most works of fiction the story would turn in that direction. That drive would have marked a turning point. Ada would have made a full recovery, K would have left her injuries behind, and together they would have started anew. All of their inchoate promise and potential would be realized, and they would enjoy some version of the successes we antici-pated when we wrote the big check to buy K. Somebody might actually want to buy the movie rights to this book.

Unfortunately, that's not the story I have to tell. This isn't a case of truth being stranger than fiction, but rather the more common situa-tion where it's simply more disappointing. Once we fall into patterns in our relationships, whether they be with animals or with fellow hu-mans, it's difficult to break out of them. Trust is hard to earn in gen-eral, and even harder when the person whose trust you're seeking is someone you've had trouble trusting in the past. The reset button can be hard to find.

It's a tough thing to go through. Ada wanted to make it work, and tried to make it work, and yet somehow, she and K never quite got in sync.

It was the complete opposite of her relationship with Cash. I'm sure it reflects poorly on me, but I began to think of D'Lovely K as D'Saster K. We considered selling K and trying again with a different horse, but of course that's often an easier plan to formulate than to execute, and it brings with it a host of transaction costs—commissions, prepurchase exams, new tack, and the like. Things in the horse world are rarely cheap or easy. Parenthood's bound to provide interruptions to your sleep in one way or another, and I spent a good many nights tossing and turning and trying to figure out what the best way out of the situation was.

I wish I could tell you that I figured it out, that everything ended up back on track, that it was as if that series of injuries and disappointments never happened.

suspect we've all got them. Places that bring on floods of memories. The old neighborhood. A school.

For me, a walk around the campus where I went to college triggers recollections of a time when my head was full of a youthful mix of confidence, confusion, and insecurity. And, of course, dreams. Some were foolish. Some came true. And some, to my occasional regret, I didn't pursue. It's a story that everyone can tell.

After I left Alex in his stall in Barn 7 at the Kentucky Horse Park, the night I had my deep conversation with him, during the Kentucky National Horse Show, I walked toward my car. It was late, the twilight was deepening, and I seemed to have the Horse Park almost to myself. My talk with Alex had put me in a thoughtful mood. I slowly started down the aisle between Barns 6 and 7 and caught a flash of movement out of the corner of my eye. I paused and looked more closely. It was a ghost. Or, more accurately, two of them.

I squinted a bit and felt a rush of recognition. One of the ghosts was me. The other was nine-year-old Ada. We were walking around the very Barn 7 where Alex had his stall. It was BreyerFest, and this was where the celebrity horses were boarded during that event.

We had not been to the Horse Park before, and we were in awe of the place and the horses. It never occurred to us then to imagine that just over six years later a horse of ours would spend a week in one of those stalls.

I watched the ghosts for a bit, then turned the corner and kept walking, my senses heightened. There we were again, two years later and still in awe, walking past the empty Stonelea Ring on our way to have a look at the start of what was then the Rolex CCI**** cross-country course. We didn't know the ring's name, nor did we suspect that in another three years Ada and her horse Cash would have one of their last trips together there.

A short way on, I nearly collided with Audrey and Melody. They were hustling through the early morning darkness to a modeling clinic at last summer's Pony Finals, with me tailing along behind.

There were ghosts nearly everywhere I looked.

It was no surprise, really. The girls had done nowhere near enough showing at the Horse Park for it not to seem like a big deal. Every visit and every show had been a significant milestone.

I've thought about that walk often since then. Those ghosts, like the ones I see at college reunions, had dreams. The girl who went to Breyer-Fest dreamed of showing at the Horse Park. The girls who got to show at the Horse Park dreamed of doing so on even bigger stages. A little time among ghosts will leave you reflecting on where you've been and where you might be headed.

Here I'm going to ask you to imagine that record needle scratch sound, the one that signifies our path is about to change.

When the call came, I was in a hotel room in Ann Arbor, Michigan, in my alternate capacity as Figure Skating Dad. It was very early, I was sick, I hadn't slept much the night before, and I hadn't had a drop of coffee. And I suddenly had to confront a situation of the sort that you don't ever want to confront.

It was Lauren, the Millcreek barn manager. Ada's horse K was colicking—experiencing severe abdominal pain caused by impaction or twisting of the intestines. It was not a mild case. Severe cases of colic can kill a horse. This one did.

It was a tragedy in multiple respects. K was the horse on whose back Ada's dreams of equitation finals would come true or not. She was the basket into which we had placed an awful lot of our eggs.

They say you shouldn't do that.

There's a clip in the movie *Harry & Snowman* where show jumper Rodney Jenkins talks about the importance of the specific relationship between a horse and a rider. For that relationship to go really well, things have to click between them. A similar idea appears several times in former US show jumping coach George Morris's autobiography *Unrelenting*. It's something that you can never quite fully explain, but that you recognize when you see it.

Ada and her first horse Cash had that. During their last summer together, they were at the height of their powers. I'm not suggesting that every round went according to plan, and he was not the world's fanciest horse. There were limits. But it was obvious that they entered the ring believing, every single time, that perfection was within reach. It was a joy to watch. I know that a father's eyes are not always clear. But a father who has been there every step of the journey knows things that no one else knows and appreciates things that no one else understands. What this father saw was a girl doing the very thing she was born to do. And doing it well.

K was a beautiful horse. But, as I've already told you, she and Ada had a partnership that was as star-crossed as any. One or the other of them was hurt for well over half of their time together, and they never managed to mesh the rest of the time. There were moments of brilliance, where they seemed on the brink of putting it all together. But some sort of setback always seemed to follow.

On the whole, the show ring was a frustrating place for them. More nights than I care to remember I would wake feeling like I had been kicked in the stomach, awash in the dread sense that I should have seen this coming, that I ought to have done something differently somewhere along the way. In the end—especially in the end—it's no overstatement to say that nothing about our ownership of K went according to plan.

K's passing was something to be mourned in its own right, of course. Untimely deaths always are, especially of those who have shared a good portion of life's journey with us. To compound things, Audrey had been K's primary rider since Ada's injury in April and had grown very attached to her. She was especially devastated.

But her passing also represented the death of a dream. It was a dream that we'd always known wasn't going to come true without good luck and the taking of some substantial risks, but luck's not always good and the thing about risks is they often don't pay off. There were lots of eggs in that basket, and it crashed to the ground.

The equitation finals were dreams for the ghosts after that phone call. They took up permanent residence at the Kentucky Horse Park, at the farms and showgrounds in Wisconsin where they first took shape, and in the ring at Millcreek Farm where it seemed, for a short while, they might actually come true.

It's not a happy story. And it's difficult even to make sense of the many layers and stages of the grieving process, let alone to put them into words more elaborate than "it sucks." As a parent the whole experience broke my heart in ways that I would never have appreciated as the child. They weren't my dreams, but I saw them form and evolve and shape every waking minute. I became invested in them. With my time, with my money, with what we might, somewhat clinically, call my emotional capital.

In the weeks that followed K's death I found myself visited by one more ghost. It was my grandfather August Hamson, a man whose memory keeps me grounded. He was a farmer for most of his life, and he held the fatalistic outlook that Norwegian farmers tend to hold. When you farm you're at the mercy of Mother Nature, and she doesn't always come through. Sometimes it rains when you need it, sometimes it doesn't, and there's nothing you can do about it. The markets are good or the markets are bad, and you've got no say in the matter. Either way you've got to get up the next morning and do what needs to be done.

By his later years my grandfather had experienced a lot of loss. As a young man he saw a brother and a team of horses killed by lightning as they worked a field. As an older man he suffered through the death not only of his wife but of an unfairly high number of children and grandchildren. He knew tough times.

His visits during that stretch featured the same reminder, a phrase I heard him utter in the face of tragedy more than once. He'd start with a word that was something like a combination of "yeah" and "yup" but that doesn't really fit into any package of letters I can string together. It wasn't quite a word, and not quite throat clearing. What was clear was that it signaled a summing up, his last word on whatever the subject might be. Here is what he'd say next: "That's the way it goes."

It doesn't sound like much. But there's an entire philosophy of life packed in those five words. One fully informed by a specific culture and a life rich with experience. Among other things, it's a shorthand way of acknowledging that life will kick you in the stomach sometimes, and there's nothing you can do to prevent that from happening, but you've got to keep going anyway, to figure out what comes next.

Because what other choice do you have?

Things blur together and we often rewrite our own histories. It's easy to judge the wisdom of our decision to buy K in hindsight, with full knowledge of how the story went and how it ended. There's a lesson I've had to continually reteach myself in my professional life, which is not to reflexively say, "Yes," to an idea that sounds good in the moment. Better, always, to take time to think things through. Making one commitment means not being able to make others. I've agreed too quickly to projects I've later regretted. I've also seen how taking a few days for sober second thought has saved me from similar regret after I've contemplated things more fully. All of which has swirled around my head as I've wrestled with whether I could or should have done things differently when we bought K. Did it happen too quickly? Did we not pause enough to think it through? What did I miss?

I know this: In the moment we all thought we were making the right decision. Everyone involved had the best intentions. Everyone involved shared the same hopes and expectations. Everyone involved felt disappointment as things unfolded the way they did. Questionable ethics are a pervasive feature of the horse world, but I have no concerns at all on that score.

The answer, I think, is more mundane: Every next step is a bet. That's as true in the world of riding as in life more generally. You try to make the best ones you can. You do your best to identify the probable outcomes, the likely costs, and the likely benefits, and you balance them against one another. Some bets are better than others but none of them is a sure thing. The best bet in the world will sometimes be a loser. You're left, always, to push your money to the center of the table and hope. Even if you've done your homework the most you can know is that there are good odds the cards will come up your way.

But they don't always come up your way. ֍

# 10

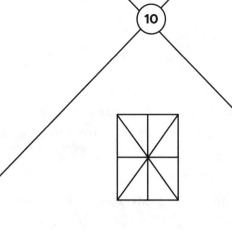

Spend enough time in the horse world and eventually you'll hear an instructor or clinician hold forth on the importance of "transitions." Applied to riding, the term refers to the change from one gait to another—walk to canter, trot to halt, and so on. Transition work can help to develop aspects of a horse's fitness. As importantly, it helps develop the connection between the horse and the rider. It's easy to continue at the same gait. It's moving from one to another where the complexity comes in, and where the rider needs the most nuance and deftness to get things right.

Transitions are important outside the ring as well. Changes are tricky, whether it's from one barn to another or one horse to another.

CHAPTER 10

A blown transition in the ring can cost you the class. Outside the ring the stakes are higher. Mess up the change and you can find yourself having lost a lot of money and a lot of time.

Yet changes are unavoidable.

Audrey and Alex's story was a good one. She brought him along from a horse easily triggered into spiraling out of control to a reliable, consistent companion—with one hitch. He was solid so long as he was in a ring where he was comfortable and the jumps didn't get too big. The Children's Jumpers, which top out at 1.10 meters high (there's that change to the metric system I told you about), seemed to be his limit. At the right show it would go very well. But it was not always the right show.

And when the jumps got bigger, his nerves returned.

I thought, or at least hoped, Audrey and Alex would work through the new challenge. Alex, after all, was my kind of horse. He was an underdog. Like Cash, he was a gatecrasher—except that for Alex the term occasionally applied literally as well as metaphorically. He wasn't pretty, and would get nowhere in a hunter class, but looks counted for nothing in the jumpers. And he had his own sort of charisma and a gentle soul beneath the sometimes-chaotic exterior. The limits seemed to be more psychological than physical. With Cash I had understood that appearance was part of the game and so he was not the right horse to fit the dream. But Alex was fast, and nimble, and able to jump high. He and Audrey had already come far, and there was no reason the progression couldn't continue. Or so I thought. It's easy to imagine the things you want to come true will come true.

Alex's final trip to the Kentucky Horse Park came in May 2017. I had a work obligation, so Lea was the parent on duty. By that point Alex had concluded that his reservations about the Walnut Ring were indeed legitimate. Things did not go well inside the ring during a particular class, and when Alex was asked to wait beside the ring for a bit, he responded by throwing a tantrum bad enough to get himself sent back not only to the barn, but all the way home, even though the plan had been to be at the show for another week.

All was not entirely lost. Serah came through in the clutch again, finding Audrey a catch ride on a horse named Goya. Together they won a championship in the Low Children's Jumpers. In that sense, at least, the lemons became lemonade.

But we had reached another crossroads. Audrey had big dreams, too, and as much as we wanted things to be otherwise, it had become clear that Alex would not be the horse to take her where she hoped to go.

Here's where resources matter in equestrian sport. Were money less of a concern, we'd simply have given Serah the okay to start looking for a new horse. Were money no concern at all, we'd have already had a second or third horse. We wouldn't have been concerned about the prospect of paying monthly board for two horses for Audrey in the event we couldn't find an appropriate new home for Alex. We wouldn't have had to count on getting something for the sale of Alex to be able to pay for a new horse. We'd have just done it. The transition could have been, perhaps, relatively seamless.

Instead, it took a year.

As I mentioned earlier, an unanticipated aspect of my family's journey through the horse world was the extent of the parallels I saw to my professional journey in law. The steps involved in learning how to ride corresponded in a rough-but-real way with what I had experienced in my development as a lawyer. The things my daughters' riding instructors did seemed, at a deep level, to be the same as things I did, or could do, in my own work as a teacher. In early 2016, I had the chance to spend the day with a lawyer named Don Verrilli, who at the time was the Solicitor General of the United States. The SG is the person responsible for representing the United States government before the Supreme Court. It's about as big as lawyering jobs get. When I met him he was, in short, someone at the top of his professional game.

We had a few friends in common, so I had a little sense of what to expect. I knew, for example, that he was likely to take me up on my offer to skip the fancy lunch reservation we had in favor of a much more character-filled Milwaukee alternative. (He did.) And as we conversed it didn't take long for me to realize that this was someone I would have loved to have had the chance to learn from back when I was a young lawyer.

Verrilli was in town to deliver the address at the Marquette University Law School's graduation ceremony. I've heard my share of graduation speeches over the years. Most are good. Verrilli's was great, and I've repeated key parts of it to new law students ever since. Its message was simple but important, and not just for lawyers: Do the little things right. It's good to have big dreams and to want to change the world. But you can't do those big things unless you're willing to do the little things, because the little things make you who you are.

When May 2018 rolled around Audrey was back at the Kentucky Horse Park, this time on a horse named Memphis Belle. Belle was not a gatecrasher. She had been to all the fancy places and shown in big classes. Like K, she had landed at Millcreek as a sales horse. Audrey had ridden her a lot and had fallen in love. We worked out a deal to buy her.

Like Alex, Belle was a strong horse. Like Alex, she was inclined to go fast. She could become hard to control, but unlike Alex, she did not have a tendency to fall apart.

One of the first things Audrey and Belle got to do together was attend a session of the US Hunter/Jumper Association's Emerging Athletes Program—the same program at which Ada and Cash had had their last rides together three years earlier. Audrey's session took place at the short-lived HITS Balmoral, a former harness-racing facility turned unsuccessfully into a hunter/jumper showgrounds.

I don't remember when or how I first heard about EAP, but I recall thinking it was a very good idea. And when Ada had ridden in the clinic with Chris Kappler as clinician and Anne Thornbury as stable manager, I'd walked away impressed. Ada, for her part, had walked away exhausted. That was true for the other participants, as well, and it's consistent with the basic logic of the program. The participants do all the work of caring for and preparing their horses themselves. Once the EAP session starts, the barn is off-limits to everyone else, save for the riders and the clinicians. No parents, no grooms, no trainers.

The program's goal, EAP program committee chair Sally Ike told me, is to help the participants become better horse people. This doesn't just, or maybe even mostly, mean better riders. Riding's a part of it, for sure, but so is all the less glamorous work, the day-to-day detail and drudgery that puts a rider in sustained contact with her horse and allows her to gain a more accurate sense of his condition and mood.

The first day of the EAP has a bit of the flavor of the first day of summer camp. There's the stress of getting ready, getting there, and getting settled in. There are the introductions and figuring out where everything is and what's expected. There are the nerves and the anxiousness that accompany any new experience.

Ada's EAP experience had been largely a solo flight. We'd trailered Cash in, I'd helped her unload and set up the stall, and then the time came for parents to exit the barn and I'd left. She was on her own. Audrey had the good fortune to be there with three friends from Millcreek Farm who were able to bring the positive, cooperative atmosphere of their home barn with them.

The session began with a message that picks up right about where Don Verrilli's graduation speech left off. As stable manager Anne Thornbury made her way down the aisle checking horses and tack, the implicit message was clear: Do the little things right. Clean saddles, clean bridles, clean horses, clean boots.

There's a safety rationale for that, of course. Clean equipment is more likely to be safe equipment. And the process of cleaning helps to uncover small problems before they become big problems.

There's another rationale too. It's the same sort of thing that leads good lawyers to obsess over spelling, punctuation, and the minutiae of language. If you haven't paid close attention to *those* things, then how can I have confidence that you've paid proper attention to the big things? Both are the products of a careful and deliberate mind. Clients usually can't tell when a lawyer has made a mistake on the law—that's what they hire a lawyer for, after all—but they can tell when a lawyer has spelled their name wrong, and they tend not to like it.

Many of the EAP attendees hoped to one day become professionals in the equine industry. Anne Thornbury emphasized that a hallmark of the most successful professionals, especially when it comes to securing sponsors, is that they keep everything in their barns in perfect condition. That doesn't mean being an unpleasant person or a snob. You can be a Don Verrilli and take the time to enjoy a leisurely lunch in a local dive. But you have to pay attention to the little things.

The little things are not glamorous. The little things are rarely fun, and they can extend an already too long day. But the big things are a lot less likely to happen when the little things don't get done and done right.

It's a useful lesson for all of us.

"Opens eyes and opens doors." That, Sally Ike told me, was the motto of the EAP.

Over the years, one of my great frustrations as a riding parent was the cost. I mean that partly in the usual sense of, "Well, there goes my lake cabin." But I also mean it in the sense that it was frustrating not to be able to provide my daughters with as many opportunities as I would have liked. We simply couldn't afford to support that much showing, and saying "no" in the face of your child's passion is never fun, especially when your child crosses paths with so many others who are able to do the all things they would like to do. (I say this in full recognition of the fact that, as both Audrey and Ada understand, there were plenty of other young riders who looked enviously at what they had the opportunity to do. Perspective is important.)

Given the opportunity at EAP, I asked both Anne Thornbury and Sally Ike what advice they'd give to someone in our family's situation. What should our focus be? Fewer but bigger shows? As many shows as we could afford? What was the right mix? Their answers differed in their particulars but were consistent in spirit.

Sally put it this way: "It's not about showing! It's about improving your skills, and the success will come. [Olympic show jumper Bill] Steinkraus characterized shows in one of his books as the test of the training. For talented and ambitious kids, my recommendation has always been to find the best help you can afford. A ski instructor once told me that I should

watch everyone coming down the mountain because of what I'd learn.
The same is true of equestrian sport; you need to surround yourself as
much as possible with the best. It will rub off!"

And as Sally reminded me: "Yes, we have people in the highest finan-
cial brackets competing at the top levels, but think about it—our most
respected and successful professionals did not come from families with
deep pockets."

It's a long way to the top no matter what your field, and the pinnacle
can seem especially distant in a world—like the horse world—where the
costs of entry alone are significant. Talent, ambition, and hard work by
themselves won't always get you in front of the eyes you hope to catch.
Luck's a necessary ingredient here, as it is most everywhere else. And
luck can take a lot of forms.

As Audrey's already very accomplished trainer Serah stood watching
the horses be unloaded and settled at the beginning of the EAP session,
she couldn't help but say to me, "I wish there had been an EAP when
I was a kid."

My point? Simply that the mere existence of the EAP is a stroke of
good luck for all those fortunate enough to take part.

Nobody makes a secret of the fact that a strong performance at the
EAP can indeed open doors. The USHJA's website and other materials
emphasize that riders who have done well at EAP nationals have lev-
eraged that into later successes. The opening meeting underscored the
point. "This is a 'show me' week," Anne Thornbury told the participants.
"Show me what you've got." It was made clear that a rider who made
a good impression in the week ahead might very well find herself with
some nice opportunities down the road.

It was a life lesson as well. As a "baby lawyer," I imagined that getting
clients involved the ability to work some sort of inexplicable magic at

cocktail parties. Maybe it does, and I just never learned how to cast that particular spell. But what seemed a whole lot more effective was doing good work for the senior lawyers I worked with and the clients my firm entrusted me with. Both wanted me to be useful, to be responsive to their needs, and to pay attention to detail. If I did that, they'd continue sending me work. And then the clients would mention my name to someone else who was looking for a lawyer, and then I'd have another client. Showing, rather than telling, is what did the trick. As far as I can tell, it's a dynamic that holds true in all sorts of circumstances.

An EAP regional session was definitely a competition for those invited to attend. But not in the normal sense. There were some sessions where no participants advanced to nationals, and others where as many as six did. But the message delivered to Audrey and the others was to focus on learning. "If you do that, you'll get noticed," they were told.

As anyone who's ever been asked, "Will this be on the test?" knows, there's often a perceived (and sometimes real) gap between learning a subject well and learning what's necessary to succeed on an exam. Here I suspect the two largely align. One of the things you could learn at EAP was, ultimately, how to be useful. How to be someone who knows the basics and is hungry to learn more, who has the judgment to handle most things on your own but also to ask for help when appropriate, who gets the little things right.

Learn all of that, no matter what your field, and you'll tend to get noticed by people who can open doors.

When I started blogging for the *Chronicle of the Horse*, I had a vague notion that I might one day use my posts as the beginnings of

a book chronicling my experiences and observations as a horse dad. And
when I told my old friend and frequent professional collaborator Todd
Peppers about my tentative book project, he asked me how much riding I'd done. My answer was, "Hardly any." Todd and I have enough of
a history together that we can say things to one another that we wouldn't
say to other people, so he pressed me a bit. Wouldn't I be better able to
appreciate my daughters' experiences in riding if I tried it myself? And
wouldn't that put me in a position to write a better book?

It was one of those moments where you hate to admit that someone
has a point. But he had a point.

As you know, it's not that I've been a complete non-rider. There were
the questionable incidents with the sheep and the cows from my days
as a farm kid. And those two times I momentarily sat on a horse in my
youth. I took a lesson at my daughters' urging once about a decade ago.
And I went on a few really long trail rides with them where I learned
about the need to dress to avoid chafing and the importance of minimizing pre-ride coffee consumption.

But it was only recently that I climbed on a horse thinking that I was
actually going to try to learn how to ride.

I don't mind saying that my first attempt went pretty well. Given
my years sitting in the cold corners of riding rings, watching Ada and
Audrey and Laura, I knew how to hold the reins and had apparently
internalized some knowledge about how to use them, and I even used
my legs a bit. Nobody said anything bad about the videos of myself at
the trot that I posted on Facebook, and a few people said some pretty
nice things, and not a single one of them was my mom (mostly because
she's not on Facebook).

When it came time to canter, though, my grasp on what I was doing
got a lot more tenuous. I started to feel like less of a rider and more of

a rag doll. My thought process went from, "Let me try making this adjustment," to "I'm bouncing around a lot. Like really a lot. How do I stop bouncing around so much?"

I didn't have an answer for myself right then. It's been a really long time since I've sat in on a lesson where someone was learning how to canter. And whatever my daughters know about riding the canter has become so automatic that they don't even have to think about it.

And so, as I sat at EAP, watching and listening to the session's featured clinician Olympian Anne Kursinski's commentary, I had two recurring thoughts. The first was that I, as a rider, was so far away from being able to think about the sorts of adjustments she was suggesting. It was mind-blowing, really, just how much knowledge the young riders before me had accumulated over the years, and how much they were able to do on the back of a horse without having to think about it.

The second was that I'd heard much of the lesson, in one form or another, before. "If you can't control your body, you can't control your horse." "Work *with* the horse, not against the horse. Anger is counterproductive. Think of the horse as your best friend." "Attention to detail in everything that you do. That's what the winners have. No stone goes unturned."

The familiarity of it all didn't surprise me, and it didn't dismay me. I'd heard and seen these things from watching my daughters ride in clinics given by eminent equestrians like George Morris, Diane Carney, and Bernie Traurig. I'd heard and seen them in Serah Vogus' lessons at Millcreek Farm. The fact that the concepts were repeated over and over suggested to me that they were important. The fact that it was necessary for them to be so consistently emphasized suggested that they were difficult to master.

I once heard George Morris characterize the process of training a horse as "like water on stone." It takes time and consistency to leave a mark. So, too, it seems, with riders. My daughters didn't learn how to do all the things they could do on a horse in one shot. It was impossible to point back to one lesson or one clinic and say, "That's the one where Audrey learned how to do a perfect shoulder-in." It was a process of gradual accumulation.

"*Feeling*, not thinking. That's what makes a great rider," said Anne Kursinski at EAP. No doubt "feeling" is the sort of thing that some people have more natural aptitude for than others. But I'm also willing to bet it's something that can be, indeed has to be, nurtured and developed over time. The journey from where I am as a rider to where my daughters are is a journey of years, of dedication, and of repetition. The journey from where they are to where they hope to be will take more of the same.

I've found it's pretty common for those of us who have reached middle age to realize that we knew very little when we were younger and thought we knew everything, and that we still know very little now that we're older and know a lot more. I have a much more sophisticated grasp of my field now than I did in my twenties or thirties. I also have a greater appreciation for just how complex it is. It's a wonder, I sometimes think to myself when preparing to teach new law students, that anyone learns to become a lawyer at all. There are just too many things you have to understand to do it well.

When Ada rode in the Emerging Athletes Program, Chris Kappler voiced a similar sentiment. He likened riding to a forest where "the deeper you get in, the more trees there are." I took his point to be that mastering riding at one level only brings with it a new set of challenges and the need for more refinement of technique. Indeed, I've heard many lifelong riders describe part of the continuing appeal of the sport as lying in the constant stream of problems it presents. *How can I get my horse to do this thing or stop it from doing that other thing? How can I get myself to do it?*

The teacher's natural urge is to want to pass on everything she's learned. I continually remind myself, with only sporadic success, that less is more. The urge when putting together a law school class is to think that it's all potentially important. As a seasoned lawyer, I can anticipate a host of situations in which some seemingly obscure concept might be useful. An experienced horse person, I imagine, has seen a million things happen for which she has developed responses. Any of it might happen, so all of it is pertinent. We want to pass every last bit of it on.

That's the challenge of a program like the EAP. The clinicians and staff collectively have several lifetimes' worth of experience at the highest levels of the sport. They know the forest, and they know the trees. Naturally, they want to share their knowledge about all of it. Anne Thornbury characterized the challenge as passing along everything she's learned in fifty years in four days. And that, of course, is impossible to do.

For the riders, it's like drinking from a fire hose. There's so much to learn, including an appreciation of just how much there is to learn. Anne underscored the point for Audrey and the other attendees by telling them that she herself always learned something new during EAP. There's always more to know, when, as Sally Ike recommended, you "surround yourself as much as possible with the best." That rings true to me. I've had the good fortune to spend chunks of time working with and around some of the top people in my field. It's always exhilarating and always leaves me feeling like I've raised my game.

A week under the tutelage of the best provides too much knowledge in too short a time for all of it to stick. There's no avoiding that. But some of it will. Some tip or trick will come in handy not too far down the line.

Some subtle shift in positioning or attitude will have a lasting and significant effect. The residue of the week, for some, will be an intensified desire to learn and to become further immersed in the horse world. It's a tremendous thing to experience, and it's pretty fun to watch too.

As with Ada's experience at EAP, the fifth and final day gave the twenty-one riders in Audrey's session, appearing in groups of three, one shot at riding a full course, followed by a critique from Anne Kursinski. Although I was sure the clinicians had already formed solid impressions of each participant, for at least some of them a strong round might be a ticket to the EAP National Training Session. There was nervousness in the air.

Moments like this I often thought about coach Herb Brooks' famous locker room speech to the 1980 Olympic "Miracle on Ice" US hockey team before they played the Soviet Union. Tailored to the situation, it would go like this: "You were born to ride horses—every one of you. And you were meant to be here today. This is your time. Now go out there and take it!"

Ada had ridden well when she had participated in EAP, and she had come home with some very positive feedback from the clinician that year, Chris Kappler. Watching Audrey's own experience three years later couldn't help but reinforce my sense that our journey had been worthwhile. It not only reminded me just how good Ada and Cash had been together, it demonstrated how good Audrey had become. Hearing an "Excellent," or a "Very good," or an "I love that, Audrey," from Anne Kursinski helped justify all her time and mine. I admired the graceful way my daughter dealt with the bundle of energy in the horse beneath her. I felt more than a little proud when I overheard another parent, one who seemed pretty knowledgeable, say nice things about her riding to someone else.

My seat had me facing the last jump. I knew the week had been tough, and nobody went without a struggle or two along the way. The course looked imposing. Yet one by one the riders tackled it, and their smiles after clearing the last fence were huge.

There was an inherent tension in something like the EAP. It was a learning opportunity, but it was also a competition. It was easy to focus on the latter and to measure success by how the final round went or whether one got an invitation to nationals. And it was easy to emphasize the portion of the learning that related directly to being a more effective competitor in the future. There was a lot to be said for Anne Kursinski's advice to the riders: "Look like a winner," and, "Constantly ask, 'How can I be better?'"

"That's what separates the winners," she explained, "always trying to get better."

Unquestionably true.

But so, too, is what Anne Thornbury told me when I asked for her final thoughts at the end of the EAP session: "Remember why you started. Too many people get hung up on winning, losing, and competing. They forget why they started."

Hard work and improvement are certainly laudable, and I like a blue ribbon as much as the next person. I'm hardly indifferent to the competition. But I also remember that prophetic moment in the horse barn at the Wisconsin State Fair when Ada was just a baby, and I, a thirty-something who had run off the farm for the city first chance he got, said to my wife after a few moments peering into a stall, "I had forgotten just how majestic they are."

A pair of highlights came for Audrey and Belle just after the trip to the EAP. They showed at the Great Lakes Equestrian Festival in Traverse City, Michigan. It was Audrey and Belle's third show together, and they were in the Children's Jumpers. GLEF was a big show with top riders from around the country. The classes were large. They were also set in the Grand Prix ring, which was considerably larger than other rings at the show and where all the big classes took place.

That Saturday the temperature was in the mid-seventies and there was, as my weather app puts it, "rain throughout the day." No doubt there was, but it dramatically understates the situation. The word "torrential" would better describe when Audrey and Belle walked through the in-gate for their class. The entire surface of the ring was a layer of water. Lea, who had accompanied Audrey on the trip as I had a work commitment, took video from underneath a canopy overlooking the ring, the action partly framed by streams of water flowing off the overhang, all the sound muted by the constant thrum of rain in the background. The rain was so loud that Audrey did not hear the announcement that the show had been put on a hold. She could have waited until the rain subsided to proceed with her round. There was no way to hear the signal from the judge letting her know that she was on the clock to start; she could tell only by looking at the countdown timer on the scoreboard.

Audrey had shown in a downpour before, on Melody at Pony Finals. That was a flat class, in a smaller ring. A course of fences presented a challenge on another level. Things, including leather saddles and reins, became slippery when they got wet. Seeing anything was a challenge, to say nothing of navigating one's way around a course of jumps. When we look now at a photo from that day taken by the show photographer, it looks more like Audrey and Belle were riding through a blizzard than a summer shower. It was remarkable that they stayed on course, and that Audrey stayed on Belle. Even more so that their round was clean and good enough for a fourth-place finish in the class. It was a moment to remember.

But they weren't done. The next day was the classic round. I confess that I've never been entirely sure what differentiates a classic round from a regular round. The entry fee is greater, and the riders usually wear white rather than tan breeches. The prize money is often higher, and usually the winner gets a cooler for their horse that memorializes the victory. So maybe they're just a little bit bigger deal only because that's just the understanding. Whatever the case, a classic is just a bigger deal.

This time the conditions provided no extra drama. The ring was dry and the visibility good. Audrey and Belle's round was clear, and they moved to the jump-off, a timed ride on a shortened course that would determine the winner. Part of Belle's magic was that, in contrast to Alex, she usually did not appear to be going as fast as she was. They often finished courses considerably faster than horses who, by comparison, seemed to be on the edge of losing control.

And so it was in this round. It was clear they were pushing, but there was no sense that things might fall apart. The ring announcer characterized it as a "blazing" time, a full two seconds better than the fastest time prior to her.

But Audrey had ridden early in the order, and there were still at least ten riders to go. All she could do was watch and hope that her time would hold up. That, as she had learned at Pony Finals, did not always happen. But one by one the competition came up short. As the last rider entered the ring a show worker tried to get Audrey's permission to put the winner's cooler on Belle so they would be ready to enter for their victory lap. Audrey declined, not wanting to jinx it.

A minute or so later it was official. They won the classic and finished as reserve champions in the division. ✿

— 11 ——————————————

U ntil we reached the point where they could drive themselves, I sat ringside for nearly every riding lesson my daughters had. I won't claim to have paid close attention for every minute of the many, many hours, but I was a pretty engaged observer. It was a fascinating experience. Part of the fascination came from watching the slow accumulation of knowhow as their skills developed over the years. Things that had been challenging became easy and eventually second nature, the sort of thing done automatically rather than as a product of thought. The process was ongoing. The old challenges were replaced by new ones as layers of previously hidden nuance emerged. Like a lot of things, riding appears to the uninitiated to be much less complicated than it actually is.

The other source of fascination came through the fact that I got to watch this progression being directed by a series of different instructors, each with their own style and priorities. My job as a law professor, I've increasingly come to appreciate over the years, involves teaching a subject where the important knowledge is just as much "knowledge how" as it is "knowledge that." It didn't take long for me to realize, as I've already mentioned in these pages, that there are core similarities between what my daughters were learning and what I teach. Just as being able to recite facts about horse anatomy doesn't make one a good rider, being able to spit out a bunch of legal knowledge doesn't make one a good lawyer. That sort of knowledge is useful, certainly, but the key skill is being able to put it to use.

It's a realization that had a profound impact on my professional life. The connection to teaching is the easiest to appreciate. All those hours sitting ringside helped me understand the value of repetition, and of emphasizing the connections between the different ideas presented in a given course and throughout the law more generally. But, less obviously, it affected my approach to the part of my job that involves thinking about, researching, and writing legal scholarship. My focus as a scholar has been on the role of judges. The topics I've considered include the sorts of things that influence judicial behavior—there's the law, certainly, but also the nature of the institutions and systems in which judges do their work, the processes by which cases make their way to them, and things like political inclinations and the various psychological distortions to which we're all susceptible. If the activities involved in learning how to ride and how to be a lawyer are similar in certain fundamental respects, then so, too, might be the processes by which human judges go about assessing the quality of riding or of a legal argument.

Let me confess that I am conflicted about some of what comes next. From my vantage point, at least, former Olympic show jumping coach George Morris was the dominant figure in the American hunter/jumper world. "Was" is a critical word in that sentence. Morris *was* the dominant figure when my family began the portion of our journey that brought us near the upper reaches of the sport, and it seems also to have been the case for several decades prior to that. A neighbor who was an entry-level riding instructor gushed about getting the chance to meet him. A colleague roughly my age who grew up riding spoke of him in reverent tones. His name and his perspectives were all over the pages of leading equestrian publications. His word, from all that I could tell, was gospel.

And yet that all came to an inglorious end. Morris received a lifetime ban from the sport based on allegations that he had sexually abused some of the young men who had trained with him in the early days of his career, a story significant enough to merit coverage in *The New York Times*. This was, for those who spent time in barns and on equestrian social media while the process unfolded, a highly controversial episode. People, as people tend to do, formed strong opinions based on very little information, and many of those people felt no hesitation about sharing them. Some were happy to proceed directly from allegation to conviction, apparently feeling no need to wait for the process to run its course. Some determined to "stand with George" simply because they could not, or would not, believe that the allegations could be true. And this dynamic has repeated itself as allegations have surfaced against other prominent members of the equestrian community. Ours is a world in which one of the more widely practiced arts is that of jumping to conclusions. We all want to draw clear lines on a reality that resists them.

One of the frequently raised complaints, and it's one that drives me crazy as a professor of both criminal and constitutional law, is that somehow the accused in these situations are being denied due process. Even worse are those whose instinct is to wonder "where the parents were," as if sexual assault is perfectly fine if the victim or the victim's parents don't take what they regard as sufficient precautions.

It's become clear in recent years that the horse world, like virtually every other segment of society, has had a problem with sexual harassment and predation. And it comes as no surprise. The power dynamics that enable such conduct are pervasive. Young riders tend to regard their trainers with extreme reverence, as people who can do no wrong. Trainers can provide access to something the riders desperately want—the best rides and the most attention. And they can ostracize the noncompliant. Yet for whatever reasons a substantial number of people are unwilling to acknowledge or deal with these uncomfortable truths and are only too willing to place the blame on those without the power in the relationship rather than on those who hold all of it.

I, of course, cannot myself claim to know whether George Morris did or did not do the things he was accused of. I can tell you that my experiences as a lawyer have led me to have close interactions with many people who did not seem to be the kind of people to do the things they very much did. I can tell you that many of those same people have no problem whatsoever denying or minimizing their conduct, both to themselves and to the world in general. I can tell you that some people are comparatively unwilling or unable to read or react to the various subtle cues that others use to express their reticence or discomfort, such that behavior that registers as problematic to most people doesn't to them. I can tell you that sustained success leads in many people to an abundance of arrogance, entitlement, and high self-regard, any of which can exacerbate the tendencies identified in the preceding sentence. I can tell you that the process leading up to a lifetime ban includes more in the way of procedural protections for the accused than those objecting appreciate, but (in my view) rightly does not include the same level of procedural protections as are afforded to criminal defendants. And that's hardly unusual. Most any professional can lose the right to practice their profession via claims of misconduct adjudicated under standards and via processes that are not very different from those that were applicable to George Morris. I can also tell you that I favor sanctions against those who abuse their positions of authority, especially when the consequences of that abuse fall heavily on specific people.

So far as I'm aware, there were no problems with this sort of abuse in any of the activities in which my daughters took part. We did our best to be vigilant. But of course the problem is hardly limited to youth sports, as we've all learned in the #metoo era. The legal profession has probably been more attentive to sexual harassment than most others, but even so one hasn't had to look far to find stories of misconduct, and I'm not happy to report that I've known some people involved. Becoming a parent wasn't the thing that opened my eyes to this set of issues, but it's certainly brought them into sharper focus. My heart now travels around in three other chests, and I'd like for it to be treated appropriately.

I try to do my part as I work to shape the next generations of lawyers. But I certainly don't have all the answers. I often think back to a moment from a Constitutional Theory seminar I taught over the summer of 2013. The class was discussing a set of readings relating to gender equality. One of the students, who was in law school after having already had a first career and who was probably only a couple years younger than I, observed, with a note of anguish in his voice, "We thought we had all this figured out. But we didn't." I can't say I ever believed we had it all figured out, but the twenty-something version of me certainly thought we'd have made a lot more progress than we did. It's probably every generation's lament. Real change takes time, and solutions are never perfect. At the moment our cultural norms seem to be shifting in real ways, evidenced as much as anything by the backlash from those who grew up with and remain attached to a different set of understandings. No doubt we'll stumble on our way to the perfect world we'll never reach. Still, it counts as progress.

For now, though, I'll ask you to set that aside as I provide a sense of what it was like to attend a George Morris clinic before the allegations against him came to light. Early on in our journey, as I came to understand his role in the equestrian world, it was understood that one should not pass up an opportunity to attend a George Morris clinic, and that—so long as one was prepared to suffer his abuse if it came—one should likewise take the opportunity to ride in one. Our arrival at Millcreek provided us with those opportunities. And so I attended several as a spectator, and Audrey got the chance to ride in one. However one comes out in one's assessment of George Morris the human being, there can be no doubt that he was both incredibly knowledgeable about horses and a person who could put on a show.

I took detailed notes at each of these clinics. My focus was less on the technical aspects of riding, because I lacked the ability to appreciate that, and more on the things he said that reflected on riding as a topic of study. What does it mean to learn how to ride well? How does one do it? What are the sorts of challenges and problems that tend to come up along the way? I was also interested in his approach to teaching. Part of that was simply the spectacle of the legendary irascibility. But more than that I wanted to be attentive to the way he approached his subject as a teacher, how he broke things down, and how he communicated his thoughts to the riders and to the audience.

I got my fill. By the time December 2015 rolled around I had audited three George Morris clinics in the preceding year. To put the profound weirdness of that in perspective, consider this: Over that same time period I sat on exactly zero horses. Indeed, if my memory is accurate, over my entire life to that point I had attended one George Morris clinic for every three times I had been on a horse.

All three clinics took place at Brookwood Farm, almost literally a stone's throw away from Millcreek. Serah rode in each one of them, and Diane Carney, who worked with Morris to put on clinics in the Chicago area for thirty years, was instrumental in connecting us with Serah. Under the circumstances it would have been odd if we hadn't gone.

I was never bored. There's something about watching an acknowledged master impart his craft that draws me in.

*"I hate teaching. It is so ... impossible. I like riding. I put up with you people."*

Morris was a showman. He had a distinct way of speaking, a cadence all his own, punctuated by an appreciative "thaaaaaaat's it" whenever a rider did something well. At times he seemed to retreat entirely into his own mind, his hands out in front as if he was holding reins, working through whatever it was that he was teaching at the moment. (I was reminded of watching Garrison Keillor wandering the stage bringing the news from Lake Wobegon, his eyes closed, lost in a world of his own creation. Curiously Keillor, too, fell from grace when he was accused of sexual harassment in 2017.)

My notes from the three sessions include plenty of quotes worthy of motivational posters. "If it's a little wrong or a lot wrong, it's the same." "Detail, detail, detail." "The horse jumps. We don't jump. We accompany the horse." "Don't practice helpless." "Rough usually has temper. Rough is not fair to the horse." "There's *always* something to do to influence the horse." "The most beautiful animal God ever created is the Thoroughbred horse." "Our goal is higher. Every rider, every horse, our goal is higher."

*"I'm not going to be nice to you, because you're paying me to get better."*

Part of the entertainment at a Morris clinic, of course, was famously of the uncomfortable sort that came at someone else's expense. For those in search of it, he rarely disappointed. "I should be a dentist. To teach you is like pulling teeth." "Your work ethic is very subpar." "You have posture like a 90-year-old." "You're the victim of a very good horse." "You young people know nothing." "You don't know what the hell you're doing." "You're such a dud." The auditors were not immune. At one point someone in the audience was texting. Suffice to say that that did not go over well.

*"The basics are simple but they're hard to acquire. This sport comes very slow."*

Perhaps the most interesting thing to me about watching those clinics was this: I understood every word that George Morris said.

I also, of course, understood none of it.

Here's what I mean: It was just like watching Anne Kursinski (herself a student of George Morris at one time) teach at EAP. There were no concepts that flew over my head, no references to movements that I couldn't imagine myself performing. At the same time, I knew full well that if I were to climb into a saddle, I wouldn't be able to put much of the knowledge to work. And even for the experienced rider, I can imagine, there is a gulf between understanding and doing.

Riding, like so many other activities (including, or so I have contended at length in the pages of law reviews, legal decision-making), draws upon something that philosopher Michael Polanyi called "tacit knowledge." Polanyi encapsulated the idea in the phrase, "We know more than we can tell." More: "The aim of a skillful performance is achieved by the observance of a set of rules which are not known as such to the person following them."

When George Morris rode, in other words, he drew on a vast well of knowledge that he could use but not fully articulate. Part of what makes a good riding instructor, of course, is the ability to put a tremendous amount of that knowledge into words, to see patterns and tendencies

in both horses and riders that others cannot, and to communicate them
to students in a way that the students can understand and put to work.

Morris obviously had that talent. But even then, toward the end of
three days of instruction, with a group of high-level Grand Prix riders,
we got: "My message, people, is you have to use your legs and use your
hands." In a trivial sense we all already knew that, even me. But what
he meant was far from trivial, and would take an entire book to fully
develop with all its implied nuance and contingency, and with all the
exceptions when what generally works isn't quite the right thing to do.
And if it's anything like law, a rider can't fully understand any specific
thing until she understands everything. The result is a vicious cycle that
can never be completed. George Morris did not lie when he said that
teaching was impossible.

When I was younger, when I thought not only that I was pretty smart,
but (worse than that) that being that kind of smart was the only thing to
be, I might have heard all this and reasoned that there was really nothing
to it. I would have heard about the importance of the inside leg and the
outside rein and concluded that there was nothing there that I couldn't
wrap my brain around.

I would have understood every word that George Morris said. But
I also would have understood none of it. And I wouldn't have been able
to appreciate that.

I've spent the past quarter-century living in the world of law. I've
gone from student to lawyer to professor, and I've now spent over half
my professional life as a teacher and scholar. Those roles have required
me to develop a deep understanding of my subject. I've come to know
quite a bit about how the law works.

Here's the funny thing. It's not the slightest bit uncommon for me
to find wisdom—true, deep insight—in a text aimed at beginning law

students, in phrases that are the legal equivalent of "Keep your heels down," or "The half-halt is a concert of aids." I couldn't possibly have appreciated the full significance of these phrases at the beginning of my career. The basics look different from the perspective provided by twenty-five years. The experienced eye can pick up on things that are beyond the notice, let alone the comprehension, of the newbie.

*"I know far from everything."*

There was no mistaking the fact that George Morris had a healthy ego. "Every horse that I ride," he told us, "is totally transformed."

But at the time it seemed there was a fundamental humility present, too. My notes didn't capture it completely, but I'm certain that at one of the clinics he said something to the effect of, "I don't know anything about horses." I would guess that most people in the audience regarded it as a bit of extraordinarily false humility, a line designed to generate a laugh rather than illustrate anything. But I think he was being quite sincere and that it was the most significant thing that he said during that clinic. It has been my experience, too, that the more I have learned, the more I appreciate how little I know.

And so, whatever I do or don't believe about George Morris following his ban from horse sport, I do believe George Morris when he says he knows nothing about horses. I believe him when he says that he spends a bit of time reading about riding each night before he goes to bed. I'm sure that he's read everything worthwhile that's been written, most of it more than once. I'm just as sure that the best of it reads a little bit differently each time, and always gets him reflecting on what he understands, and what he doesn't, and what he might want to start thinking about when he wakes up the next morning.

One of the highlights of the first clinic I attended with Ada and Audrey was discovering that one of the horses involved was one that Ada had recently been riding in her lessons. The horse was giving his rider a bit of trouble, and midway through the session, Morris got on him. The transformation was amazing, and evident even to one with eyes as dull as my own. Toward the end of his time on that horse, having demonstrated his magic, Morris remarked simply, "That's the clinic."

It was a great demonstration, and it certainly seemed to have been the thing that stuck with most of the people in attendance. But I think the true lesson, the bit of wisdom that best puts one in a position to get to the point of being able to perform that same sort of magic with a horse, is that George Morris, and I'm sure it is true to this day, believes—no, *understands*—that he knows nothing about horses.

"That's hot." Those were George Morris's first words after dismounting from Audrey's horse Belle on the third day of the last of his clinics I attended, this time with one of my daughters as a rider. He paused a few seconds, his gaze shifting from the mare to the audience as he unbuckled the chinstrap on his helmet, then repeated, "That's hot."

He did not mean the phrase in the sense made famous by Paris Hilton.

We had already seen Morris teach three times before Audrey rode with him. We all knew what to expect. Neither fools nor inattention would be suffered gladly.

For Audrey, the decision to attend was easy. In part because it was an honor. This clinic, in particular, was one you couldn't just sign up for. And in part because of the challenge. I'm sure she was nervous, but she was just as eager to prove herself. I debated whether I ought to attend, by which I really mean I wondered whether I'd be able to sit through it if things went poorly. People tell me I'm stoic, but I've got my limits.

In reality, of course, there was never a question. I would go.

There wasn't any doubt who was in charge at a George Morris clinic. "I talk. You don't talk," he told the audience when folks failed to settle down as things got underway on the second day. "Don't tell me you 'agree' with me," he responded to more than one rider who acknowledged his comments. "To say that you 'agree' with me implies that you might disagree."

He reserved most of his venom, however, for the parents in the room, together with schools and colleges. We bore the responsibility for today's "soft culture," one sadly bereft of discipline, concentration, and the word "no." The world we had created was too afraid of leaving its comfort zone, too focused on bling, VIP tables, and hoopla. "In my day, if you had it, you did not show it. I don't care about the VIP table. I do care about shoulder-in."

Our responsibility for the decline of America must have been by proxy, however, because the clinic participants, Audrey included, were generally at the top of their games. The "thaaaat's it"s and the "very good"s well outnumbered the reprimands to pay attention or to stop riding one's horse like a "constipated cat."

"It's not magic," Morris told us. "It's called well over seventy years of riding horses." And: "The repetition gives you the habit." "Have the courage to make mistakes. Mistakes teach us." "Good teachers don't teach in the comfort zone. They teach just out of it."

I'll have some things to say about the harsher edges of his teaching techniques, which I think are often counterproductive, a bit later in these pages. But I can't deny an affinity for aspects of Morris's old-school mentality. I'm deeply skeptical of those who proclaim their expertise too loudly. I do not much care for hoopla or bling, and I prefer to avoid the VIP table if I can. The horse world, like the world more generally, often strikes me as too focused on image and appearance. Give me the ones who have it but do not show it.

Somewhere in the midst of the second day, as he was bemoaning the influence of money in the sport, Morris offered up this: "Luckily you can't buy a seat. You have to earn a seat. You can't buy legs, you have to earn legs. You can't buy feel, you have to work. You can't buy the things that count. Thank God."

I hoped that was right. Because there was a lot we couldn't buy. There were no fancy equitation horses for our girls, and no trips to the Winter Equestrian Festival in Wellington, Florida (where thousands of well-heeled hunter/jumper riders migrate each year), or indoor shows. For us it was nothing more than a handful of shows each year and opportunities like the Emerging Athletes Program. What my daughters had, and have, is grit, and intelligence, and a work ethic like you wouldn't believe. The things you can't buy.

That, and in Audrey's case at this clinic, a wonderful, hot horse.

Audrey was the only one in her group of seven clinic riders who was not a professional. She more than held her own, and Morris had plenty of nice things to say about her riding over the course of the weekend. For my money, the best came during the trip she rode right after Morris got off Belle, right after he searched for a good ten seconds to say something other than, "That's hot."

"I'll tell ya, she and this horse click. This is a very hot, strong...she rides this horse very well."

You can't buy that either. You have to earn it. She did. ❀

# 12

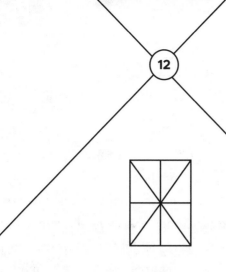

K's death marked a transition point for Ada. In an obvious sense it was abrupt. One day she had a horse, the next day she didn't. But in another it was the culmination of a long, difficult period.

Compatibility's a funny thing. You ever have two friends who couldn't stand each other? It's weird. You get along well with each of them. But whatever it is that makes your relationships with them work doesn't translate between them. People with lots in common can rub each other the wrong way while people with nothing in common can speak for hours. Sometimes the desire to make a connection gets in the way. Maybe you find yourself riding in an elevator with Bob Dylan. Maybe you're looking to ask your crush to go to prom. What you get is tongue-tied. Human relationships are hard to predict.

The same seems true with animals. Dogs walking down two sides of the street might ignore each other, or they might immediately want to fight or play. They've seen each other for only a few seconds and yet, somehow, they've formed a strong impression. I've seen horses who couldn't be let near one another, and other situations where they become deeply attached.

No surprise, then, that relationships between humans and horses exhibit the same quirks. It's not hard to find stories about horses that go well with one rider but not others of equal skill. It's hard to say why, and it's hard to predict, but it's certainly true. What seems good in theory doesn't always work out so well in practice. I don't have enough knowledge of riding to offer developed thoughts about why one rider's talents might not mesh so well with a specific horse. But I suspect that any story that any of us could tell would be incomplete.

One thing's for sure. Whether it's humans, animals, or a combination of the two, once a relationship starts off down a certain path it's difficult to put it on a different one. First impressions are huge.

Ada's relationship with K got off to a bad start, and try as she might to form the necessary connection, they were never able to reach anything approaching the compatibility she had with Cash. In a sport where little things often have huge effects, that's a devastating place to be.

Their last show together followed the same basic script as their first. It leads a parent to do funny things. I'd watch each round from a different spot, hoping to find the lucky one, always hoping to distance myself from another spectator who either wasn't catching on to or was just ignoring the fact that I didn't want company just then. I stood along the rail. I stood under a tree attempting to summon the spirit of Cash to guide them flawlessly around the ring. I stood on a hill. I videoed. I didn't video. The only constants were the knots in my stomach and the fact that none of it worked. There's nothing fun at all about seeing someone who not so long ago entered the ring with all the confidence in the world suddenly struggling to find a foothold, especially when that someone is your child.

Ada's last round at that show came on a different horse. It wasn't a perfect round, but it was clean, and pretty good given the way the day had gone. The underlying talent, the feel that Chris Kappler had identified, remained. It just never meshed with K. It somehow clashed, instead.

There was another problem: somewhere in amongst all the injuries and struggles and disappointments, the trip to the barn had lost its magic.

That was, I'll admit, disorienting. In fact, it was worse than disorienting. Things with K had gone about as poorly as they could have. We'd done the best we could, always taking the next step that seemed like the right one. But still I would wonder. *What was the red flag I missed? What should we have done differently? What now? Do we push through it, or take a different approach? Is this, ultimately, my screwup? Or a screwup that I could have prevented?* I sacrificed more than a few hours of sleep to these questions.

It's a tricky subject to raise. People tend to take it as a cue to provide reassurance. "You're a great dad," I've seen people on social media say to others whose parenting skills they're in no real position to assess. They certainly don't respond by agreeing, "Yeah, you probably did wander off the right path back a ways." Which, to be fair, would be an assessment best left to close friends and family, anyway.

All of that's fine, though I'm not terribly interested in reassurance. Whatever impressions to the contrary you might be inclined to take from this book, I've got a strong enough self-conception to admit to and try to grapple with my mistakes without facing any sort of existential crisis.

I've had a pretty successful career. I'm aware enough of the limits of self-awareness to at least try to avoid imagining that I'm especially self-aware. (The people who tell you they're self-aware? Usually, they're the people who most clearly are not.) People seem to value my instincts and judgment. Part of that stems from my willingness to assess my decisions, and part from my recognition of what I take to be the basic fact that none of us really knows what we are doing. It's good to have a sense of your limits, and of the limits of your knowledge. It's denial and doubling down that cause the most trouble. Seems to me it's the people unwilling to admit the possibility they may have made a mistake who are carrying around the most insecurities. Show me a person who won't admit fault and I'll show you a person who can't be trusted.

Over the years I've come to appreciate just how much of a difference luck can make. Grit and talent matter, but so does being in the right place at the right time. "You pays yer money and you takes yer chances," as the saying has it. And then? There's another saying for what comes next: "You win some, you lose some." We can plot and plan and agonize all we want. But some things are beyond our ability to control.

In the wake of all this, Ada made a decision. She wanted to try dressage. It seemed like an easy enough thing to make happen. She was a dedicated, experienced, and talented rider. Surely there would be an instructor eager to take her on.

It turned out that while there were plenty of dressage instructors around, few of them were located in a convenient place. A barn near Millcreek was in a transitional period. Ada had one lesson with an instructor who thought she'd have access to a horse that Ada would be able to ride, and then that horse became unavailable. Experience and talent in one discipline doesn't automatically open doors in another, particularly when you don't have a horse.

What seemed like it would be easy was not. This would take a while. ✺

— 13 —

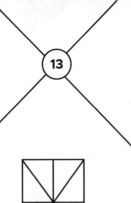

L ike most horse parents without their own background in the horse world— indeed, like most parents whose children take up an activity they're not familiar with—I have to take a lot of what I encounter on faith. Even after well over a decade of fairly intense involvement, my first impression of a horse tends not to be "good mover" or "nice bascule" or "hangs his legs" or the million other things that I've come to learn about. It tends instead to be something more basic. Like, "Look! A horse!" I'm not that good at identifying specific horses, even when I've seen them many times before. My eye just isn't that developed. Many of their obviously distinguishing features don't resonate with me.

CHAPTER 13

I've missed a lot from my spot in the corner of the ring, and not because I've had an obstructed view. It's that there's so much nuance. So many small things that have such a big effect.

The fact that I can't see it doesn't mean that it doesn't exist, of course. That's where a trainer comes in.

Of course, to have a trainer you've got to find a trainer, and that, too, can be a difficult thing. We parents find trainers by relying on word of mouth and various sorts of proxies, same as we do whenever we look for someone to do a job that we don't have the expertise to do. *Who has a good reputation? Do I know someone who says good things about this person? Who has a track record of results? Does this feel right?*

And it *should* feel right. Horse and rider training, like lawyering, is ultimately a service profession. The most knowledgeable horse person in the world will not be a good trainer if she cannot effectively communicate her knowledge to others, or if she doesn't really enjoy teaching and does it only to support her riding career. It's important to remember that the rider-horse connection isn't the only one on display during a riding lesson. There's also the connection between the trainer and the rider.

And here we've stumbled onto a piece of the puzzle that I can very much relate to and assess—and that I've mentioned before.

As a lawyer I figured out quickly that simply *telling* my clients that they should trust me because of the diploma that I never quite got around to putting on my wall was the strategy of the insecure professional. Better to *show* them that they should trust me by letting them see that I understand and appreciate where their questions and concerns are coming from and explaining—patiently and as many times as necessary—why it makes sense to do things the way I advise.

Effective teaching—or so it seems to me as someone who spends a lot of time at the front of a classroom—requires something similar.

I'll concede that the teaching I do doesn't perfectly parallel what a trainer of riders and horses does. I'm often standing in front of sixty or seventy people at once, and even my smallest classes are well beyond the size of the largest group lessons I've seen. I am not able to give the sort of focused, individualized feedback that a riding instructor consistently provides.

But in a core sense the tasks are the same. The teacher, hopefully, has knowledge that the student does not. The job is to pass that knowledge along to the student so that the student understands it and can put it to effective use.

Doing this well isn't just about speaking clearly. It requires knowing one's audience. And—this may be the hardest part—knowing oneself. Being able to communicate effectively to students requires putting yourself in their position. Which in turn requires—and this I've mentioned before, too—remembering how much you once didn't know. And since those who become teachers tend to be those who were very good students, the need may run even deeper than that, because they have to imagine a version of themselves that had a different aptitude or interest level. It's a really hard thing to get right.

Couple this with the fact that every student—every rider—is different. Each has different strengths and weaknesses. Some take in information very well when it's delivered one way and not so well when it comes in another form. Some have thick skins, others do better with a softer touch. The existence of these differences can be a really hard thing to grasp on a basic intellectual level, and even harder to put into practice as a teacher. Each of us can see the world only through our own eyes, and each of us tends to imagine that everyone else is like we are. It seems relatively easy for the skilled horseperson to understand that every horse is different, that some are sensitive while others need tough love and so on. Only the very best consistently recognize and are able to act on the insight that the same is true of our fellow humans. Too many seem to fall into the trap of thinking that one size fits all.

We all have our strengths and weaknesses, of course, and I'm not making any claims to having found the key that unlocks every student's understanding. A fellow named Karl Llewellyn, one of the brightest legal stars that ever burned, routinely cautioned incoming students that each of their professors would be "lopsided." This lopsidedness was, Llewellyn continued, both a bug and a feature. "We feel it well that you should be exposed to a series of lopsided men, to the end that you learn from each his virtues and see in each his defects. For you the balance, for you the rounding out, for you the building of a legal equipment better than that of any one of us." It's the student's job to take that lopsided information and turn it into a balanced whole.

There are two things worth highlighting here. The first is that it's unfortunate that exposure to different trainers and different disciplines isn't more of a routine thing. Every pair of eyes sees different things. Trainers, like law professors, are lopsided, and any rider can benefit from input provided from multiple sources. A clinic with a different instructor can help, but the longest of those, such as the sessions of the EAP my daughters participated in, provides only a few days of new perspective.

The second is that there's a final piece of the puzzle. For real learning to take place the student has to do her job, too. I once heard George Morris talking about some folks who had worked for him early in their careers and who had gone on to become prominent trainers in their own right. I don't recall the specifics of the discussion beyond the punch line: "It's what I didn't teach them that they learned." It was the time *outside* the lessons when they were experimenting with and extending what they had learned *in* the lessons where they truly gained the knowledge that set them apart. Ada learned things in a basic sense when she and I attended the Frank Madden clinic together, and then learned them more deeply on those nights where she worked through the exercises on her own.

It's a complicated business, teaching and learning. My own attempts at riding have taught me that watching lesson after lesson provided me with a sense of the basics, but also that what I learned from watching was a far cry from what my daughters learned by doing. I haven't really learned all that much about riding. But I have learned a lot about teaching.

There are all sorts of ways in which every horse farm is the same. There's a barn, an outdoor ring, and an indoor (or at least covered) ring. There are paddocks for turnout and there's a place where the manure gets stored before it's spread or hauled away. Inside the barn there will be stalls situated on an aisle, a tack room, and a familiar set of tools and implements. There's a place where the hay is kept and a place where the feed is stored. Usually there will be a dog or two wandering around. Always there will be at least one cat, though the demands of mice patrol often require more. (There's a very good chance that one of the cats will have just showed up one day and never left.) There will be spots where the barn regulars will gather before and after riding. Sometimes they'll talk about life outside the barn, but usually the focus is on horses. Especially when the weather is nice, there's a good chance that a bottle of wine will appear.

At the same time, every barn is different. Some are larger and some are smaller, of course, and each has its own quirks of configuration. Every barn has its own distinct smell, some of which are more powerful and distinctive than others, but all of which are apt to linger in clothes and hair. Some of the differences are of the sort that suggest something significant about the place. Wealth reveals itself in the flooring, the type of wood used for the stalls, the fanciness of the fixtures, the luxuriousness of the viewing area. And, of course, in the horses. All of it contributes in ways perceptible and imperceptible, to a barn's atmosphere.

But the main source of difference is a product of the humans inside the barn, and the tone is set at the top. Sometimes the barn owner and the head trainer are the same person and sometimes they're not. But whether they're one person or two, everything flows from them. Some of this is apparent to the visitor. How tidy is the place overall? What sorts of things are tucked away on ledges or other out-of-the-way places and just how dusty are they? Some of it can take a while to figure out. You can get a sense of a barn's vibe from a visit, but there's always a danger that it will be a mirage. One of the most toxic people I ever worked with was extraordinarily good at seeming congenial and easygoing during casual interactions. It took time and exposure for the good first impression to dissipate. It can be that way with a barn. Something about human nature makes most people inclined to say good things to a prospective lessoner or boarder even when they've just spent the preceding twenty minutes complaining to a barn mate.

It's become clear to me over the years that being a trainer is a uniquely difficult job. There are the obvious parts related to teaching that I've discussed in various ways on previous pages. But to understand the difficulty of teaching is just to scratch the surface. The trainer is usually running her own business, which undoubtedly brings with it all sorts of details and administrative headaches that a person drawn to the barn would prefer to leave behind. She's also caring for a barn full of horses and managing a staff and thinking about the logistics of getting to the next show. And she's in the sort of business that involves an unusually close relationship with her customers. If they're boarders she sees them most every day.

Whether they're boarders or not they'll have an unending string of questions. *How should I handle this? Where can I find that? My horse feels like he's moving a little funny, could you come take a quick look at him?*

The people who can do all those things well are rare. And we haven't even talked about what might be the hardest part. Clients are rarely just casually invested in what goes on at the barn. Horses are their passion. They have goals and dreams and they're looking for expert advice on how to achieve them. They have days when things go well and days when things go poorly. There will be tears, and those tears won't always be the result of something that happened at the barn. The trainer has to be able to deal with all of this.

For better or worse the trainer is the focal point of her barn, whatever its size or shape, or the discipline it serves. She sets the tone and provides the example. Young riders, in particular, look up to her, take their cues from her, and treat her every word as gospel. To an extent that she may sometimes fail to appreciate, she is a large source of their self-conception. Her critical comments can cut deeply. Whether young riders believe in themselves or not often turns on whether they think she believes in them. Indeed, whether they are able to make their best effort to have their dreams come true depends on her. It's an enormous responsibility.

Over the years I've seen many lists of tips on how to be a better riding student. They often get widely shared on social media, usually by trainers, and for the most part they seem to contain good advice. What I've never seen is a list of tips on how to be a better trainer—or how to recognize a good one. Having long contemplated the subject myself, I solicited input from a range of people, both trainers and riders, and came away with some good suggestions. If you're a parent or a rider, these are things to look for. If you're a trainer, they're things to take to heart. For the most part, they generalize into other youth sports and beyond.

_____*Remember that nobody makes mistakes on purpose.* Running coach David Roche says, "Throw 100 eggs at a wall, and a few might not break. If a philosophy forms around the approach of those unbreakable eggs, we may think that the secret is going full speed into a wall. That's why the first thing I look for when thinking about training is whether there are graveyards of shattered shells lying around." Too many trainers throw eggs at walls and conclude that it was only the ones that didn't break that have what it takes to be successful riders. It's a large and important topic, and I'm going to return to it in a few pages. For now I'll just note that this is a point that holds especially for trainers working with riders in the early stages. Some people respond well to being driven hard, just as some people signed up for clinics with George Morris knowing what they were in for. Those are different situations.

Harsh methods can also be counterproductive for trainers if they drive clients away. Dressage trainer Jeremy Steinberg has written some perceptive pieces on this subject and other parts of the equine industry over the years. In an essay on abrasive approaches to instruction that appeared in *The Chronicle of the Horse,* he put it this way: "It makes absolutely no sense to make fun of, put down, shame or humiliate not just the hand that feeds us, but the people who are the patrons to the art we love." The approach he decries is one that can cause an awful lot of unnecessary collateral damage. Better to recall that students are almost always doing the best they can. As one trainer put it, she strives "never to make them feel like a victim in their lesson. I always follow a correction with an explanation."

_____*Good trainers don't gossip, especially about their own clients.* One of the things that was drilled into me from the beginning of my legal career was the importance of keeping client confidences. That has always made intuitive sense to me. In order for me to be able to do my best work for you, you need to be able to have complete trust in me. If I'm telling other people your secrets (and it's best for me to assume you want me to treat everything as a secret) or saying bad things about you behind your back, you'll lose trust in me quickly. And rightly so. It's a breach of one of the most fundamental professional obligations.

Now imagine you're my trainer. First, imagine that I hear you talking about another client when she's not around. You're criticizing some mistake she's made while riding, griping about some request she made of you, or disclosing something that she likely understood herself to be telling you in confidence. I can't help in that situation but imagine that I'll be the one under discussion when I'm not around. That's going to undermine my confidence in you. I'll be less likely to tell you things or ask you things—especially the sorts of things I'd prefer not to have everyone else know.

And, of course, if (when) you do end up saying things about me, it's likely to get back to me. And depending on what you say, my confidence could easily be undermined. You're the one who's supposed to be building my confidence, and instead you're tearing it down, because now I've got to walk around the barn knowing that everyone else has heard your opinion of my riding. With Junior riders in particular, who are at a naturally difficult time in their lives as it is, this can make for a toxic environment. What should be a refuge from the troubles of everyday life can become anything but.

The better approach is the lawyer's, and also the parent's. When I was practicing law, I tried to make it clear to my clients that there were two distinct roles I played. One required me to be perfectly straight with them when it was just us. The other required that I have their back when it came to dealing with the rest of the world. The same with my kids—at least when I was doing it right. Critique is a private affair and has no place elsewhere, whether it comes to the world at large or simply one sister versus another. It's Leadership 101. Praise in public, criticize behind closed doors. It's both intuitive and something that we all struggle with.

_____*No favorites.* Here's another lesson from parenting that applies just as well to trainers. I'm fairly certain there have been times when each one of our daughters has felt we've singled her out for poor treatment. That's certainly never been the goal, and I think we've done a fair job of treating them all equally, all things considered. We certainly tried. But equality is one of those concepts without an agreed-upon definition, and what seems like equitable treatment to one will often not seem that way to another. The risk of creating that sort of perception was always on our minds. The gymnast Kathy Johnson Clarke once Tweeted this, which gets it exactly right, for parents and trainers alike: "Note to coaches. Throughout your career you will have MANY teams. MANY athletes. Please remember that each ONE of those MANY athletes has only ONE career. ONE pass at that journey, dream, ultimate goal, or chance of a lifetime. Your actions [and] decisions matter."

There's a corollary to the No Favorites Rule, which involves not letting people get away with things. It's remarkably easy for people to perceive their situation as more compelling than everyone else's, and to conclude that they're entitled to an exception. And it's easy for those responsible for setting the tone to give in to that. I've been there as a parent, and I was often there during the period when I served as a law school administrator. Everyone wants the squeaky wheel to stop squeaking, and sometimes it seems easier to give in than to provoke a confrontation. Somebody's always late for lessons, or doesn't always do a thorough job cleaning up and putting things away, and usually someone else will step up. But that can be counterproductive. Sometimes a confrontation is necessary.

_____ *Honesty.* I'm happy to report that we've never once had a concern about whether our trainers were dealing with us in an ethical manner. But the equestrian world is filled with ethically challenged conduct. The incentives to engage in it are real, whether doing so means engaging in shady behavior at a show, marking up the cost of services provided by others, influencing the way a sale takes place, or providing a young rider and her parents with an unrealistically optimistic assessment of just how far she might be able to advance in the sport. Here, too, Jeremy Steinberg offers a pointed and appropriate critique of his fellow trainers: "I think we do more harm than good telling kids their horses are not good enough to take them to the levels to which they aspire." Why? Partly because it's often advice that's strongly influenced by the trainer's interest in sale commissions. Partly because it's not the approach most conducive to getting a rider to develop her talent to the greatest degree. The development of high-level skills, he contends, does not always require a high-level horse. The upshot for trainers is this: What might be easy enough for you to justify in the short term can have long-term repercussions.

_____ *Good trainers have a plan.* When a young rider with big dreams walks through a trainer's door, what should they hear? The trainer's incentives all point toward saying, "We can make that happen." Doubly so if the trainer is young and out to build a reputation. That's understandable. I certainly wasn't about to turn away business as a young lawyer just because it might have been a bit beyond my experience level at the time. But then I had a couple hundred senior colleagues I could lean on whenever I found myself in uncomfortably deep water.

What I'd look for as a parent is a clearly communicated, realistic plan, projecting out however many years necessary into the future, and attempting to account for the anticipated ways that things might go well or might go poorly. In most situations, young athletes and their parents don't have any idea how negotiating the levels of the equestrian world (or those of any sport) works, so it's on the trainer or coach to spell out what the path might look like and, among other things, how much it is likely to cost. In the horse world, especially, it's possible, and indeed even likely, that a family may quickly realize that the "big dreams" are simply beyond their means.

Ideally everyone will also understand that a given trainer may not be the one to make those dreams come true. A good coach may be able to accompany a rider on only a portion of the journey, and there may be a point where she needs to be handed off to someone with the right sort of experience for a different discipline or stage of development. Bernadette recognized this. Her reaction when I told her the girls were moving to Hidden View to ride with Charles was to emphasize her role in getting them started. Charles and the others at Hidden View were likewise gracious as Ada and Audrey took their next steps. None of that was foreordained. And so maybe the right message is that there are skills a rider (or any athlete) needs to develop given the level she's at, that the priority should be to develop her talent to the greatest extent, and that only then will it become appropriate to talk about bigger goals.

_Acceptance of feedback._ We'd all like to imagine that we're doing a great job all the time. I never teach a class thinking that I'm going to do a subpar job of conveying the material, and frankly it always comes as a little bit of a surprise when something that's perfectly clear to me—and that I would have thought I had just explained in a perfectly clear manner—didn't come across so clearly to all of my students. That's not always on the teacher, of course. But sometimes it is. We've all got weaknesses and blind spots. A defensive reaction is natural, but it's best avoided. An inability to admit weakness is just an admission of a different sort of weakness. I've won a teaching award, but I still take a couple deep breaths before I open the packet of teaching evaluations I get at the end of each semester. I might find some pointed critique, and that wouldn't be fun. But it can also help me to see a way in which I have fallen short.

A trainer's clients, and the parents of her clients, may include people who have been quite successful in their lives in various ways. They may also be flawed and limited people, inclined to imagine they know more than they do. They might be missing something, or they might simply be wrong. We seem to be living through an epidemic of parental mis-behavior in youth sports, and I'm certainly not suggesting that they're always right. But they'll at least sometimes have useful feedback, and the fact that they're missing something might just mean that a trainer didn't make that thing as clear as she thought she did. Not all feedback is good feedback. But a lot of it is, even when it's not fun to hear.

*Respect for clients' time and money.* As a lawyer in practice, I had to account for my time in six-minute increments, and I had to be prepared to explain myself further if what I had written in the bills didn't satisfy my clients. I didn't always like it, but I understood it was part of the job, and that part of being successful at the job meant doing it well. It seemed like the right thing to do anyway, and certainly appealed to the farm kid conditioned to avoid waste.

Like the practice of law, training and coaching horses and riders is a service business. Clients pay for time and attention. A trainer should respect that, by (for example) being on time and staying off her phone during lessons. She should understand that her clients, and her clients' parents, have lives and expenses outside the barn. This is not to suggest that coaches should be available at all times, but they should strive to respond promptly to every text and email. Ideally, they'll have a list of charges for various kinds of services and will only provide those services in situations where they have been approved or are absolutely necessary. They shouldn't get defensive when asked to justify a bill or a charge.

_____ *Always learning.* As I've already discussed, it seems to be a universal feature of human knowledge that the more someone learns about a topic, the more the person comes to understand just how much she doesn't know and to appreciate just how complex even the basics truly are. There's always more to learn, both about a topic and how to convey it to others. I'm in my nineteenth year of being a professor. Each time I return to material I've taught many times before, I appreciate it in a different way and see connections I haven't seen before. Each time I re-read something I first encountered early in my career and thought I understood, I realize I have grasped only a portion. Those who tell you they've learned everything there is to know about a topic are really just telling you they've reached the limits of their imagination and aren't able to ask better questions. A coach or teacher who feels like she's stopped learning has likely lost her passion, and it might be time for her to consider stepping away.

This list of qualities when searching for a trainer or coach for oneself or one's child is undoubtedly incomplete. It is a process that requires the exercise of good judgment, which is not a quality that everyone develops to the same degree. Some seem never to develop it at all. My list may simply reduce to the fact that a trainer should "be a decent human being who follows the Golden Rule." Most people do. But it's never everyone.

A person hears things at horse shows. Perhaps especially if that person looks like a dad who isn't quite sure of what he's doing or where he's supposed to be. It's almost like being invisible, I've found. Because, believe me, I've heard things. Parents saying things; judges saying things. One time I heard the mother of a well-known rider attempt to carry on a conversation with a judge *while her child was riding in a hunter class being judged by that judge.* A pretty obvious ethical violation on both ends.

Among the many things I've heard, the thing I've probably heard more than any of the other things is yelling. I'm using the word "yelling" here in a fairly broad way. The raised voice kind, for sure. But also the more insidious kind. The kind of comment that might not require a raised voice, though it can certainly involve one, but that's clearly designed to cut uncomfortably close to the psychological bone. The kind that demoralizes.

Once at a show I was just sitting there minding my own business—because let me be clear that I don't seek this stuff out so much as find a place to sit and wait for it to appear—when I found myself part of the audience to a conversation between a trainer and one of her students. The student had clearly just had a tough round, and the trainer was trying to build her back up. Saying nice things, being encouraging, and so on.

But then the girl started crying. Not little tears, but a full-on, shoulders-heaving cry.

The part I'll never forget is that the trainer reacted to this by saying something along the lines of, "Are you crying because you can't believe I'm being nice to you for once?" And then proceeded to colorfully outline how she *could* respond through yelling if that was what the girl preferred.

As it happened it seemed like a nice moment. But as I thought more about all that likely led up to it, I was less sure. Don't get me wrong here. I'm not advocating in favor of participation trophies, lowered expectations, and rainbows over every horse show. Horses are large and potentially dangerous, and students need to understand that they've got to be attentive to what they're doing at all times. There's a place for high standards and firm expectations. There's a place for the raised voice.

It's a fine line that separates "old school" from "gratuitously cruel," and "high standards" from "abuse." Or perhaps more accurately, a hazy one. I grew up in a time and place that valorized coaching behavior that's hardly extinct but increasingly suspect. I was on some very good high school teams without having coaches who fit that mold, but it was the screamers from neighboring towns who tended to be regarded as the best at their jobs. For a time I accepted that. I've since modified my views.

This much seems clear: yelling's effectiveness can be illusory, and its users are likely to be fooled into thinking it's a more effective tool than it is. Here I'm drawing on an insight from the Nobel Prize-winning psychologist Daniel Kahneman, who developed it when asked to consult on a project for training pilots. A trainer, whether of pilots, riders, or something else, is most likely to yell after a student has done something abnormally poorly. Which means, because it was abnormal, that the student will almost certainly do it better the next time. By the same token, a trainer is most likely to give praise after a student has done something abnormally well. Which means the student will almost certainly do it less well the next time.

The punch line is that all of that would be true without either the yelling or the praise. A student who does abnormally poorly on try Number One is very likely to do better on try Number Two, even if the trainer isn't paying attention at all. A student who does abnormally well on try Number One is very likely to do worse on try Number Two, even though the trainer has been giving her full attention and feedback. It's simply the law of averages in action. But it's very likely to give the trainer a false sense that the yelling worked ("It got better!") while the praise did not ("It got worse!").

An example might help. Imagine you are an okay-but-not-great dart player trying to hit the bullseye. Suppose that you'll hit the bullseye once in every twenty throws and miss the board entirely just as often. The remaining eighteen throws will end up somewhere in between.

You throw a dart and miss the board. Whether I yell at you or not, your next throw is almost certain to be better. Yet if I've yelled at you, I'm likely to imagine that your next throw was better *because* I yelled at you.

That's an illusion.

Then you throw a dart and hit the bullseye. Here, your next throw is likely to be worse no matter what. But if I've praised you for your bullseye, I'll conclude that my praise didn't work because you didn't hit two in a row. Which is also, though less obviously, false.

There's much, much more that could be said about this. Humans are complex enough by themselves, and in the equestrian world we're talking about situations where there's another creature with a mind of its own involved. My point for now is simply that I'm uneasy with the need for and effectiveness of some of what I have heard as I've made my way around the horse show world. Raised voices are sometimes necessary—hurtful comments only rarely so. I can't draw a precise line between them, but as a first cut I'd ask whether they're delivered from a place of empathy or not. There's a difference between a tough exterior that masks a big heart and one that does not. Either way, while high expectations are great, they rarely require a sharp edge. I've spent lots of time around trainers who are vastly more positive than negative, and I've seen that it works. A lot of the rest of it just seems like unnecessary cruelty. ✺

—14—

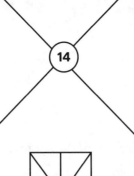

A show day is always a big day. In the early years it was a big and rare enough day that bedtime always took a little longer. It's hard to fall asleep when tomorrow ranks right up there with Christmas. Sleep came more easily in the later years, but the thrill of competition never went away. Most days you're in familiar surroundings, riding the same jumps in the same ring, working to improve, the inevitable bad day seeming to be just part of the cost of getting better. Most days you are simply riding against yourself. On a show day you're riding against others, in front of an audience, and usually in a relatively unfamiliar location. The competitors are typically a mix of the familiar and the unknown,

CHAPTER 14

sometimes from distant parts of the country. When you don't get the chance to show often, this is always a big deal. Shows are the dates you circle on the calendar, the goals you work toward. Shows are often where memories get made.

Every now and then there's the chance to ride against someone who's developed a reputation. It doesn't have to be a big reputation for that to seem like a big deal. Once, in the schooling show days, a particular young woman found herself farther down the placings than she liked, and her sportsmanship coming out of the ring was, shall we say, not ideal. "She's used to winning everything," I overheard one spectator say to another after one of these incidents. (On this day she was not winning everything. The trophies that she thought herself entitled to came home with us instead.)

Sometimes it does end up being a rider with a big reputation. Once, in Kentucky, Audrey and Alex rode in a class that included essentially a who's who of prominent Junior riders. Both Ada and Audrey have had their moments of success against people who have gone on to do notable things.

Show days usually start early and end late. They feature bursts of tension and excitement surrounded by hours that can easily become tedious. The food options are often limited, and the perennial challenge for a parent is to convince your child to actually eat something so she's not running completely on empty when she rides into the ring. Her nerves, of course, are usually providing her with the opposite message. Experience teaches you to try to focus your efforts early, before the nerves are pronounced and while there's still time to digest. "Hangry" does not make for the best performance.

The day will be shaped by what takes place in the ring. Winning the right sort of ribbon helps a lot, but it's of course not the only ingredient. Much can depend on what happens during the downtime. The right group of companions makes all the difference. Some show days pass uneventfully and quickly fall out of memory. Others quickly take on their own significance. It might've been a specific thing that happened. *Remember the first time we saw that pony that could jump the moon?* Or it might've been more atmospheric. *There we all were, sitting on a hill above the ring on a beautiful summer evening, taking in the last classes of the day and talking about nothing in particular.*

Occasionally the conversation takes on some of the sport's bigger questions. The world of horses, perhaps as much as any subculture, reflects the full range of pathologies afflicting contemporary American society. *Are the sport's governing bodies too concerned about the elite and not enough about their members more generally? Is everyone too focused on the short term—riders on ribbons and awards, trainers on doing what brings the most recognition, show managers on making money—to the long-term detriment of quality in the sport? Why are so few of the best horses bred in the United States? What should be done about all the unqualified and/or unethical trainers out there? Why is judging so problematic? Why is there so much cheating and why doesn't anyone seem to take it seriously? Why isn't there more diversity? What's the appropriate response to the sexual harassment and abuse of authority that has long been prevalent?*

As in society, there's general agreement that there are real problems, that the system is broken, that something needs to be done. As in society, there is nothing close to general agreement about how to fix these problems or even about whether some of them are problems at all. As in society, social media brings out the worst side in nearly everyone. Online exchanges generate lots of heat and very little light. Change will inevitably come, but it might end up happening because the system has collapsed under its own weight rather than because it has productively changed from within.

Underlying most of these controversies is this undeniable fact: There are massive wealth disparities among participants in the sport. It's true at every level. I grew up in modest enough circumstances that any sort of serious riding, even at the most basic level, would have been out of the question. There was no money to devote to any kind of private instruction in anything. No doubt there are plenty of kids who can get no closer to riding than what they can find in a book or TV series. Even at the entry level, it's expensive.

And then, always, at every level, there is someone with more. The improbable trajectory of my life has led my path to cross those of literal billionaires on several occasions, and the horse world is one of the places it's happened. It's no surprise that many of the sport's top riders have names you've heard: Gates, Bloomberg, Springsteen. Near-infinite resources may not be necessary to success, but it's hard to argue with the idea that they help an awful lot.

So, I recognize that it was a privilege for my daughters to have been able to participate at all and to have shown as much as they were able to. The concept of "haves" and "have nots" in the equestrian world is very much a relative one, because nearly everyone involved is a product of some form of privilege or other. My daughters understand that they have been extraordinarily fortunate to get to do even as much as they have. At the same time, it's impossible to look around and not feel somewhat envious of those able to do more.

There are pressures that a rider of comparatively modest means feels more acutely than her wealthier counterparts. Consider Audrey's round in the downpour at the Great Lakes Equestrian Festival. Several of her fellow competitors simply scratched that class. It was one class at one show and they went to many, therefore it was no big deal. Certainly nothing worth getting wet for. They had probably shown the week before, and they'd likely be there the week after. A missed class or a bad round is not a big deal when you're able to look at it from the perspective of, "There will be others."

It's different, though, when a show is one of the handful you'll get to do over the course of the year. Scratch the class, or have a tough round, and you've put yourself in a tough spot. Hunter/jumper competitions are unforgiving. No matter how perfect the rest of a round might be, a single mistake—just one dropped rail, no matter how fluky, or just one distance that's not quite right—is fatal. You won't win the class, and you might not even place, and there's no way to recover from it. You could still compete for the championship, but the battle is uphill. That alone creates pressure. That pressure is magnified when you go into the ring knowing you won't have the chance to do it again for weeks or months.

A natural response to all of this is to say that it shouldn't be about placings and championships, that the reward is in the experience and in the resulting improvement. And, of course, there's truth to that. There's *lots* of truth to that. But it's not the entire truth, and it's the rare competitor who enters the ring truly not caring how it goes and truly indifferent to placing. Placings and championships are a way to measure one's advancement. I once saw a rider upset with her placing throw a ribbon in the trash. Bad form, no doubt. But I understand, and to a degree even admire, the sentiment.

People often resist the role that good fortune plays in equestrian sports. "You still have to be able to ride 'em," as the saying goes. And that's true, but it's not as compelling a point as it's often thought to be. No doubt a talented rider on a good horse will consistently beat a considerably less-talented rider on a great horse. But that's rarely the matchup. The range of the talent level in a given class narrows as one moves up the ranks. It's not that there aren't still more- and less-talented riders as the fences get bigger, but that the difference in raw talent between the strongest and weakest riders in a class gets smaller. When everyone is evenly matched, or close enough to it, small enhancements can have significant effects. In the horse world it can be a difference in resources that provides one rider with access to enhancements unavailable to another. One rider has more and fancier horses, gets the sort of training that enables her to make small but significant refinements to her technique, shows often enough not to have to worry about whether any given class goes well or poorly. Take two riders of equivalent talent and drive at age sixteen and give one of them access to a pool of top horses, the best training available, and the opportunity to show every weekend, while the other gets one horse, a trainer with no national reputation, and the ability to show a handful of times a year. Ninety-nine times out of a hundred the first rider will beat the second at age eighteen.

So far as I can tell, nobody in the horse world denies the basic truth of what I've just said. It applies in other sports, too. The common reaction seems to be a combination of pointing out that life's not fair (so get used to it), that's how it's always been, and that one-rider-in-a-hundred proves that it's possible for the rider without resources to succeed. It's a classic rhetorical move by those who have advantages and want to preserve them. "Sure, we get to take a well-traveled road to the top of the mountain while others have to climb a steep and unforgiving slope with no clearly marked path. But some of them make it, and that proves that everything is perfectly fair. You just have to want it badly enough."

Every kid would like a pony, but not every kid will be able to get one. That's how the world works. But to focus on the unfairness of life and to suggest that inequalities in equestrian sports are just another manifestation of how things are is to miss an important point. Fairness unquestionably is a core component of legitimate athletic competition. It's not truly competition if the winner is mostly determined in advance. Events with insufficiently level playing fields might better be called exhibitions than competitions. At some point the advantages are so thoroughly embedded that the label "sport" is no longer appropriate.

It's notable in this regard that there simply aren't surprise winners in hunter and equitation classes. Other sports of course see underdogs win all the time, whether it's an upset in a specific game or a team that just happens to get hot at the right time and makes a deep and improbable run in a tournament. There's no obvious reason to expect things to be different in riding. A top rider or horse can certainly have an off day. An unknown should be just as able to catch lightning in a bottle. But that never happens, to the degree that it's widely understood that a rider can't expect to place well at a national competition without a well-known trainer standing at the ingate. That this reality is a source of shrugs rather than scandal is no credit to the sport.

None of this is to deny that disparities have always existed or to contend that they should completely go away. Simply owning a horse is a luxury unavailable to most. Even so, the magnitude of the gaps within the sport seem to have increased alongside inequality in society more generally. To prove possibility—to show that one or two kids from modest backgrounds have succeeded—is not to prove fairness. The truly exceptional runner will win a race even if she starts from well behind. The rest who start behind will lose even though they are faster than many of the runners who started in front. Tempting as it might be for me to imagine that my own life story is a product simply of talent and hard work, I know that I'm as much the beneficiary of luck as anything.

At the outset we had no idea just how stratified the hunter/jumper world is. There were riders who had grown up at Appy Orse and gone on not only to ride in college but also to make it to nationals as collegiate riders. That sounded impressive to our ears. We didn't appreciate the differences between NCEA teams (which are fewer in number but tend to draw almost exclusively from the elite ranks of young riders) and IHSA teams (there are hundreds of them, and they provide opportunities for all levels of riders). We instead imagined that things worked largely as they do in conventional sports. There are plenty of opportunities for the talented and motivated basketball (or soccer, or baseball, or whatever) player to get noticed even when she doesn't have a high-profile background. The equestrian world, we naively assumed, would be no different.

But there are significant differences. The influence of wealth, as we've already seen. But there's also this: Coaches in traditional sports generally don't have an incentive to deliver messages of false hope to athletes who have reached the limits of their talent. Their goal is to win, and their motivation is accordingly to work with the players who put the team in the best position to do that. They're often volunteers whose income doesn't depend on what happens in the coaching portion of their life.

The incentive structure is different in the equestrian world. Trainers need clients to pay the bills. Show managers want to maximize their revenues—which, it bears noting, is nowhere near the same as having an incentive to maximize the number of people showing. (Because the national governing bodies restrict the amount of competition between shows, show managers effectively operate as monopolists rather than participants in a competitive market. The price of showing reflects that.)

The effect is to muddle the messaging, to make it easy for riders (and their parents) to perceive possibility where it doesn't truly exist.

These might sound like controversial assertions, but they are not. Flip through the pages of a leading equestrian publication or browse a website devoted to horse sports. The conflicts of interest are real, acknowledged, and almost entirely unaddressed. Money flows freely in the upper reaches of the equestrian world, and there are plenty of people eager to siphon off a bit of it for themselves.

I recall a moment from early in our adventures on the "A"-circuit. The big dreams of riding in events like the Maclay Finals still seemed realistic. I sat in an overflow parking lot at the Kentucky Horse Park working on what would become one of my first writings for the *Chronicle of the Horse*. Our car faced the Alltech Arena, where the Maclay Finals take place, and the symbolism seemed significant. We planned to end up there; I could already feel my heart pumping and my hands shaking, my body contorting with each jump, hoping for a clean round and a clear-eyed judge.

Those dreams reached their formal end on the morning that K died. Audrey never pursued them. In neither daughter's case was it for lack of talent. Both held their own with the Maclay crowd when given the chance. Nor was it for lack of effort. But nothing worked as planned when it came to K, and both of Audrey's horses were jumpers to their core, neither one the sort to support the picture of effortlessness required in an equitation class. There was no room in the budget for a second horse, or to do the amount of showing that we now know would have been required.

What I didn't appreciate until after the conclusion of the 2019 Maclay Finals was just how unrealistic our dreams had been. We had crossed paths over the years with a number of the 2019 Maclay competitors, and so I casually followed along as the day unfolded. And then I got curious. Just how different was their situation from ours? How much more would we have to have done to level the playing field?

I pulled the United States Equestrian Federation (USEF) rider reports for every rider who made it to the second round for the period from September 1, 2018, through August 31, 2019 (the qualifying period for the that year's Maclay). And then I started counting.

For context, during that same period Audrey rode in thirty-four classes over five shows. Thirty of those trips were on her horse Belle, and she got the chance to catch ride one other horse in four classes. All of this was uncomfortably expensive. Had we stretched we might have been able to fit in one more show.

Here's what I found: The average rider who made it to the second round of the Maclay Finals had shown nearly twenty-one horses in 336 classes at thirty-one shows. The median numbers were fifteen horses, 289 classes, and thirty shows. The lowest numbers in the three categories were four horses, 112 classes, and twenty-one shows. (And because you're curious, the highest were fifty-nine horses, 930 classes, and forty-five shows. Neither the highest nor lowest numbers in all three categories belonged to the same rider. That is, the person who showed fifty-nine horses was not the same person who rode in 930 classes, and so on.)

What's more, every single one of these riders rode during that year in at least one of the following: the 2018 Maclay Finals, the Washington International Horse Show (District of Columbia), the Winter Equestrian Festival (Florida), and the Devon Horse Show (Pennsylvania). I selected these shows specifically for the simple reason that from our perspective, they all seemed like once-in-a-lifetime, destination events. Eleven of the competitors rode in all four, and nine more rode in three.

There were no Cinderella stories in the second round of the 2019 Maclay Finals. Nobody was an underdog who happened to catch lightning in a bottle.

This, of course, is not conclusive proof of anything. It's one year in the careers of one group of riders, and it's no surprise that riders with that much experience on those sorts of stages had developed the talent necessary to rise to the top. The rider reports for the 154 who did not make it to the second round no doubt show a greater range of show experience. An analysis taking into account a greater period of time would undoubtedly be instructive as well.

Still, the results are suggestive. Even in that early moment in the parking lot facing the Alltech Arena, when things seemed to be on track, I had recognized the possibility that the pursuit of the Maclay Finals might turn out to be a fool's errand. Truly, though, I had no idea just how much of a fool's errand it was. Perhaps I'm alone in being so naive, but I doubt it. I understood that others are able to do more, but I hadn't grasped the magnitude of *how much more.*

The cost of showing as much as these riders had is unimaginable. We could have devoted our entire household income to the project and still not have kept up. It's hard to know how to react when you've uncovered a truth like this. Part of me felt foolish for having admitted the dreams out loud. And for having believed in them at all. A different part of me begrudged the riders of great means and their parents nothing. The riders were still unquestionably talented. And, as a parent, if I had the resources necessary to provide such opportunities, I would use them. Everyone within the system—riders, parents, trainers, show managers, judges—is, as far as I can see, generally responding rationally to the incentives they face. The problem is less with the people and more with those incentives and the industry structure that creates them.

The problem's not limited to the horse world. For better or worse, increased specialization in youth sports is the order of the day, and it's fostered by niche coaches with whom a kid can spend a portion of their summer learning to be a better version of whatever it is they are, whether that's a quarterback, point guard, or pole vaulter. Few people defend this state of affairs. At the same time, no one quite seems to know what to do about it.

In some sports this sort of competitive imbalance would lead an innovative coach to find a fresh approach to the game, a way of doing things that's both effective and different from how everyone else does it. Better to zig when everyone else zags than simply to do a merely average job at what everyone else is doing. Perhaps the equitation world is just waiting to be disrupted by a trainer who focuses on taking kids and their OTTBs to out-of-the-way shows run by a show manager who's willing to set difficult courses at legitimate heights, who minimizes the money spent on travel and keeping up appearances and maximizes her clients' ability to get show experience. It'd be a great story, but I won't hold my breath. It's still a world in which it's an open secret that it matters who's standing at the in-gate. That innovative trainer would be a gatecrasher, which is a tough thing to be in a judged sport. And so, the equestrian world seems to be locked in a place in which most potential participants have no realistic chance of rising to the top, because of economic considerations that bear no relation to talent, and because of a culture that resists bottom-up innovation.

As I've suggested, these sorts of imbalances threaten the integrity of the sport to the point where the label "sport" may no longer legitimately apply. That no doubt *is* a controversial take. But I'm not sure it should be. A recreational activity in which only the one percent can realistically hope to participate at the highest levels hardly seems worthy of the designation.

There's another problem with equestrianism as a sport, and it is particularly acute in hunter and equitation competition. The structures and procedures for judging are, by comparison to virtually every other sport with judges, primitive and outdated. (Only competitive dance seems to have a less-well-developed judging regime, in part because it simply hasn't existed for all that long.) Understand that I'm not simply repeating the standard claim that judging is subjective. I don't think that is true, at least not in any strong sense. It's imprecise, but that's not the same as subjective, and I think if we simply write it off as subjective, we allow ourselves to excuse too much and blind ourselves to the possibility that things might be improved.

Recall that in my day job I study the sort of judging that takes place in the legal system—how judges ought to decide, how they actually decide, what the legal system does to attempt to bring those two things into alignment, and how we might be able to do them better. I will ask you to trust that I've given a considerable amount of thought to this sort of thing.

We'll start with a basic distinction. Some sports are scored. The key questions are technical, and determining the score involves asking questions about things like whether a ball crossed a line or went in a hoop or goal. There are often judgment calls for the officials to make along the way, but not when it comes to scoring. It's quite easy to play those sports without officials, in the form of "pickup" games. Other sports are judged. In those sports a score doesn't exist except as a product of a judge, who must draw upon some base of knowledge to assess each competitor's performance. Judgment, in other words, is at the heart of things. And that's where the notion of "subjectivity" comes in.

So, let's explore for a moment what truly subjective judging might look like.

Imagine if I were to judge a couple classes and do so based on nothing more than what I happen to like—my subjective preferences. For example, we've had some bay horses that I've been pretty fond of. And even after all these years a horse that jumps flat (without much bascule over a fence) strikes me as way more sleek- and efficient-looking than one that jumps round (with a lot of bascule), like it's more apt to catch whatever it is we're hunting. If I judge based on these subjective preferences the results on my scorecard will surely look quite a bit different from those of an actual licensed judge. You could rightly call me a bad judge.

Let's come at it from a different angle and think about what I would have to do to become a better judge. I could try starting with the rule book, which would get me pretty far in a lot of sports, such as baseball or football. It'd even do the trick in the jumper ring. But the rules will get me almost nowhere in the hunter ring. Consider, for example, the language at the heart of US Equestrian Federation Rule HU 122, which defines the concept of "performance," on which hunter classes are to be judged: "An even hunting pace, manners, jumping style together with faults and way of moving over the course." That's not a lot to work with. Same for equitation. There the core idea is in USEF Rule EQ 104: "Rider should have a workmanlike appearance, seat and hands light and supple, conveying the impression of complete control should any emergency arise." It sounds good, but the language alone provides very little guidance.

That the rules aren't all that precise shouldn't surprise us. There are too many variables involved for it even to be possible to capture in precise words what an ideal hunter or equitation round looks like. This sort of imprecision is a common phenomenon in judged sports, including gymnastics and figure skating.

But—and here's the key point—the fact that the rules are indefinite doesn't mean that the horse show judge gets to make it up. The rules don't tell her all that she needs to know, but it's understood that she can't simply favor flat-jumping bay horses, even if her instincts happen to run in that direction. She has to draw on something to fill out the rules' lack of specificity, but that something has to come from her years of experience learning about horses and riding, and more than that, what's regarded as excellence within the sport itself.

This is reflected across judged sports in the design of the systems for deciding who even gets to be a judge, and after that, who advances to the highest levels. There's a period of practice judging and a requirement that the aspiring judge demonstrate that her placings are sufficiently similar to those of existing judges. Advancement to a higher level in turn requires demonstrating the ability to conform to the judgments of those at the next level.

For me to become a judge, then, would mean learning to suppress my personal preferences, and to replace them with the collective tastes of the hunter/jumper community as evidenced by my ability to emulate the preferences of existing judges.

Of course, this system is not perfect, and there's room for slippage. We know all too well that there are conflicting schools of thought when it comes to what a strong hunter or equitation round looks like, and there are members of those different schools judging at horse shows even as we speak. There's no guarantee that any two "R"-rated judges (the "large R" is the highest judge designation in the hunter/jumper world) would place the same class in the same way. Doesn't that make it subjective?

What that makes it, I'd suggest again, is imprecise, which is not the same thing as subjective. The difference matters. To be an acolyte of Famous Horse Person A or Famous Horse Person B, and to judge accordingly, is still to follow a developed set of ideas rather than an idiosyncratic set of preferences. In an ideal world we'd all agree on everything, but the existence of competing schools of thought is still well short of "anything goes." That's part of why the innovative trainer I mentioned earlier would be unlikely to have success.

But there's one big worry remaining. This imprecise world is one in which it is quite possible for subjective factors to get smuggled in. Because the line between a "good hunter round" and a "better hunter round" is never so clear as the line between "no dropped rails" and "a dropped rail," there's always the possibility that a judge could choose to decide based on something entirely improper—such as a preexisting relationship with one of the competitors—while thinking she could justify it in terms of her school of thought's preferences. Or, even more likely, she might not even realize that her past favorable impression of a horse or rider affects her perception of the round taking place in front of her in the moment. Truly subjective factors, in other words, can still find their way in.

Indeed, there is plenty of evidence from studies in other judged sports such as figure skating and gymnastics to support the conclusion that these improper factors do have an influence. Unsurprisingly, judges have difficulty maintaining the same standards over the course of an extended competition, and those competitors who appear later in a sequence tend, on average, to receive higher scores than those who appear earlier. Judges who work in panels, and who are able to see one another's scores, tend to converge toward a shared standard. Reputation, affiliation, and a judge's past experience with a competitor can also influence scoring. (It bears emphasis that these things are all tendencies rather than things that inevitably occur. That's part of why we're so often blind to them.)

None of this is surprising to me as someone who comes to these questions from the legal world, where there are rules and procedures that at least attempt to address analogous influences. The audiences of legal judges I have spoken to over the years have, for the most part, been receptive to the suggestion that they should account for the possibility that their judgment might be unwittingly distorted. Indeed, when one looks to other judged sports one sees that they, too, have taken steps to attempt to mitigate some of these concerns.

So, let's talk about the sorts of things the horse world might do, in a no-idea-is-a-bad-idea, "let me see if I can provoke some thought" sort of spirit. In doing so, I am drawing on my study of how judging is structured in law and in other judged sports. (In other words, each of the suggestions I offer is done by at least one judged sport that appears in the Olympics.) Not all of what I suggest is workable, for various reasons, but I think, even in those circumstances, a concept is worth discussing, nonetheless. I hope judges in the horse world will accept this sort of discussion as graciously as judges in the legal world.

_Tightening up the consensus._ One way to achieve greater uniformity is to reduce the scope of disagreement over what counts as excellence. Doing so would increase the level of consistency across judges while also making it more likely that spectators and competitors would agree with judges' placings.

This is a tall order. It would require achieving greater consensus across the sport, and a reduction in the number of schools of thought. Pulling that off would involve more regimentation of the sport than seems likely to happen, including perhaps the implementation of a much more structured process for becoming a riding instructor. If you can't become a judge until you've become a certified instructor, and you can't become a certified instructor unless you've demonstrated that you understand and are on board with a specified set of ideas, a more widely shared sense of "the right way to do things" seems likely to result. There are obvious drawbacks, of course, not least of which is cost. Still, other sports do things along these lines, including figure skating, so the idea shouldn't be dismissed out of hand.

*Making the rules more explicit.* Consider Rule 430.f of the International Skating Union: "Officials must ... not show bias for or against a competitor on any grounds; be completely impartial and neutral at all times; base their marks and decisions only on the performance and not be influenced by reputation or past performance; [and] disregard public approval or disapproval ..."

There is not, so far as I can tell, any truly analogous provision in the US Equestrian Federation rule book. GR 1033 (1) provides: "A judge serves three interests: his own conscience, exhibitors and spectators. He should make it clear that the best horses win." And 1033 (6) adds, "The decisions of each judge constitute solely his individual preference ..." This language leaves room for the sort of truly subjective judging I have disparaged, and the conflict of interest restrictions in GR1038 are so narrow as to provide little real counterweight.

In a sense, I'm not surprised. For me, one of the more striking parts of reading George Morris' autobiography *Unrelenting* was his more or less open acknowledgement of a phenomenon I've already noted, that in a Maclay or other "Big Eq," high-level equitation class, it matters to the judge who a rider's trainer is. That's not—but ought to be—scandalous. If the goal is to determine which rider had the best round on a particular day, then that sort of information should play *no* role at all. Instead, one should expect that the favorite will sometimes fall short, and that occasionally a little-known rider will have the round of her life, same as happens in other sports. Formally endorsing this in the rules wouldn't solve all the problems, but it would be a significant start.

_____*Judging panels.* Another difference between the equestrian and figure skating worlds is the latter's use of panels of judges (usually five) at even the lowest levels of competition. It makes sense. The use of multiple judges brings multiple perspectives, certainly in terms of the knowledge and preferences the judges bring to their task, and also potentially in terms of their physical location around the ring. The result is that the collective views of the panel are more likely to represent those held across the sport as a whole. My experience in the figure-skating world was that there was generally broad agreement among the judges, but also quite a bit of variation in their specific rankings. That was also my sense at Pony Finals, which, like some other top equestrian events, use multiple judge panels. Yet the bulk of judging, especially in hunter/jumper competition, is done individually. Broader use of panels would be a major change; it would also likely entail a shift to volunteer judges.

_____*Banning communication among judges.* Twice I've found myself sitting near a panel of judges working a class. In both cases the judges were talking with one another as they were judging, and in both cases it was obvious to me that it was affecting how they were judging. In one situation one of the judges was quite clearly simply acquiescing to the conclusions of the other, with the dominant judge offering her proposed score while the round was taking place, adjusted downward but never upward depending on how things progressed, and the other judge contributing little more than variations on "I agree." In the other instance, the judges in a Big Eq class at the Kentucky Horse Park were exchanging their views on some of the riders—the ones that had already developed a reputation—as soon as the riders entered the ring. Among the things I learned were that one rider "never could get her heel position right" and another "just wasn't quite as good as her sister."

Mention these things to someone who's been in the hunter/jumper world for a while and you'll get a shrug. But this, too, ought to be scandalous. These conversations completely undermined the value of panel decision-making. Most, if not all, of the other sports that use panels of judges expressly prohibit judges from communicating with one another during a competition. The horse world should follow suit.

_____ *Compensation.* Another very striking difference between the figure-skating and horse worlds is that in the former all judges, from the lowest levels to the Olympics, are volunteers who are compensated for their expenses only. I'm not familiar enough with the workings of how horse show judges get paid to speculate on how it might affect their incentives, but I've lived long enough to appreciate that whenever there's money changing hands the potential for corrosive effects exists somewhere, and not only in situations where the show manager who's writing the judges' checks has a family member competing. I'm confident that it would be no problem at all to find a sufficient number of people in the horse world to judge on a volunteer basis. At the same time, I'm under no illusions that this change is coming any time soon. The more general point is that things such as who hires the judges and how and under what constraints they do so can have very real effects on how those judges go about their jobs, and it's worth considering whether any adjustments might be made to further the perceived integrity of the sport.

_____ *Mental breaks.* Horse-show judges often have incredibly long days in which they must attentively watch dozens of rounds, often in what can't be the most comfortable circumstances. Meanwhile, it's beyond dispute that each of us has only a limited amount of mental energy and that our minds don't work the same when that energy is depleted. I try to be especially mindful of this when grading exams, and I take breaks and otherwise structure the process in ways designed to prevent an inadvertent drift in my standards as I make my way through the pile. Figure skating recognizes the phenomenon as well. There the panels of judges are swapped out and reshuffled from one event to the next. The days are long, but they include frequent breaks.

Ways of doing things become entrenched and seem natural if not inevitable. People understandably worry about the consequences of change, both intended and unintended. But I don't think I'm alone in being concerned that people so casually regard horse-show judging as subjective in the full sense of the word, and that everyone just sort of gives a "what are you gonna do?" shrug when someone openly acknowledges that it matters which trainer is standing at the in-gate. Those aren't the hallmarks of a robust and legitimate sporting community. It doesn't have to be like that. ✸

—15————————————————

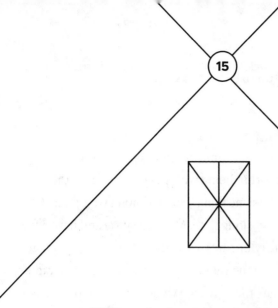

Back when I signed Ada up for her first riding lesson I didn't imagine myself to be doing anything more than that. She had been deeply in love with horses for over half of her short life. Riding lessons were the inevitable next step. I appreciated on an intellectual level that it would lead somewhere.

That it would lead to the development of a set of skills was no surprise. The extent to which it would immerse us in a community was. I've often thought of that community via the metaphor of a river, always the same, yet always changing. It's wide, and it's deep, and it's been running for a long, long time. It has many tributaries, and a powerful current, and you needn't get too far in for it to pick you up and carry you along.

CHAPTER 15

You meet people on the river. Some of them took their first steps in when you did. There's comfort in being with people who have the same questions and are learning the same things, and you bond with them. Others have been in the water for a long time. Many are wise and have a feel for things, and if you're lucky one or two will guide you. They'll teach you how to read the surface of the water, let you know where the rapids are, teach you how to navigate them. After a while you develop your own knowledge and share it with those who come after. Just as a large part of learning to ride involves internalizing intangible knowhow, so, too, does learning how to make your way around an unfamiliar community.

The river has its twists and its turns, its rapids, and its places where people sometimes get hung up. There have been wrecks on the river. People talk about those, analyze what went wrong, think about what they would have done differently. There are stretches of fast water, interludes of beauty, and long pauses where things move slowly and nothing much seems to happen at all. A look back, however, reveals that those slow times hold some of the more meaningful moments.

At times you might think you know where the river will lead. But you learn that it will take you where it takes you. Luck and the current defeat most attempts at navigation. You will go where you will go.

You learn to emphasize the journey over the destination.

We've been on the river for a while now, my family and I. We've reached a point where from a newcomer's perspective we're among the old hands. We've seen some things, made some mistakes, acquired some knowledge. We've shot some rapids and enjoyed some stretches of simply floating along. We tried to navigate, with only partial success. We've ended up where we've ended up.

I don't know what lies ahead, and given our journey so far, I'd be foolish to predict. The river will lead where it leads. These days I tend to look back more often than I look ahead. And when I glance backward it's often the small moments that I see—the things that didn't seem all that significant when they happened but that now sit in my memory as crystallized encapsulations of the entire experience. The moments in the barn aisle helping Ada, Audrey, or Laura brush a horse, or at a show providing as much reassurance as I could. The winter nights we had a farm to ourselves, the outside shrouded in cold and darkness as we went about our business. The drives and the stops for food. The time together.

often recall one beautiful late summer afternoon at Appy Orse Acres in Fredonia, Wisconsin, the farm where it all began for us. The horse was named Sunny, and we had leased him for Ada. Our first lease. Still early days on the river.

It might've been planned, it might've been spontaneous, but either way Ada ended up taking Sunny for a ride on the farm's network of trails while Audrey, Laura, Ada's friend Sara, and I followed along on foot. We walked, and we talked, and we paused to pick apples.

Somewhere along our way things went from merely pleasant to that certain kind of perfect—the kind where you remind yourself to look around and soak in as much as you can, hoping that you'll absorb enough of the moment to one day remember more than just a fragment.

After a while we came to a mulberry bush, and Ada got off Sunny. Right about then Audrey and Laura found a toad and began to discuss what they would do with it.

I had the presence of mind to take out my phone and get a picture. This was before smartphones, when phone cameras were somewhat primitive. Before we documented all the moments of our lives.

The photo is nothing special at all. Yet it is among my all-time favorites. It does the work that a photo is meant to do. It serves as a small reminder of an ordinary day that became an extraordinary day. It reinforces for me the idea that sometimes the little moments are the biggest ones. Posed photos and big events are nice. But so much of living takes place in between them.

Years later, I'd been on the river long enough to know that sometimes you've got to ask for help.

When Ada decided to take a break from jumping and give dressage a try, we struggled to find her a trainer. I got lots of recommendations, but for each one something—usually geography—got in the way. Just when I thought I was out of ideas I had one more: I would reach out to Tori Polonitza.

Tori was a dressage trainer, Florida-based but in Wisconsin several times a year to cross-train a group of primarily hunter/jumper riders at several local barns. Ada had ridden with her many times while at Hidden View Farm and always loved it. Tori was one of the most gifted instructors I had ever seen. She was an excellent communicator, able to clearly convey both techniques and the rationale behind them. More than that, she was able to assess the skills and needs of riders and horses and, as it's fashionable to say in education these days, "meet them where they're at" by providing instruction appropriate to their needs.

Tori, I knew, had some sense of the lay of the land in our area, and it was only natural for me to seek her advice as I tried to help my oldest daughter. I explained that with all that had happened, with K and injuries and disappointments, riding had stopped being fun for Ada. Tori was quiet for a minute, and then she said, "I have an idea."

A couple days later I was at my dining room table talking on my phone again, this time with Patty Van Housen. I had known of Patty and her sister Barb for years. They were fixtures in the southeastern Wisconsin horse community and owned a facility called Split Rail Stables, but we had never met.

Tori had connected us, thinking it might be possible for Ada to find a spot at Split Rail. And as Patty spoke, she used words and phrases like "everybody pitches in" and "try different things" and "we focus less on appearance and more on what works"—and, yes, "fun." She could not have known it, but she was speaking my language.

Life in the horse world teaches you not to get your hopes up too high. But I allowed these conversations to elevate mine a bit. And looking back now, my phone conversations with Tori and Patty remain among the most meaningful and consequential of my life.

Over the following months Ada lessoned intensively with Tori when she came to town and taught at Split Rail. She rode, and she showed. And we both did chores and helped repair fences and played with dogs. Our family fell in with a group of people who had spent their lives on the river, who had picked up knowledge and perspective, and who shared it freely. And we have continued to travel with them, grateful each day for their friendship, wisdom, and generous spirits.

One of the big events on the Wisconsin equestrian calendar is the annual Wisconsin Equine Derby Weekend. It's the event where Ada had her fateful ride in front of Diane Carney and a place where you can expect to cross paths with most all of the regulars in the Milwaukee-area hunter/jumper community. The summer after our introduction to Split Rail, Ada, Audrey, and I attended as spectators, there to see and support friends both old and new.

About midway through the day, we found ourselves seated under a tent with Heidi Modesto, Debbie Knuth, and Charles Zwicky. This was most of the core of the Hidden View show team, reunited. We shared some inside jokes. We watched Hidden View barn manager Kelly Doke show her longtime horse Red in the last class of his career, an emotional retirement party for an unsung hero, a horse all of my daughters had ridden along the way. And we quietly enjoyed one more, brief taste of the connection we shared.

was in my office when my phone started buzzing. It was Ada, who now had her license and had driven with Audrey down to Millcreek Farm, where Audrey continued to ride.

It was hard to make out what she was saying. Then she put Audrey on the phone who wasn't speaking any more clearly. I heard the word "fall," but I couldn't tell whether Audrey was laughing or crying.

It was laughter. But the situation turned out to be not entirely funny. The horse she was riding stumbled, a freak thing, and Audrey's foot got caught between the horse and the ground before the horse popped back up. The vet who happened to be present had said he "didn't need to have her jog to conclude she was definitely lame," but he also didn't think anything was broken.

A few hours later the swelling was still severe, so Audrey and I were off to urgent care. An x-ray revealed a small fracture. She would be in a boot for at least a month.

There was an interesting pattern in how our horse friends responded to her injury. The longer they'd been at it, the more likely they were to follow their expressions of regret by immediately offering helpful suggestions to enable her to ride anyway.

"There's nothing wrong with a month of no-stirrup work," as one of them put it.

The first full summer that Ada competed in dressage, we went to a small local show. The horse she was riding was talented but emotional. The mare reared as Ada tried to get her from the warm-up ring to the arena. (I didn't see it, but those who did say she was close to going over backward.) I heard the commotion and turned around just in time to see Ada on the ground.

Their day together was done. But because it was a local show, Ada could ride the test on a different horse. She gathered herself together and turned in a round good enough to earn the blue ribbon. Perhaps twenty minutes later, as Ada and I stood outside the barn, the show announcer approached. We did not know her name and our paths had never crossed before. We will likely never see her again. The woman had seen everything and simply wanted to let Ada know how much she admired Ada's willingness to get back on and keep riding.

The best moments are not always on the biggest stages.

The April of Ada's senior year in high school, she and I made the drive to Madison to attend the Midwest Horse Fair. This was a major annual pilgrimage in the early years. We would stay in a nearby hotel so we could arrive early and stay late, making our way through all the exhibition halls, wandering down each aisle of every barn, me holding Ada up at each stall so she could see inside, watching as many clinics as possible, attending the rodeo or "Night of the Horse" or whatever the evening's entertainment happened to be. At first it was just the two of us, but then we were joined by Ada's friend Madi Segrin and her grandma Deb, or by some or all of Audrey, Laura, and Lea. Usually we would run into several people we knew. Always we would come home with a new Breyer horse, the result of a process that involved lengthy consideration and multiple trips to the various booths that sold them.

We had fallen out of the habit somewhere along the way. But both of us knew there might be just this one last easy chance to visit the event that was such a large part of those early years. My birthday often coincides with the dates of the Horse Fair, and this year all I wanted was to make that trip again, to try recreate the magic of a horse-crazy childhood, to chase a few more ghosts. It was just a day trip this time, but we fit it all in. We walked the aisles and watched some clinics. We saw a few friends. We remarked on what had stayed the same and what had changed. We stayed for the rodeo. We canvassed all the usual booths, and then we bought a Breyer horse.

"I hope that's not the last time we do this, " I said to Ada as we drove back to Milwaukee.

"Me, too, Dad."

These are just snapshots—moments I've pulled out of our box of memories. There are so many I've left out, each significant, each a part of this adventure that has shaped our lives, each connected to this larger community of "river people." Those connections inevitably grow deeper with time. I can't remember when we first learned that Olympic great Beezie Madden grew up in greater Milwaukee, but at the time the knowledge was abstract, her presence near but distant. She had been a part of a world that was still foreign to us. Then, every time we went to Hidden View, we found ourselves driving past the barn where she rode growing up. We came to know people who had ridden with her as kids, who knew her family. We learned about other high-profile riders who had called Southeastern Wisconsin home for a while. What seemed distant became closer. Eventually, Ada and Audrey each found themselves riding with Olympians, even if just for a week. Our world became both larger and smaller.

My family's presence isn't the only thing that ties these moments together. I've included some names, but there are many, many others. It's surprisingly large, this group of people whose lives intersect in various ways and different times, all part of this great, meandering river. They're people who've left marks on one another, often without really appreciating that they've done it at all, let alone how much of an impact they've had. We're connected not only to those who we've met and interacted with along the way, but with those whose time was before ours and who are known to us only by name and reputation. We'll share the same sort of connection with those who come after. It's been a fascinating and rewarding thing to be a part of. And it's all because of an animal. ✿

—16—

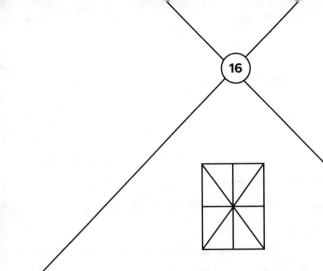

As I write this it's been fifteen years since that first lesson at Appy Orse Acres. As the pages between then and now attest, a stretch like that will supply a lot of memories. The first lessons, the first horses, the jumps that once seemed huge and now look small. The talked-through nerves, the signals for when it was okay for me to approach between rounds, the "here's what I'm gonna dos" that actually got done. A nice collection of ribbons. The smiles, and laughs, and summer nights sitting ringside in the setting sun watching my daughters do the thing they love to do.

Of course, not all of those memories are happy. There were falls, and refusals, and placings that seemed to make no sense at all.

CHAPTER 16

There was frustration, and tears, and offered hugs that only sometimes got accepted and only sometimes seemed to help. There were show bills and vet bills and trailering bills. There were bets that did not pay off.

There was colic.

I've left some things out of the story, of course. There were moments where people, very much including me, were not at their best. From what I can tell our story has had fewer of those moments than many, but they were there. Barn families, like real families, or law school faculties, or any other group of human beings, have people who tend to rub others the wrong way. They have their simmering resentments, petty frustrations, and lost tempers. Certainly, there have been moments when I've felt let down and due an apology or expression of regret that never came. I can't claim to have read every situation correctly, and there's a good chance there are people who feel I've wronged them in ways I'm not aware of. (It happens. I once got an email from someone who was angry at me for failing to take action in a situation that I hadn't even realized I was in. I try to give people the benefit of the doubt when something like that happens, but not everyone does.) The bad moments were rare, though, and I think I remain on good terms with nearly everyone we've crossed paths with.

Even so it's a mixed bag, this world of riding. And when you hit those patches filled with difficulties and setbacks the questions that always lurk in the background start to push their way forward: *Why do we do this? What have we gained? Is it worth all that we sacrifice in time, money, and opportunities to do other things?*

It seems I'm not alone in this. My Facebook feed regularly includes links to some parent's list of reasons for supporting a child's riding habit, some attempt to identify what it is that makes it all worthwhile. Those lists get shared a lot, and they garner their share of likes. To me that suggests that people aren't quite sure. Because you don't often see posts justifying choices that people are confident about, like, "Here are seven reasons I encourage my children to eat their vegetables." Some things are clear. Getting deep into the equestrian world is not.

The lists of "pros" include things like learning how to handle winning and losing with grace, being responsible, working hard, developing a skill, and so on. They're valuable lessons of the sort that riders undoubtedly pick up, and I certainly understand the impulse to embrace the message. It's natural to want to believe our actions were justified.

But there's always a little voice in my head that says something like, "Well, yeah, but you can learn those things from other sports, too, and usually a lot more cheaply." In fact, I've seen very similar lists posted by parents of figure skaters. Once the exact same list of reasons appeared in my feed on consecutive days. Exact same, that is, save for the fact that one of them said "wrestling" where the other said "riding." Wrestling, I can promise you, is *a lot* cheaper than riding.

And yet here I am. So, what's my justification? Why didn't we just send our kids out for soccer or softball instead?

I've tried to puzzle my way through that. Just what was it that my daughters got from riding that wasn't available somewhere else? What's the added value? I can't say that I've got a complete list, but I think I've managed to identify a few things that are more effectively learned in riding even if they may not be unique to the sport. It's not a long list. And not all of the lessons are happy lessons. But I think they're good lessons.

*A fuller slice of life.* I often come back to a moment in the tack room at Hidden View Farm. We had just returned from a show, and there were several other members of our barn family there, representing a broad range of ages. The post-show work was mostly done, and people were in the final stages of cleaning the last bit of tack or organizing their trunks for the return to routine. It would soon be time to go home and rejoin normal life, but the group was hanging on for a few more minutes, not quite ready to move on.

One of the riders proposed that each person around the room identify a thing she was thankful for. Everyone else had showed, and they all talked about what they or their horse had done well. I hadn't shown, of course, but they looked to me for an answer anyway. I spoke from the heart: "I'm thankful my daughters get to do all of this with all of you." I meant it then, and I mean it still.

Part of the reason has something to do with a dynamic that might be unique to riding. Most sports are played with kids of the same age. That was certainly true in my youth. There were adults around, of course, but as coaches and parents. The adults were "them," and definitely not "us." They sat in the front of the bus and, understandably, kept their distance. We were okay with that.

It's a different story in the riding world. The barns we've been fortunate to call home have all been places where the riders ranged from the quite young to the more mature, and the arrangement seems to foster a different sort of relationship between kids and adults. Ada and Audrey have in significant ways related to the older riders in these barns as peers and friends—as "us" rather than "them." Some of my favorite horse show memories involve moments when women who were decades older sincerely asked for, and then followed, my daughters' advice.

Beyond that, the barn has provided mostly good role models and great exposure to adult interaction. It hasn't been entirely drama-free, but in a world in which growing up is hard to do, that sort of thing is invaluable.

      *Life's not fair.* No doubt there are occasions in any sport where it's appropriate for someone to say, "That's not fair." On the whole, though, sports are designed to minimize the influence of anything other than the competitors' ability. The best shoes in the world won't turn a pretty fast runner into a really fast one, and in most sports once a certain piece of equipment starts to provide too much of a boost, it usually ends up getting banned.

Things are different in the horse world, and not just at the higher levels with the fancier horses. I understand, of course, that horses are athletes rather than mere equipment. And that in any sport involving team competition it's possible to surround oneself with the best possible teammates. Still, as I suggested in earlier pages, I think there are senses in which the hunter and equitation portions of the hunter/jumper world, in particular, are close to being better regarded as "exhibition" rather than "sport." The imbalances at the upper levels are simply too great to regard the opportunity to compete as meaningfully open to more than an extraordinarily thin slice of the population. Make no mistake, though. The dynamic exists to a degree throughout the equestrian world. The awarding of nearly every ribbon to a Junior rider, to some greater or lesser degree, could be accompanied by the statement, "Congratulations on your parents' income, and their willingness to devote a large portion of it to this."

For several years I had the honor of being the emcee for the Wisconsin Hunter Jumper Association's annual banquet. Each time I made a point of asking the (mostly) girls in the room to thank their parents for making their participation in the sport possible and reminded them that there were even more girls *not* in the room who would love nothing more than to be able to be there, but who couldn't be.

It's a cycle that repeats itself at every level. The girl with no chance to ride at all envies the girl at the schooling show, who envies the girl at the

"B" show, who envies the girl at the "A" show, who envies the girl with the fancier horse, who envies the girl with four of them. There's always someone with more money and the willingness to spend it.

And unlike running shoes, it often matters. A talented horse can offset a rider's talent differential in ways that don't hold in other sports. We've already talked about the advantages of having a brand-name trainer standing at the in-gate. These things often seem deeply unfair. It's far from the ideal way to design a sport, but as life lessons go, it's pretty good practice for the road ahead.

_____*Price is not the same as value.* While spending more money can make a difference, there are certainly no guarantees. The adage that you get what you pay for sometimes holds true only in the sense that what you get is the appearance of having paid a lot.

My assessment of the relative value of the horses we have owned bears very little relationship to the prices that we paid for them. And while some of this is no doubt the Midwestern farm kid in me shining through, you certainly won't convince me more generally that "most expensive"—whether we're talking trainers, show clothes, equipment, or whatever—is even roughly synonymous with "best."

It can be a tough lesson to learn, and one look around at the ostentatious displays of wealth at certain showgrounds will tell you that not everyone agrees it's a good one. But I'm standing by it.

_____*The usual lessons—with passion.* Those lists that I mentioned make the rounds on Facebook? The ones that get shared *a lot*? Writing this has given me a new perspective on them. My daughters have, after all, learned many of the same lessons that I learned playing high school sports. And while it's easy to say they might have learned those lessons much more cheaply playing soccer or basketball, it's of course not the same. You don't get up from those falls, or work through the difficulties, or even get frustrated to the point of tears, unless it means something.

A sport teaches best, I suspect, when you care deeply about that sport.

So, for me, the best answer to the "Why do I do this?" question is simply this: I couldn't *not* do it. When your child becomes obsessed with horses at age two, when every book you read her and every toy she wants and seemingly every moment of every day is devoted to thinking about horses, and when that obsession doesn't go away, you do what you can. And when a second daughter catches the bug, you keep on keepin' on. The lessons follow naturally, and they mean more, because it all means more.

There are lessons for parents, too. I've often been asked whether there are things I'd do differently, or what it is that I wish I had known before starting out on this journey. There are certainly plenty of things I'd do differently. There are things I wish I had said and things I wish I hadn't. There are options I wish I had explored and paths I wouldn't go down a second time. There are people whose advice I wish I had sought and people whose advice I should have discounted. Much of it is unique to our situation and to my own quirks and shortcomings. But some of it may hold value for others. What follows is not entirely a list of things I wish I had known. Some of it I sort of knew but now appreciate more. Some of it I've seen other people struggle with. Some of it really doesn't fall into any of those categories. An awful lot of it is simply my opinion.

*Your job at horse shows is mostly to stay out of the way when it's time to go into the ring.* It's probably more accurate to say that your job in general is to stay out of the way as much as possible, and for all the usual reasons that over-involved parenting isn't a great idea. What that means turns out to be very context-specific, and what's appropriate as the parent of a five-year-old often won't still be appropriate when the next five years have passed. And staying out of the way doesn't mean not being involved. I was generally involved and often around and no doubt sometimes got in the way despite my best intentions. But I tried to understand that there were moments when it was best for me to walk away from whatever was taking place in the ring. I loved the fact that, especially in those early years, the barn was often "our" place, but I also understood the importance of it being, ultimately, "their" place—a spot where my daughters were the ones with the expertise and the privileges that go with being a member of a community.

The proper contours of the role of show parent will vary a little bit from one barn to the next. At my most involved, I've been a water-and-crop-carrying, last-second boot cleaner, and at my least involved, just a person in the stands. What I've pretty much always done, and what you should probably do, too, is kept my mouth shut. If you can't be a quietly supportive presence near the in-gate, then the odds are good you shouldn't be a presence at all.

_____ *Steer clear of the gossip.* Earlier in the book I characterized gossiping by trainers as committing the cardinal sin of professionalism. I think it's best if parents avoid it as well. You can find gossip pretty much everywhere you go, and the horse world is certainly no exception. I'm not going to pretend that I've never taken part. But it's corrosive, especially when it involves members of a barn community saying negative things about another member of that same community. Plus, it seems a safe bet that if a person's in the barn aisle talking to you about someone else one day, that person's likely to be talking *about you* to a different person the next day. It can make trust a little hard to come by. Best to avoid it if you can.

_____ _Lots of people are confident of the right way to do things. They just don't agree with one another._ I can't count the number of times I've heard someone proclaim, with all the conviction of the guy who's been sitting at the end of the bar all day, that there is one, absolute, single right way that some horse-related thing should be done, only to later hear someone else assert with equal conviction that the first way is the exact way not to do the thing, and that some other way is the truly correct way. Occasionally, in a truly fun twist, these two people are actually the same person, with the strongly held opinions separated by a few weeks or months. Lots of people, for whatever reason, make the mistake of equating confidence with correctness. I think that's a mistake. There's usually more than one effective approach, and rarely a single approach that works in all situations.

_____ _It's hard to know what the goals should be._ Setting goals is important. It's good to have both short-term goals, the sort that are just at the edge of a rider's current ability, and longer-term goals that are well beyond the reach of the moment but not outside the realm of possibility. The trick comes in figuring out that they should be. If you're an outsider to the sport, as I was, it's really hard to figure out what's realistic, and thus how to steer your kid in the right direction. I still don't have a great answer, other than that it seems best if the goals are the sort that are intrinsic to the activity—getting better at doing something and enjoying the process of doing so—rather than the sort that depend on getting a specific ribbon in a certain place. Too many things can get in the way of even making it to that specific place, let alone earning a specific ribbon once there.

That's not to say that the latter sort of goal is inappropriate, but I suspect if that's all there is, then something is missing. The writer George Saunders made an observation that rings very true to me:

"Accomplishment is unreliable. 'Succeeding,' whatever that might mean to you, is hard, and the need to do so constantly renews itself (success is like a mountain that keeps growing ahead of you as you hike it)." It's an endless quest, and it may never lead to satisfaction. Wining that specific ribbon may just lead you to start thinking about the next one.

_Be chill with respect to whatever the goals are._ Your daughter wants to go to the Maclay Finals? That's cool. So did mine. She's a really good rider? Same here. Is that going to be enough? Not by itself. As I've shared, it's almost certain to take a lot of money, maybe more than you've got to spare, and at least a little bit of luck. You'll need to find the right horse, and it and your daughter will have to stay healthy, and things can go wrong with respect to every single one of those ingredients.

Setting expectations around something specific like going to the Maclay Finals runs the risk of setting up disappointment, especially if you don't have a realistic sense of what's all involved in getting there. I'm not denying the value in setting ambitious and tangible goals. As a parent, though, it seems better for your expectations to be nothing more than that your young rider give her best effort, and to make clear that you'll be happy with that, wherever it leads.

_There's always someone with more._ Look, the fact that I can write a book about my daughters' experiences riding and showing horses suggests that, in the scheme of things, we're incredibly fortunate. There are lots of people who would give anything just to have a taste of this world. It's a point that's easy to appreciate at an intellectual level, even as we look across the way and see someone else who's doing more showing of more and better horses and think to ourselves that it's not fair. And it's not, at least in the sense that most of us wouldn't build these inequalities in if we were designing a sport from scratch. But it seems unlikely to change so best to be as zen about it as possible and take whatever life lessons from it that you can.

_Relationships with horse trainers are different._ Riding requires being at the barn a lot. Trainers are also at the barn a lot. Shows frequently require out-of-town travel with lots of downtime together. There is no off-season. For these reasons and more, trainers come to play a much greater role in their clients' lives than coaches in other contexts tend to. "You come to think of these people as your friends," a trainer (whom I consider to be a friend) once explained to me. But there's also a business relationship there, he noted, and that can create a tricky dynamic on both sides. This is especially true if things go poorly, as things sometimes do.

_There are other horses in the pasture._ Buying a horse is exciting. And unless you've got money to burn or a taste for risk, it's also an exercise in abject terror. With luck, a child will find just the right horse, and everyone will live happily ever after. But that's not always how it works out, and of course you can't know at the front end what the result will be.

It's also understood, as I've mentioned before, that the world of horse sales is filled with deeply unethical behavior. Kickbacks and hidden commissions are reportedly prevalent. I've seen several articles suggesting that horse sales ought to be regulated more, like real estate sales are. I worked for a time in the real estate world, and I can't say I came away impressed with how ethical everyone was. The fact that people would offer up the way real estate is sold as an improvement tells you something pretty significant about just how bad the horse world can be.

My main piece of advice is that you not allow yourself to get pressured into buying *this* horse *right now.* If it doesn't feel like the right horse, or things seem to be moving too quickly, don't be afraid to hit the "pause" button. At the very least take a day or two to give yourself space to truly reflect on the decision. We're wired as humans to emphasize the positive aspects of reaching a conclusion we want to reach while at the same time minimizing the downsides. The fact that the horse is there in front of you and that she looks pretty and that she has a good pedigree is all the sort of thing that can make a questionable decision seem like a good one. "We'll just sell her if it doesn't work out" may seem like good reasoning in the moment, but even setting aside the costs involved in the transaction, there's the difficulty of getting to the point of even *having* a transaction. Horses are easy to buy and hard to sell. There are lots of them out there. They're just as beautiful. You don't want to be so skittish that you don't go forward at all, but be cautious, because the only one you can know for sure has your interests in mind is you.

_____ *You will make mistakes.* I have an acquaintance who claims never to second-guess any decision he makes. I'm not built that way, and I don't think I'd want to be. One of the themes running through this book is that as a parent you're constantly making decisions against a backdrop of deep uncertainty. This is doubly so when you had no prior experience in this world. Are the goals we've set the right ones? Is this the right horse to achieve them? The right trainer? And on and on.

You won't always make the right decision. Sometimes you'll get lucky anyway. And, of course, even good decisions can have bad results. You'll find yourself wishing you could go back and take a mulligan. It seems to me that it's appropriate to dwell some on your mistakes, in the hopes that you can avoid making them in the future—but also that you shouldn't dwell on them too much. "Moderation in all things" is just as hard to achieve here as it is anywhere else, but it's the right approach.

_____ *Don't just take my word for any of this.* I'm just one person, with one set of experiences, and with values and preferences that may be different from yours. Your mileage may vary, as they say. Ask around; get as much input as you can. Do more of that than I did. If someone who has no incentive to be anything other than straight with you suggests that you do something, or seems to be waving you off doing another thing, give serious consideration to that person's input.

Sooner or later the non-horsey parent faces a critical question: How do I interact with these people? (As in "horse people.") Here's my take, with specific reference to the situation where the question appears in its starkest form: the barn holiday party.

Several years ago, I met a fellow professor who, like me, had grown up on a farm. We got to talking about how we came to know that we weren't cut out to be farmers, and he told a story about being out in a field of cows and calves with his dad, who was calling them each by name.

Eventually, after his dad had greeted yet another calf by name, my befuddled acquaintance asked, "Dad, how can you tell?"

His dad, himself a little befuddled by the question, said, "Well, she looks just like her mother!"

In most ways the barn holiday party is just like the office holiday party. There are, of course, the barn regulars. The people who see each other all the time and have relationships with one another. Those people fall into easy conversation. And then there are the hangers-on—the spouses and the kids who don't know each other or many of the other people there.

For those latter folks the barn party can be awkward in all the usual ways. The inner monologue's the traditional mix of: *Who can I talk to?*

*What can we talk about? Please, please, please don't start talking about politics!* But at the office party there's at least the likelihood that nobody's going to want to talk about work all that much, so the conversations will at least tend toward topics that are accessible to everyone.

At the barn party it's exactly the opposite. Because, from the perspective of a horse person, how great an opportunity is this? Nobody's off riding or grooming or doing anything else that might distract them from the ability to talk about horse stuff. This is even better than dinner with the group after a day of showing because *everyone's* here! After we exchange gifts of horse treats and grooming supplies and that belt that's really fashionable this year, we can pull up horse videos on our phones and pass them around! We should totally do this more often!

In the early years, as a non-horse-person at a barn holiday party, you're like me and my professor friend in the midst of a crowd of people who can all tell the cows apart. Except the cows are horses. And they don't look the same at all, and how could you possibly confuse Contessa with Cabernet, because Contessa's got a blaze and Cabernet's got a stripe? And what's more they don't move the same or jump the same and all of this is obvious to everyone but you.

That's not all: Some of the horses apparently do look like cows sometimes, and you'll infer that that's not a good thing. Others look like llamas sometimes, and that doesn't seem to be a good thing either. Sometimes they're "light" in the front and sometimes they're "heavy." They can "fall in" and "fall out," neither of which involves falling down. And also, they bend, but you have to ask them to. Usually. Evidently there's something called a "daisy cutter," too, and you make a note to check that out at your local hardware store because it seems like it'd be a pretty good gift idea given the way everyone's talking about it.

After a bit you'll be tempted to look around for a TV, hoping there's a game on. Or at least find someone who you can talk about football with.

My advice? Don't do it. Sit there and take your lumps. Try to smile in the right places. Don't tell the story about the one time you rode a pony as a kid. Remember that they've heard it. Generally, don't speak at all unless spoken to. Listen. Attentively. You're a visitor to this land, one whose mission is to try to figure out the language, to understand this strange new place in which you find yourself.

Why? You're not there unless your kid is one of them, and if you want to understand your kid (which I recommend) you should try to understand these people. It turns out that another thing those horses can do is talk, in a language that only some can hear. Your kid is one of those people, and, for her, that language is one of the most beautiful things of all.

This party, for you, might seem no different from your spouse's office party, a thing you've got to go to because that's just how it is. For your kid, especially in the early going, this is a big deal, a highlight of the year, a chance to spend some time with the grown-ups and, even better, the older kids, talking about the thing they all love. The trainer will be there, and you'll notice a certain, almost cult-like devotion to her or him that's never on display quite so much as when the entire barn gets together. These people, or people like them, are going to end up as important role models for your child, shaping her view of the world in all sorts of ways.

And if you listen, patiently and attentively? After a few months parts of the conversation will start to make sense. After a couple years most of the conversation will make sense, and you might even start to look forward to the barn party. After a few more years you might start to ask yourself, "Would it be weird if I went even after my daughter's gone off to college?" ✿

—17—

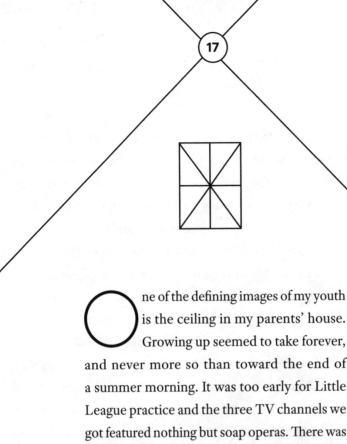

One of the defining images of my youth is the ceiling in my parents' house. Growing up seemed to take forever, and never more so than toward the end of a summer morning. It was too early for Little League practice and the three TV channels we got featured nothing but soap operas. There was absolutely nothing to do. And so, I'd find myself staring at the ceiling, sometimes dreaming of where life might lead and sometimes just wallowing in the sheer endlessness of youth and the seemingly infinite supply of time stretched out ahead. Everything moved too slowly. None of the milestones came quickly enough.

I imagined parenthood unfolding on a similar scale. I'd have all the time in the world to pass along all the knowledge I wanted to pass along. I might not have the degree of influence I once imagined, but surely I'd be able to equip my kids with the information they needed to avoid some of my mistakes and to otherwise take advantage of things I'd learned along the way. There was no need to rush. We had all the time in the world.

There are probably no childhoods like that anymore. The internet swapped the infinite supply of time for an infinite supply of distractions. Kids tend to be more scheduled. Boredom no longer has the same meaning. And, of course, life just moves at a different pace when you've reached middle age. Reality has narrowed the scope of possibility. More doors have closed than remain open. Time becomes alarmingly finite. A day passes in an instant. The years, somehow, have accumulated, and at some unknown point the number in the pile becomes greater than the number to be added. I did my best to be mindful of this, and to live in as many moments as I could muster, knowing that it would one day all exist in the past tense.

And now it does.

I t sinks in after a while. No matter how things might once have seemed, the sky is not actually the limit. The lucky breaks that might have led to the Maclay Finals did not happen. That life turned out to be for other people.

We've already talked about the elusiveness of success, and how reaching even that sort of goal tends only to breed other, loftier goals. Our expectations are malleable and are shaped by what we think is possible. "If I can do this," we're apt to say to ourselves, "then why not the next thing as well?" The quest for external measures of success is never-ending.

There's a happy flip side to this dynamic. We can adjust our goals in other directions as well. I've come to terms with the fact that I won't achieve the sort of prominence as an academic that I once quietly hoped for. I won't be the Bob Dylan of law professors. But I can and do continue to take great pleasure in the work of thinking and writing about law, and in teaching newcomers to the profession. External recognition is nice, and a kind word from the right person can go a long way, but so much of the reward is in the doing, and in the being able to do, this thing that I deeply enjoy.

Ada and Audrey's careers as young riders, their time in the category that the hunter/jumper world labels "the Juniors," have passed. Their resumes have some nice entries, including things that are well beyond what we could have reasonably expected if we'd had the knowledge to form reasonable expectations when we started. But the biggest dreams they formed along the way, as we've seen, went unrealized.

Ada's taking up dressage was, in a sense, a process of starting over. It's a different way of riding, and a different culture with different norms and expectations. For one thing, in the hunter/jumper world a dad can pretty much park himself wherever along the rail he wants when it's his daughter's turn to show. They don't like that so much in dressage.

In the first year or so she worked with a variety of horses, none of them strictly dressage horses, and learned a ton. Dressage consistently demands precision. There remains a need to be reactive and improvisational, but on a smaller scale and within tighter constraints than when one is jumping a course. The tests are the same from one show to the next, the inside of each ring a blank page on which the rider is to inscribe a specified design as meticulously as possible.

Audrey and Belle continued to show and continued to develop, though the end of their time together mostly consisted of helping Belle recover from a lingering injury. We sold Belle in the summer of 2021, and Belle, too, began a transition to dressage. Over the years Audrey became a crucial part of the fabric of Millcreek Farm, serving in a working student role, assisting the veterinarian when he made his rounds, and riding every horse she could. Once she got her license, she drove herself. A trip I used to make several times a week suddenly became a trip I hardly made at all.

I tried to do a bit of riding myself. Never any formal lessons, just a few sessions under watchful eyes. Not enough to be good at it, but rather enough to know just how truly difficult it must be to be good at it. I used to sit ringside hearing a trainer repeat an instruction to a rider—sometimes one of mine, and sometimes not—for something like the millionth time. "Carry your hands higher." "Heels down." "More leg!" (There is almost never enough leg.) And I'd wonder why they couldn't just do it. "She's telling you to carry your hands higher. She's been telling you to carry your hands higher for approximately forever now. *I've* been carrying my hands higher. Why is this so hard?" (All thought rather than spoken, of course.)

And then I got on top of a horse named Handsome. It wasn't a repeat of that trip around my cousin's yard as a kid. At least, not entirely. I'd had years of expensive training by that point, though of course it was all secondhand. I knew about all the things I was supposed to be thinking about, and I tried to think about them. But then Handsome kept moving, and I had to keep adjusting. I'd focus on my heels and lose track of my hands. I'd try to think about both heels and hands at the same time and somehow inadvertently give the signal to canter. Then I'd have to focus on not running into something—or someone. I managed some minor successes, one of the coolest of which was reaching a point where I could get him to turn simply by shifting myself in the saddle and without using my hands at all—at the walk, of course. But I also understood just how big a task it would be for me to actually "get good."

If I had an infinite amount of time, or at least knew that I had a lot more time, I'd definitely work to develop my skills. But one of the minor themes of this book is that two decades can pass quickly. My list is long. I don't need a lot to get my horse fix. I still help with chores at Split Rail a couple times a month, and that seems to do the trick. And I still watch Ada and Audrey ride when I'm given the chance, which, for now, happens less often.

As you've no doubt come to realize, I tend to get a bit nostalgic. It's no surprise, then, that I clearly remember a lot of the "last times." I can still imagine my seat toward the back of the bus the team had chartered to take us to my last high-school football game. We had made the state tournament for the second year in a row, and for the second year in a row we had lost to the same team. It was a bitterly cold day, the sort where your skin starts to hurt a bit as it warms back up, and I can still see the field as we sat for a few minutes on the bus before beginning the long trip home. A few months later I sat in a locker room in Blue Earth, Minnesota, commiserating with a wrestler from a nearby town after we had both just reached the end of the line with losses in the district tournament. Later that spring I hit a single over the second baseman in the last at-bat of my baseball career. We had been two wins away from the state tournament, but our early lead had evaporated, and my contribution was too little, too late.

Don't misunderstand. I wasn't some great high school athlete wrapping up his glory days. But each one of these last times came in a setting where a win would have meant another game or another match, and a loss brought an abrupt end. Each represented the last time I would ever compete in a sport that had been a significant part of my life to that point.

The equestrian world's not quite like that, of course. Aging out of the Juniors or the Young Rider division marks a significant transition, but it doesn't mean the end of competition.

I understood that on an intellectual level in late summer 2019 as we prepared for Ada's last show before she headed off to college. But there's sometimes a difference between what you know and how things feel. My own experiences told me that this was a significant moment. It felt like this long journey was coming to a close. What began with a quest to find toy horses in Oklahoma City would end in a ring at Lamplight.

It wouldn't be the ending we had once imagined. Whatever the fate of those dreams in any alternative universes, Fortune did not smile on them in this one. That's the way it goes, as my grandpa would say.

Although Ada's dressage career had an unsteady beginning, Fortune, perhaps feeling a bit badly about how things had gone before, provided her with the opportunity to ride a horse named Ruudi, a talented and experienced Dutch Warmblood whose own resume included an appearance on the cover of *Practical Horseman* magazine. Ruudi had most recently belonged to a woman named Ingrid Wallin whose life was taking her from away from greater Milwaukee to her original home in Sweden. She placed Ruudi with Patty at Split Rail, and Patty graciously offered Ada the chance to ride and show him.

The initial plan had been to compete over the course of the entire summer, but things didn't line up that way. Rather than a steady progression it was a concentrated dose. Five weeks, four shows, two different trainers. (Many thanks to Bonnie Bowman and Nicole Trapp, and three cheers for cooperation!) Dressage showing involves riding prescribed "tests" at increasingly complex levels, which begin at

"Introductory" and end at "Grand Prix," with levels designated "First" through "Fourth" sitting roughly in the middle of the progression. The plan was for Ada and Ruudi to start at First Level and, if things went well, end showing at Third.

Things had gone well. The week-to-week and ride-to-ride improvement was clear even to me.

And so here we were. Final show of the summer, Third Level debut. A mere three days separating the last minutes in the saddle from the first moments in a new dorm room. My work schedule meant that I could be there only for the week's concluding ride. There was no way I was going to miss it.

It had been a while since we'd been to Lamplight, long enough that all the original goals had still been in place. What might have been Ada's best hunter/jumper show took place there. But so had the injury that truly kicked off the run of bad luck.

As I walked around, burdened with the sense that this was the end of the line, I once again saw ghosts. I couldn't help but remember those prior shows. I couldn't help but hear the voices of all the trainers and barn managers and friends whose various contributions had brought us to this moment. Phrases came to me in bits and pieces, with two floating to the top, the entirety of all those years distilled into two phrases: Bernadette Ruckdashel's constant injunction in those beginning years to "be a rider and not a passenger," and Charles Zwicky's simple, consistent, and enthusiastic last words to his riders as they enter the ring: "Have fun!" The recipe for a good ride and a good life.

Soon enough it was time to ride. Was I kind of a wreck? Maybe. Did I cover it up? Well, I did make a point to walk in front of everybody else on the way to the ring. And, you know, there was lots of dust and pollen and stuff in the air.

Ada and Ruudi warmed up, I took a few pictures, and then it was showtime. Nicole Trapp sent her in the ring with the injunction, "Ride it like you stole it," and off they went to tackle Third Level, Test 1.

It was a good ride. It might have been the strongest one of the summer, though by no means the highest scoring. Ada clearly felt good about it, flashing the big smile she wore most every time she came out of the ring on Ruudi.

I don't remember whether I walked in front or behind on the way back to the barn, but I know I walked alone. And that my thinking, still clouded by the various ends of my own high school athletic careers, was basically a stunned, "That's it. It's over."

We got back to the barn, Ada hopped off Ruudi, and I gave her a hug. Then she untacked and led him to the wash stall, where I, once again, stepped in to hold the lead rope and attempt to keep him from squirming around too much while she hosed him down. We took lots of photos, same as we did at other milestone shows over the years. Meanwhile, I tried to make sense of it all. We were doing something we'd done countless times before, but it was different now. We had reached the conclusion.

But then a funny thing happened. Ada started to talk about "next year." Andrew Weniger, a friend I've made entirely as a result of writing about my family's life with horses, stopped by to say hello. We stood in the barn aisle and talked about what the future might hold. There was more of the same on the drive home. *Next year. When we do this again.*

I had been dreading college drop-off. Too many of my friends had told me how difficult it was, and I expected it to be the same for me. I'm not saying it was easy. But somehow that last show, by so clearly being *not* the last show, made it less difficult to say goodbye when we left Ada in her dorm room. We'd turned the page to a new chapter, but we were still reading the same book.

And the journey indeed continued. Ada joined the equestrian team at the University of Minnesota. I made it to one of her shows during her freshman year, the first IHSA show I'd been to as a parent, and it struck me as I stood in the crowded area beside the ring that there were more people attentively watching the action than at nearly every other show I'd been to. Among other things, it made the collective gasp when someone fell especially striking. And it provided me with a special sort of reassurance. They announce the riders by number only. My distance vision isn't great even with glasses, and of course every rider wore a helmet and was otherwise dressed the same, and so I was worried that I wouldn't immediately be able to tell which one was Ada. I needn't have worried. I've seen more than enough over the years to be able to instantly recognize her profile on a horse.

That first collegiate season, like so much else, got cut short by the COVID pandemic. But Ada returned home for the summer and resumed riding Ruudi. They managed not only to get some showing in, but also to earn Ada's USDF Bronze Medal by collecting sufficiently high scores from different judges at the First, Second, and Third Levels. We even managed to come through on the plan to return to Lamplight during the Festival of Champions, where Ada and Ruudi brought their summer to a close by making their debut at Fourth Level.

And now, all three of my daughters are in college. Ada is a co-captain of the equestrian team at Minnesota, and Audrey has joined the team at the University of Virginia. I write these words in the immediate wake of a weekend in which they both had successful shows. Laura is at Fordham University's Lincoln Center campus, taking full advantage of all that New York City has to offer. Here in Milwaukee the nest is empty. Soon enough, the challenge will be to find times when we can get the entire family together at once.

I take solace through all of this in a memory from an early morning during Ada's run of shows in the summer of 2019. We were at Silverwood Farm in Camp Lake, Wisconsin, and had finished the morning's first bit of work. We sat outside Ruudi's stall easing into the morning when a truck drove past and parked about fifteen yards away. A rider emerged, a woman who looked to be a few years older than I. So, too, did a woman who appeared to be her mother. The rider was dressed to show. The mother was dressed to support. They got to work without exchanging a word, each knowing what needed to be done.

The message was a hopeful one. We could be at this for a long time to come.

I stand ready to do my part.

Over the years there have been a number of times when people have suggested that I was doing something extraordinary. That never seemed right to me. From my perspective, I was simply doing my job, taking advantage of the fact that I had a career that allowed me the flexibility to do the driving and to "be there." Of course, it was nice to hear anyway, and one moment stands out. It was the Sunday of Memorial Day weekend, the day of the annual Willow Hill Riding Club Show, and at that point in our lives, one of the biggest days of the year.

For most of the day at the show, the indoor arena served as a warm-up ring. But over the lunch hour it became the setting for the costume class. Most of the spectators moved in to watch. We were usually too last-minute in our preparations to place high in the class, but one year we made it a priority. Laura wore a Snoopy costume atop her ride that day, Zipper, who sported a doghouse costume fashioned primarily out of a large cardboard box and swaths of red felt. Audrey wore a frog costume, with her horse Max playing the part of a pond, complete with lily pads. They finished first and second.

The costume class had come to its conclusion and the crowd lingered a bit before moving back outside. I found myself standing next to a woman who for the preceding few months had been on a schedule similar to ours. She had a small pony with a lot of energy and was often riding or lessoning on nights when I had the girls at the barn to ride. We struck up a conversation on a topic I've long since forgotten. Small talk of some sort, no doubt.

Then she said something that was, for her, probably a throwaway line, just a casual observation. Partly because of that, because there was no sense that she was trying to curry favor with me in any way, no sense that she was being insincere, it's stuck with me as one of the nicest things anyone has ever said to me.

"I wish I had had a dad like you."

That, for a dad, is some awfully powerful stuff.

It wasn't, of course, a solo parenting effort by any means. Lea's relative absence from this book should not be taken as an effort to in any way minimize her contributions. It was a team effort, but the nature of our family and our respective responsibilities meant that we were usually parenting solo when it was time to head off to whatever the calendar held on a given evening. The story I've told is the story as I experienced it. I took the lead as the horse parent in part because it was an easier role for the former farm kid to assume. But I took it mostly because I wanted to, because something drew me to it. The farming gene that I didn't think had been passed down to me might just have expressed itself in a different way.

Whether I've lived up to the compliment I got that afternoon after the costume class is not for me to decide. I focused my attention on what seemed important to my children during a critical period of their lives. But when you focus on some things you might be missing others. So, I'm certainly not about to claim that all the "World's Greatest Dad" mugs are rightfully mine. If it's true that the better part of success is just showing up, then I'll claim success to that extent. I showed up. I tried to teach and I tried to learn. I tried to be helpful where I could, and I tried to stay out of the way where I couldn't.

I didn't always get it right, but I gave it my all. ⑨

—18———————————

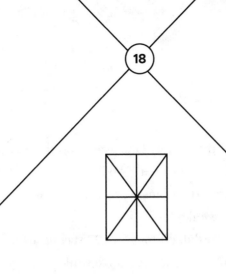

n January 2020, while Ada was home from college on break, I contacted Bernadette to see whether we could pay a visit to Appy Orse to watch a lesson. I had just reached a formal agreement to write this book, and I wanted to shake loose as many memories and images of those early days as I could.

But I also wanted to observe an anniversary. Fourteen years had passed since I first spoke to Bernadette on the phone to set up our visit to watch that first riding lesson.

It had been some time since we had returned. That hadn't been our intention. We had planned to be present often, and to stay involved, and for a while we followed through. But two careers and three active daughters leads to a shortage of time. Appy Orse wasn't on the way to anyplace we'd normally travel, and though life would occasionally take us along the stretch of Interstate 43 that runs near the farm we hadn't found a way to travel the last couple miles for a visit.

This time, though, we did. We took Exit 97, staying in the left lane and following Highway 57 as it continues north while the interstate curves off to the right toward Lake Michigan. I made sure to reduce my speed quickly, remembering that there would often be a police officer tucked in behind the trees just after the interchange, and we proceeded a short way north before making the turn in onto Willow Road.

There's a small dairy farm at the corner that's still operational. Fourteen years earlier a pair of horses lived in a small pasture on that farm, right alongside Willow Road. We had often wondered about them as we drove past. Did the farmer like horses? Was there a daughter who did? We never saw them being ridden. They were simply there, together, until one day there was only a single horse in the pasture. That led to a new round of questions. What happened? Was it hard for one horse to stay when another left? Horses, Bernadette drilled into her riders, are herd animals. They do not like to be alone.

Now there were no horses, and no fence, and no obvious sign that they had ever been there at all. There was another layer to the small mystery that had once entertained us, another reminder that time marches unsympathetically forward, paying no mind to whether we've managed to puzzle our way through all the things we'd like to get figured out.

A short way down the road, at the crest of a small hill, we turned once again into the Appy Orse drive. Just as when we had first driven past, I tried both to stay on the road and catch glimpses of the farm to see what was the same and what had changed. We spotted Bernadette's unmistakable profile—a thing that certainly had not changed—as soon as we passed her house. She wore a full-body black snowmobile suit, as has long been her winter custom. We parked, put on the rest of our cold weather gear, and made our way across the yard. Bernadette greeted us both with hugs.

It's hard in a moment like that to keep track of everything taking place. On one level it's a conversation with an old friend, an effort to fill in years-long gaps in a short amount of time, to see what might have changed. The talk is all about the time that has passed. Meanwhile the familiarity of the surroundings invites you to imagine that no time has passed at all. You're back home and ready to pick up where you left off. The brain struggles to triangulate the space between itself, the past, and the present.

Overall, the farm and the barn looked almost exactly as they had when we were regulars. The barn's wood remained weathered, with few traces of any paint that might once have been there. The horses, still living outside in a large herd, were largely huddled under the covered area next to the barn, their long winter hair caked with mud. I stood in spot where I'd stood a dozen or so years before, trying then to imagine where all this might lead.

We stepped into the barn and I remembered a moment in the aisle when a young woman, home from college on break, returned for a lesson. She attended the University of Wisconsin and was a member of the equestrian team. Bernadette asked Ada if she might one day want to ride in college. It had seemed so abstract and hypothetical. And now, somehow, Ada stood in that same aisle, an adult, and a member of a college equestrian team.

I excused myself to use the restroom, as always a port-a-potty just inside the door to one of the hay barns. On the way I paused at the small paddock where Bernadette would leave Sunny and Ozzie on the nights

I would bring Ada and Audrey up to ride. The hay barn looked only slight-ly rearranged from when I'd last been in it. If Bernadette had walked in and asked me to move some bales from one place to another, I would have got right to it.

I stepped into the port-a-potty and willed it to be a time machine. Maybe if I paused there for a minute, closed my eyes, and wanted it really badly I'd step out and find that it was 2007 and my six-year-old daughter was standing there waiting for me. I opened the door. She wasn't there. The car parked outside was still a 2015 model.

I'd have to try again on a different day.

I returned to the barn. Ada stood talking with Bernadette as three young women got their horses ready for the lesson. Two of them, Bailey and Kate, introduced themselves at Bernadette's request as they and their horses walked past on the way to the indoor ring. The third, Camille, remained in the barn to finish getting ready, telling us as she stepped into the tack room that she had just started riding at Appy Orse. She closed the door behind her. That was the rule in the winter, because the tack room was the only place with heat.

Just then Marina Lee, a local artist and long-time Appy Orse client, walked into the barn. We spent a few minutes catching up, remembering how it was, and generally lamenting the passage of time. Marina offered a memory or two of the little girl I had brought to those first lessons.

To this point our visit was completely predictable. Powerful, certainly, but not much different from what we had expected. Life at Appy Orse, it seemed, had continued on much the way it always had. The lesson we were about to watch would be the same as the lessons we'd seen and ridden in before. I had no sense that we were about to see something inspiring.

As the minutes piled up, Camille remained in the tack room, and Bernadette called out to remind her that it was time for the lesson to begin. And then she provided us with some background. Camille is 26, Bernadette told us, and is severely disabled, the consequence of illnesses suffered in infancy. She had ridden before coming to Appy Orse, but in what was more of a therapy setting, the sort of thing where she sat on a horse and was simply led around by someone walking with a lead rope. She had come to hope for more—she wanted to *ride*—and was finding it at Appy Orse. She had gone into the tack room simply to get her helmet, which Bernadette had set out for her. It had already taken several minutes, but she would have to find it on her own.

Camille finally emerged, and we walked to the indoor.

The "Sound Voice Before Entering" sign that captured my attention years before was faded almost to the point of invisibility. My memory of walking through that door for the first time remained vivid, when the very next thing we saw was a dramatic fall, when Ada wanted to watch for as long as she could, when her interest was rewarded with the chance to get on a horse and ride it around the ring. Not to be led, but to do it herself.

Having to do it yourself, to "be a problem-solver," as Bernadette routinely phrases it, is a nonnegotiable part of the Appy Orse culture. Everyone is welcome to ride there, and there seems to be a way to make it work even for those who couldn't otherwise afford it, with the sole condition being that the child (or the adult) be willing to put in the work necessary to keep the enterprise going. So far as I can tell the only thing that will get you turned away is an entitled mentality.

I had, I thought, seen this from Bernadette before—raising the bar for a young person who had encountered false limits imposed elsewhere. A trainer who thought this was a kid who simply wouldn't have enough talent or attention span, or was "disabled" and therefore unable to be anything other than led around a ring. At times it seemed as though Bernadette took these situations as a personal affront, or at least as a challenge. I had long taken her "We don't say 'I can't'" mantra as one of empowerment for her riders. I had missed the extent to which it serves as her personal mission statement.

We walked to the same corner where we sat that first day and took a seat on a wooden bench. The bench hadn't been there when we first came, and neither had the platform it sat on. Both were built by the grandfather of a rider somewhere around the midpoint of our time there, both part of Appy Orse's "everyone pitches in" ethos. Some of the details were different. The footing in the ring had changed—sand rather than the wood-chip based footing that was there when we left—and the jumps were more brightly colored and differently arrayed from how they had tended to be in past winters. But the vibe remained unmistakable. More of the past washed over me, the lessons, the shows, the nights where it was just Ada, Audrey, and me in the indoor, working on basics and dreaming of what might come to be. I could have sat for a while just taking it all in, but the lesson was about to begin.

Camille's mother Kara, who had been waiting in her car, took a seat next to us and introduced herself. As the riders warmed up, she explained that Camille could not read or write and was largely unable to function independently in the world. Their presence at Apply Orse, much like ours, happened almost by accident. They had taken a family road trip to Michigan's Upper Peninsula and had promised Camille a trail ride while there. That had turned out to be more difficult than they anticipated, and Kara had been left to call barns on the fly as they worked their way back to their home in Illinois. It's hard to schedule a trail ride on short notice. But it didn't surprise me one bit that Bernadette had been willing to do it.

"I had just assumed that Camille would go on a trail ride for an hour, and we would continue on our way home from vacation after that," said Kara. "We met Miss Bernadette and...she explained that she boarded horses and gave lessons on Sundays. That's when I looked at my phone to see how far we were from home... one-and-a-half hours. I could do that. So, I proceeded to tell her all about Camille's epilepsy and her cognitive level, and Miss Bernadette didn't blink or hesitate one bit. I was shocked. To be perfectly honest, most people struggle dealing with special-needs people with one disability, but you add in a medical issue and they want nothing to do with your child. And here was this woman in her seventies looking me straight in the eye and telling me that Camille could start lessons next Sunday morning."

And now, not five months later, Camille sat atop a horse named Jenkins, an old soldier who just happened to be the horse I rode in the only formal lesson I'd ever taken at Appy Orse. There was no one leading her, and indeed there was no one close to her. She had instead led Jenkins into the ring, mounted by herself, and now was, as I had assumed when she first walked past us on her way into the tack room, just another rider, guiding her horse around the ring.

Camille and Jenkins walked, trotted, cantered, and ultimately jumped small jumps. She struggled, at times, to execute instructions completely, especially when it came to remembering a short course of jumps. But her response to each request was a cheerful "I'll try!" And then she would not only try but succeed. Even if it took a few attempts.

Most of us wouldn't have the patience to pull this off. We would have walked into the tack room to hand Camille her helmet after she had disappeared for a while. We would have succumbed at various points when Camille struggled to do something. Shortcuts are easy to justify. We're in a hurry. Other people are waiting. There simply isn't time.

Bernadette held firm. She didn't intervene, or in any way do anything for Camille beyond repeating instructions as many times as necessary until she figured out how to do what she was being asked to do. Bailey and Kate waited patiently. This is how it works at Appy Orse. They would get their lesson's worth of jumping when it was their turn.

Kara was clearly thrilled by and proud of what her daughter had proven able to do. She admitted that their experience with Bernadette had led her to rethink some of the assumptions she brought to her own job as a special education teacher.

"It's made me think that we don't expect enough out of our students," she said. "If Camille can do this..."

After the lesson we stood in the barn aisle talking, the conversation a mix of further reminiscing on Ada's early years and reflections on what had just transpired. We compared histories. Neither of Camille's parents were horse people either. She was simply drawn to horses in that way that some people just *are*. And her parents had done what they could, because that's what you do.

"I've gone on trail rides with Camille in Colorado and Wyoming," Kara said, "hanging on to the reins and squeezing those poor horses with my legs, vowing each time that it would never happen again."

Kara and her husband had provided their daughter with regular chances to spend time with horses as a child, but the family had drifted away from the barn as they struggled through adolescence. "Now we are trying again," noted Kara, "and this time succeeding. It's been nice to see her so happy!"

Camille clearly felt a sense of accomplishment. And as she sat on a mounting box, struggling with her spurs, she offered an assessment of her new trainer: "Berndatte has a warm heart on the inside, but she can be strict on the outside."

It was as concise and accurate a read of one human being by another that I've ever heard.

We had left Appy Orse Acres to chase dreams, some of which hadn't even yet taken shape when we pulled out of the driveway after the last lesson there. The intervening years brought bigger jumps and bigger dreams. We crossed paths with Olympians and billionaires, and Ada and Audrey both were able to ride some fancy and talented horses in beautiful settings. We did what we could, because that's what you do. We had neither the bank account nor the luck to secure a place in the big time, but we've had a few tastes of what it's like. It's always pretty on the outside, and less consistently so on the inside. As an "A"-circuit groom once put it to me, "I've seen people at their best, and I've seen people at their worst." The mix, it seems to me, tends more heavily toward the unflattering the higher up the ladder you go. The journey has, at times, made me cynical.

I arranged our visit to Appy Orse in the hopes of refreshing my memory of the place and of our early adventures in the horse world. Getting to meet and watch Camille was a bonus, an important reminder that much of what is pure and good and even powerful about horses has nothing to do with how fancy they look or how well they show, nothing to do with ribbons or awards, nothing to do with traveling to showgrounds in exotic locations. Simply getting to ride, having the ability to get on a horse and make him go where and how you want him to go, can be one of the most enjoyable and important things in the whole world. It was a solid reminder of Anne Thornbury's injunction: "Remember why you started." And it suggested a corollary: Remember *where* you started. You might leave a place behind. You should never forget the lessons you learned there. ✺

# EPILOGUE

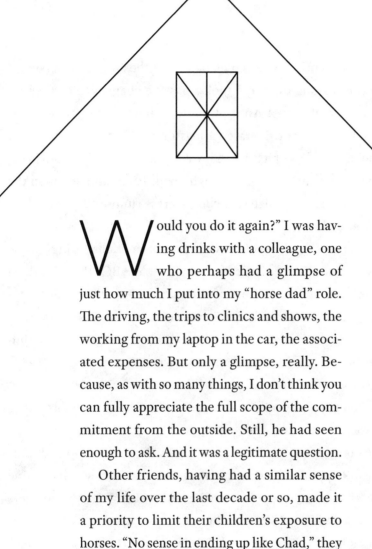

W ould you do it again?" I was having drinks with a colleague, one who perhaps had a glimpse of just how much I put into my "horse dad" role. The driving, the trips to clinics and shows, the working from my laptop in the car, the associated expenses. But only a glimpse, really. Because, as with so many things, I don't think you can fully appreciate the full scope of the commitment from the outside. Still, he had seen enough to ask. And it was a legitimate question.

Other friends, having had a similar sense of my life over the last decade or so, made it a priority to limit their children's exposure to horses. "No sense in ending up like Chad," they never quite said out loud.

**EPILOGUE**

The investments of time and money aren't the only ones, of course. Several times along the way I took a pass on chances to further my professional ambitions. And, of course, there was a tremendous emotional investment. I shared Christopher Hitchens' line about parenthood already, but it's worth invoking again: "Nothing can make one so happily exhilarated or so frightened: It's a solid lesson in the limitations of self to realize that your heart is running around inside someone else's body."

That heart has experienced a broad range of emotions during its time in the horse world. That classic line from the old ABC "Wide World of Sports" opening about "the thrill of victory and the agony of defeat" captures a lot of it. But there's also pride over accomplishments and growth. Worry over decisions and emotional states and the health of both children and horses. The happiness and satisfaction that come from seeing your kids find something they love to do, and from being able to support them in doing it. The regret that accompanies foregone opportunities and decisions that didn't work out.

None of this is unique to the horse world. Pick your sport and there are plenty of opportunities for spending time and money in increasing amounts as a kid moves up through the ranks. Though maybe not *quite* as much money. (Once I was at a figure skating competition where a vendor was selling a t-shirt that read, "Skating Dad: Broke and Ignored." I paused to take a photo. The person standing next to me chuckled and gave me a sort of "I know, right?" look. My thought process was more along the lines of, "Ha ha ha, they have no idea.")

In the early portion of our days on the "A" circuit I had this idea that sooner or later we'd make it to show in Florida for the winter. That's where all the cool kids end up—the talented, the wealthy, the ones drawn to wealth for whatever it is that proximity to it provides them. And I'd be standing ringside and leaning against the rail when another horse dad would take the spot next to me. We'd get to talking and we'd discover that we both came from backgrounds where all the pomp and the luxury and the pretentiousness that surrounded us might as well have existed on another planet. But we had daughters who were drawn to horses. We'd remark that it was pretty strange, when you think about it, that a couple guys like us would end up in a place like this, and that we were starting to feel a little uncomfortable just talking about it. One of us would suggest that there's gotta be a dive bar around here somewhere, a place where we might fit in a little better.

And then, fellow horse dad Bruce Springsteen and I would get in my rental car and drive off in search of cheap beer and a good juke box.

That didn't happen. I'd have mentioned it already. A lot of what I imagined might happen did not. What *did* happen is that I helped parent three daughters to adulthood. It's hard to express the depth of my pride in who they have become. Each is an extraordinary young woman. As individuals and as a group they are a joy to be around, and they have pushed me—sometimes intentionally—to become a better version of myself. The first word I'd use to describe being their dad, and I am being quite sincere, is "fun." It has been a joy, and the great honor of my life.

For a while during high school, Ada worked at a local tack store. One night she got home from work a little later than usual. She'd had to keep the store open, she explained, because just before closing a dad came in with his young daughter. They were there to buy her first pair of paddock boots. A big moment.

Ada asked the girl the standard question, "Where do you ride?" The answer came back, "Appy Orse Acres."

It was one of those stories that'll catch you even if you're ready for it. *That*, once upon a time, was us. And in that moment, I wanted nothing more than to go back to being a dad with his daughter out to buy her first pair of paddock boots. ֍

Would I do it again?
*In a heartbeat.*

Thanks to Bernadette Ruckdashel, Charles Zwicky, Tori Polonitza, Emily Elek, Heidi Modesto, Serah Vogus, Diane Carney, Bonnie Bowman, and Nicole Trapp, all of whom taught my daughters how to ride, but not only how to ride, and who taught me plenty of things as well; to Kathy Happ, Barb Van Housen, Patty Van Housen, and the barn families at Appy Orse Acres, Hidden View Farm, Stonewall Farm, Millcreek Farm, and Split Rail Stables for providing welcoming and supporting environments for my daughters and for allowing me to feel like I was part of the team, too; to Kelly Doke and Lauren Carter for gracefully handling the difficult role of barn manager; to my colleagues during my time on the Wisconsin Hunter Jumper Association board, who welcomed me and patiently brought me up to speed; to Molly Sorge for agreeing to add my voice to *The Chronicle of the Horse's* stable of bloggers; to Rebecca Didier for an outstanding edit; to Robyn Louw for the periodic emails of encouragement; to Todd Peppers for keeping me on task in the occasionally profane way that only a truly good friend can; to Bonnie Thomson for her insights, advice, and good humor; to everyone who has offered a kind word about my writing; to the many people I'm privileged to call friends as a result of our connection to the horse world; to all the horses we've met along the way; to my wife Lea for being the best possible partner in parenthood; and most of all to my daughters for making it look as if we knew what we were doing. ✺

Chad Oldfather has ridden horses just enough times to appreciate how difficult it is to do well. He has also mucked stalls, cleaned tack, stacked hay, helped fix fences, logged hundreds of hours ringside as his daughters have taken lessons and ridden in shows, and served on the Board of Directors of the Wisconsin Hunter Jumper Association. By day he is a professor at Marquette University Law School where, among other things, he teaches classes on and writes about judicial behavior, constitutional law, and the jurisprudence of sport, and serves on the Board of Advisors to the National Sports Law Institute. His non-legal writings have appeared in *The Chronicle of the Horse,* the *World Equestrian Center Magazine,* and *Harvard Magazine.* ⦾

————— ABOUT THE AUTHOR —————